M000213137

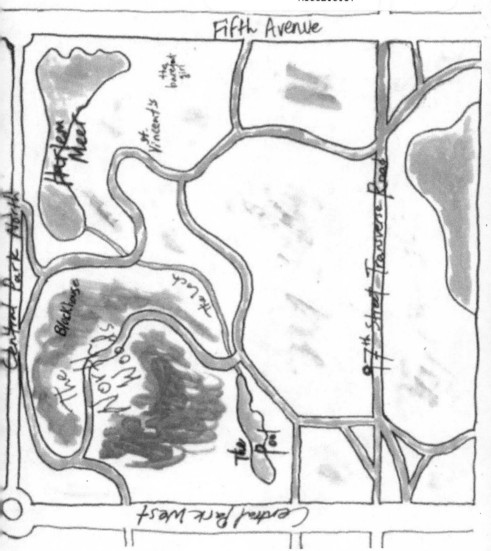

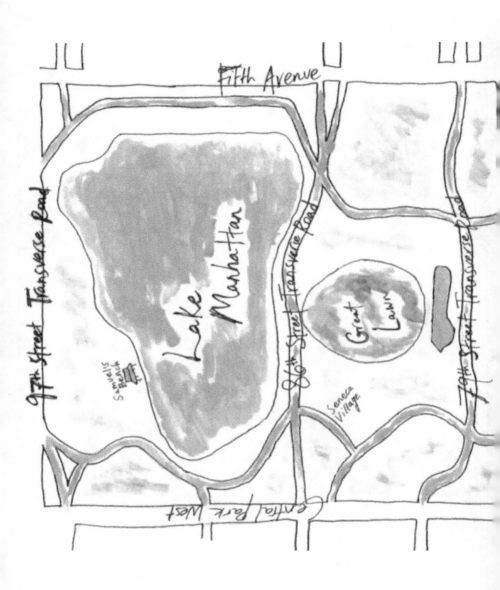

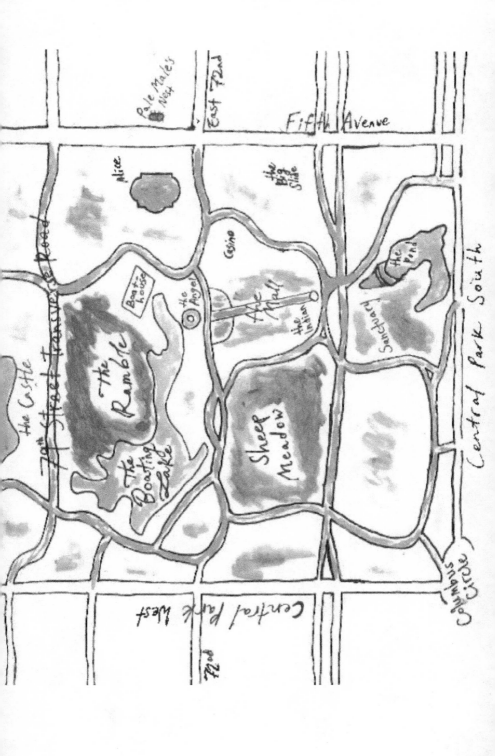

CENTRAL PARK
LOVE SONG

Wandering Beneath the Heaventrees

PRAISE FOR

CENTRAL PARK LOVE SONG

Adopted New Yorkers—those who have with romantic intention come to live for good in the metropolis of their dreams—sometimes feel compelled to express with words their profound love for what E. B. White called "this mischievous and marvelous monument which not to look upon would be like death." In *Central Park Love Song*, Stephen Wolf, editor of *I Speak of the City: Poems of New York*, is as rhapsodic as White in prose where nostalgia and knowledge are skillfully combined. This book about an enduring enchantment with place will resonate with all who find in the city's green heart a special world of their own.

—ELIZABETH BARLOW ROGERS, author/editor of *The Central Park Book*, author of *The Green Metropolis,* first president of the Central Park Conservancy, 1980-1996.

Stephen Wolf loves the city & its green sanctuary as Frank O'Hara did its streets, cafes & museums, as Nelson Algren sung about Chicago's Janus-head & gritty heart, as James Joyce celebrated the lives of work-a-day Dubliners. *Central Park Love Song* is a hand-guided tour of the world's most famous & beautiful park from the purview of a master story teller & street smart historian. Everywhere you look there is wonder & beauty & the everyday real people who populate the place. Along the way, wandering beneath the heaventrees, you will most certainly fall in love.

—KEVIN COVAL, author of *A People's History of Chicago*, *This is Modern Art*, editor of *The Breakbeat Poets*.

Stephen Wolf's *Central Park Love Song* is an intimate historical and personal portrait of perhaps the world's *most* beloved urban park and the city surrounding it. It is a meticulously researched and beautifully written homage to Olmsted and Vaux's man-made paradise. Here you will meet the people who inhabit the park, and learn the stories behind the statues, fountains, bridges, ponds, meadows and landscapes that have existed from Civil War times to the present day. There is much more to NYC's Central Park than meets the eye and this wonderful book reveals it all!

—DAVID SMITH, New York Public Library's "Librarian to the Stars"

Printed in the United States of America
First Printing, 2018

Cover Image "New York Skyline with Central Park"
watercolor and pencil on paper, 19.75 x 26.12 in.
by American Artist Fairfield Porter 1907–1975
© Courtesy Estate of Fairfield Porter

Photos by author: 13, 27, 31, 45, 63, 132-133, 155, 193, 214

Book Design: Marvin LLoyd Larson

ISBN: 978-0-9993153-6-1
Library of Congress Control Number: 2018934802

Published by Griffith Moon
Santa Monica, California
www.GriffithMoon.com

CENTRAL PARK LOVE SONG

LOVE SONG

Wandering Beneath the Heaventrees

STEPHEN WOLF

Griffith Moon

CONTENTS

Part Three

Epilogue

Prologue

One night soon after the ball dropped in rowdy Times Square for 1977, we began our journeys to Central Park. Bo sniffed only a few cold yards ahead keeping close on the unfamiliar blocks of Bleecker Street. It was well named, Bleecker, though surrounding streets were as badly wounded. Much of the city lay in shambles then, aluminum gates ripped from empty storefronts, dark brick walkups crumbling, trash on sidewalks and in stairwells and gutters, graffiti's mad, white lines over everywhere: in the distance far downtown, the slender shafts of the World Trade Center glittering between the gaps of the potholed cross-streets.

Just before descending the stairs to the Broadway/Lafayette subway station, I fixed Bo on a short leash. From my coat pocket I removed a thin, white, fold-up cane with a bungee cord running through it that snapped open long and straight, put on a pair of Roy Orbison-style sunglasses, then tapped my way downstairs; this late at night fewer people would see us if anything about my plan went awry. The white cane's red tip touched just to the left and crossed over to the right, always low to the ground to detect a rise or drop. Everything was so dark in these glasses.

We passed the drowsy attendant in the booth as I tugged Bo slightly toward the turnstile and, in character, fumbled a little with the token while seeking the slot: fifty cents a ride back then. Once through, we moved to the uptown tracks, descended the stairs with steady taps, and waited on the empty platform, Bo patient and curious though never having seen anything remotely like a New York City subway platform. Someone hunched in a pillar's shadow along the downtown side, never looking at us.

Bo was a border collie the color of graham crackers, with a muscular white chest, lively brown eyes, and a floppy ear torn in a fight he picked with Cerberus. He ran free on a college quadrangle fastened to

Illinois soy bean fields when he adopted me a decade ago. He's run free ever since until a few nights earlier when I romantically landed us on a battered street of New York's Lower East Side with no other plan than the next few beats of my restless heart. Though past his prime Bo still needed more than a walk around the block twice a day, so we headed to Central Park. When I felt the cold air pushed through the tunnel by the incoming train I rubbed Bo's flank, his fur soft as talcum: "It's okay," I said just when the leash grew taut as Bo pulled forward, prepared to protect me from any challenge. I had worried he might be skittish as a rapid subway rushed toward us, but when the D train burst from the dark tunnel, then slowed with a screech, stopped, and the doors gaped opened, Bo confidently guided me inside.

Only a few people were in the car though I couldn't really look around since I was blind. As the subway clattered and clanked, shimmied and sparked, I saw myself in the reflection of the subway door's window: wavy brown hair needs trimming, worn black coat, could be taller, and looking unconvincingly blind despite the dark glasses, white cane, and handsome dog.

Soon the train came to a gradual, jerking stop at Columbus Circle, the southwest corner of Central Park. The doors opened and a bundled man grudgingly made way as I tapped by. Along the platform were other travelers of the night, in couples or alone, and once off the train I vigorously rubbed Bo along his strong neck.

"Good *doggy*!" and he leaned his weight into me.

I tapped along a trash-strewn, foul-smelling corridor, then down another, wadded, wet newspapers along the rank gutters. Ugly lines, mad and thick, covered cracked, tiled walls, every poster for six-packs and cigarettes, every subway map made useless, and each ethnic group biting into Levy's rye bread.

I was heading for any exit when suddenly Bo hesitated, narrowed his eyes and sniffed the air, then pulled me in a different direction. Down another dreary, piss-reeking corridor, a lone traveler never glancing at us as Bo kept pulling toward a darkened corner of the station where from a stone staircase cold, fresh air descended. He was heading for Central Park. All exits at Columbus Circle Station lead to the streets above but only one directly to the edge of the park, and that was the one Bo found; he could smell it. We walked up the steps into the cold night, the city bright and churning but a vast plain of darkness to our left which we entered at the first opening in a low stone wall. I broke down the cane and slipped it into my pocket, removed the sun glasses to see better that New York night, then freed Bo an instant before he scampered for a thin grove of trees and I lost him in the dark.

Together we made dozens of visits to Central Park: without him, I another five thousand. This book is what I found in those wanderings.

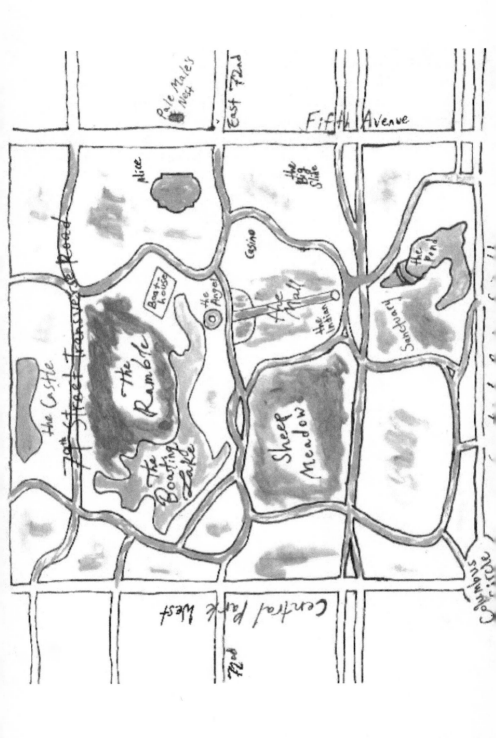

Part One

"To an ecologist, New York is most interesting as an ecotone, a place where natural worlds collide."

Anne Mathews,
Wild Nights:
Nature Returns to the City

CHAPTER ONE

Passage Though the Wall

The greatest urban park in the United States and a model for many parks to follow was designed by a young man from Connecticut who had never designed anything before, a landscape architect lured from London by a doomed horticulturist living sixty miles up the Hudson River, and an Austrian who had once tended the gardens of a king. A moody ornamentalist from Chislehurst, England, sculpted the park's most enchanting artifacts, a woodworker from Hungary created in his Brooklyn shop the park's rustic, rugged shelters, and thousands of Irish laborers who hauled a million wheelbarrows of earth, drained the swamps, and dug tremendous pits miraculously transformed into ponds and lakes demanded that no African-Americans work those acres and got what they demanded.

From a wealthy family on Manhattan's Upper East Side, a young woman would sculpt the model of her lover into an angel, the park's iconic image. Though it was the only statue intended for the park, gradually there would be many more, most of them incidental, some terrible, the payment for one assisted by a benefit performance of Shakespeare's *Julius Caesar*: included in the cast, a man who would murder our greatest president. And there was the capable ax man from Savannah, Georgia, a Union artillery captain during the Civil War who failed as a farmer on the rich, black earth of Illinois but heard of work for able-bodied men clearing land for a vast public park in New York City. One day at the job site he watched transfixed as a co-worker molded the head of a wolf in wax, and this began a journey that led him to become, self-taught, the nation's most celebrated sculptor of animals.

Where any other great metropolis displays in the center of town its most arrogant buildings or lofty monuments, New York planted trees, for Central Park's enlightened designers were inspired by their era, one that found the Creator's spirit not amid the rigors and right angles of the artificial city but in Nature's simple splendor. Central Park was a blessing to New York before the skyscraper and subway, before millions lugged their dreams through Ellis Island or a single steel cable looped from one epic tower of the Brooklyn Bridge to the other. When wealthy New Yorkers displayed themselves in fine carriages along the park's undulant roadways, Times Square was a remote, scarcely populated stretch of cobblestone streets known as Longacre Square where those carriages were made. And just as with the towers and streets that now surround it, Central Park's forests and rolling meadows, its ponds and streams were never here; it's all been created with the same care and effort as the Sistine Chapel ceiling or Wagner's *Ring* or the odyssey of one man's day and night in Dublin. Yet to this day most visitors still believe as did Horace Greeley when seeing the park after its official opening in 1873. Utterly charmed by the illusion, the renowned editor of the old *New York Tribune* said of the park with satisfaction, "Well they have let it alone better than I thought they would."

On that late night early in January I knew none of this. Never had I heard of Frederick Law Olmsted and Calvert Vaux, Andrew Jackson Downing, Jacob Wrey Mould, or Elizabeth Barlow, but the instant Bo and I first entered Central Park the city had quickly fallen away, parallel streets and perpendicular avenues left at the tree-line. The landscape dipped to a dark, gentle valley or rose to a ridge, and even the constant hum of traffic and blasts from car horns, all but a distant siren somewhere in the vast city beyond the trees faded as I followed Bo deeper into the park. Often I lost sight of him since the globes of nearly all the lampposts had been shattered, but after a whispered call he returned, only to wander off again as I followed him up black, ridged rock face where I could see the park rolling and barren and dark.

Now, everyone knew the park's reputation; "Last night it was so quiet in Central Park," Johnny Carson once quipped at the time of my first wanderings, "you could hear a knife drop." But I was fit and Bo a fierce protector, and muggers tend to avoid targets with big dogs. Besides, I felt lucky. "No one should come to New York to live," wrote E.B. White in *Here Is New York*, "unless he is willing to be lucky."

So this book is also about the city that needed and created Central Park, a city with the chutzpah to place a park so big in the center of an island this small. And on that first night in the park the city pressed all along its edges, light from surrounding buildings dangling like jewels through the bare trees. But Manhattan's midnight shrouded us with invisibility as if I wore the magic tarnhelm, prowling unseen the valleys and rocky ridges; even Bo's white chest dimmed to a soft-furred grey. It was a thrilling night.

East First Street in the Lower East Side resembled the street where Dylan and Suze Rotolo are cuddling on the cover of *Freewheelin'*, and here in a five-floor walk-up I rented two rooms on the second floor. Laid out long and narrow, it was known as a railroad apartment, half the width and the entire length of the old, cranberry-colored brick building with a black, zig-zag of a fire escape bolted to its exterior. In the front room, two dirty windows faced a tattered street, lively each day but Sunday and loud on Saturday nights when the Puerto Rican social club in the storefront blasted salsa that set the wood floors trembling to the beat. Another, more narrow room led to the kitchen in the rear, and in the walls of this narrow room, ingeniously, windows for light and air.

The kitchen stove resembled the grill of a '55 Buick Roadmaster, and since the pale yellow Frigidaire had no handle I had to pry it open with my hands. Cracked, yellow linoleum on the kitchen floor and two windows looking down upon a small, bare backyard enclosed by a chain-link fence. A large, leafless tree grew in a corner, and behind the fence, wide East Houston Street, traffic moving crosstown from river to river.

There was a bathtub along the kitchen wall with a little sink at one end of it. Above the sink, a bathroom cabinet. Beside the sink, a narrow closet with a toilet inside with "the chain thing" and wooden box like the one where Michael found the gun Clemenza had taped behind it. East First Street, a fitting place to begin life in New York, so I signed a year's lease for a $150 a month. The apartment needed a good cleaning and places in the walls patched, all four windows were grimy inside and especially out and I also must open a bank account, hook the phone and power in my name, find a good veterinarian close by, God forbid, and soon a job. But here in this city of promise and possibility there must be at least one copy editor or proof-reading position, and I would find it.

First I must make some semblance of a home in these ragged rooms where for weeks I'd wake for a confused moment in the night before realizing where I was, Bo snoring on his rug beside the bed. And after the old apartment was swept and mopped, sponged and plunged, scraped and swept and mopped again, before some patching work and sanding and long before enough off-white paint covered the bumpy walls, we headed back to Central Park. I had kept thinking about our visit there a few nights before, how I felt both thrilled and calm at once, so I put on my heavy black coat as Bo's head rises, ear perked, and as I reached for the white cane he raced for the door.

Before fleeing the Midwest I had mulled over ways to get my old dog to Central Park, nearly four miles from the apartment I had rented. A taxi might not even pick up a big dog, especially after wading in water or strolling through mud as Bo liked doing. Besides, taxi were expensive and I had low funds and no prospects. With confidence in the one bold option, I headed to the medical supply store off campus for a guide-dog harness.

"A dog must be fitted for one," the pharmacist told me. He was elderly, thin, serious, and I knew Bo would never fool him enough to pass the audition.

"May I see that?" I asked, pointing between the bedpan and catheter at a white cane with a red plastic tip in the display case.

I was confident after our late-night ride to take the subway during the day when many more people did the same; I felt their eyes on me far longer than they would if I could see, which, of course, I could. I kept my gaze fixed ahead of me, even tilting my head back slightly like Stevie Wonder, and we were left to ourselves. At Columbus Circle Station the way parted for us again, and again I tapped for the dark stone staircase where we entered the park at the first opening in the low stone wall.

Only then did I see how the park was as badly battered as the city. Once off the leash Bo again headed for the valley to our left, dry and dusty, the exposed tree roots resembling thin hands, skeletal and desperate. Most benches lining the walkways had splintered rails, as were the planks of a gentle bridge above a bridle path, its cast iron lace rusting. Like the city, graffiti was everywhere: on lampposts, benches, across the great shelves of black rock. It was like Mississippi kudzu; if I stayed still long enough someone would graffiti me. And none was exciting graffiti sprayed with skill on a crumbling wall or the exterior of subway cars winding like colorful dragons through dark tunnels. Graffiti scarring the park was the kind *inside* the subway, initials and bizarre signs making you edgy, like constantly being yelled at.

Off the walkway I followed Bo, his keen snout skimming the soft rise and fall of the hard, cold land. I called him back when he headed up an embankment towards a roadway where cars sped through the park. We entered a tunnel under the road, a crescent entry to a rank, sour passageway, a bundled figure huddled along a crumbling wall; at the other opening, rolling, barren landscape, curving walkways, and so few people despite the mild winter afternoon.

When we visit Central Park today the groves are green, benches mended, graffiti blasted clean, walkways lit and flower-lined. There are bike tours and walking tours and tours of famous movie scenes (no tours for fiction or poetry) that occurred in Central Park. There are long lines at bathrooms and cafes, for row boats and drinking fountains, walkways often as visitor-thick as Times Square. The restoration from those dusty meadows to today's luscious lawns took decades, as the abuse and neglect had taken, and to know Central Park is to experience those changes, its seasons and migrations, the animals struggling to survive within and to share the park with people who love it for reasons as varied as themselves. And so, as in our memory and dreams, the past and present often entwine in this story, merging at times into something both remembered and imagined. What I thought would give Bo a place to wander besides the streets of the Lower East Side soon cast a spell over me; I imagined the park while away from it, like a good book on a nightstand, beckoning despite the tattered pages.

My old dog was always eager for a walk, but after only two visits to Central Park he spun in a circle like a puppy when I reached for the collapsible cane; if I tarried, he scratched at the front door. Again we rode the D train to Columbus Circle, Bo in the lead and I with a cane and sunglasses, and we did this several more times before I noticed chiseled on the park's wall the words MERCHANTS' GATE.

More than fifty entrances are cut into the park's stone perimeter though only twenty were intended, and each has a name carved into the wall; there is a "gate" for artists, artisans, children, farmers, inventors, saints, strangers, warriors, women, woodsmen, and more. They serve as both portal from the turbulent city into the quiet park and greetings to each group, with a thematic statue nearby. Today only two remain: Samuel Morse at INVENTERS' GATE (Fifth Avenue/72nd Street) and a bust of Friedrich Wilhelm Heinrich Alexander von Humboldt at NAT-

URALISTS' GATE (aka EXPLORERS' GATE at Central Park West/ 77th Street). Why it took so long before I noticed the friendly greeting and acknowledgment is that here at Columbus Circle the city boldly declares its pomposity.

In 1892 a seventy-foot tall pillar rose in the center of the 'circle' for horse-drawn busses to turn around before heading back downtown where Broadway, West 59th, and Eighth Avenue converge. Commemorating the 400th anniversary of his invasion, Christopher Columbus stands atop the pillar gazing down Eighth Avenue, and here all distances from New York City are measured. Soon after Columbus arrived so did a concrete bow of a boat just as we enter the park. A woman stands in the boat, her arms outstretched to us, while muscular, naked figures lounge along the port and starboard sides. Behind the boat rises a tower where at the top a golden woman holds a victory wreath in one hand and the reins of gold, charging horses in the other; it's as if we're in Rome's Hippodrome or the Coliseum.

This is the *Maine Monument* for the ship that exploded in Havana in 1898, igniting the Spanish-American War. On the back of the tower, lower right, a piece of iron from the shattered ship. The names of all 266 Americans killed on board are carved along the sides of the tower and have faded far less than our memory of why they died. Financed largely by *New York Journal* publisher William Randolph Hearst (who many believe bullied the nation into the war), this forty-foot high, overwrought, allegorically confusing hulk was originally planned for the prow-shaped intersection where a straight Seventh Avenue and a meandering Broadway cross 45th Street in Times Square, a place known as the Bow-Tie. Once Hearst financed a memorial in Central Park, his competitor from the *New York World* Joseph Pulitzer wanted to finance one also.

With the southwest corner of Central Park now resembling ancient Rome, the park's south corner along Fifth Avenue on the East Side is New York's version of the Place de la Concorde in Paris. The stately, pale Plaza Hotel is here —our own Grand Hotel like a French Renaissance chateau: across from it, the large basin for the Pulitzer Fountain where a pale nude cradles a fruit-filled basket between her thighs. Just to the north, a life-size, gold-leaf statue of the brilliant, brutal General William Tecumseh Sherman astride his horse led by a winged goddess of victory; the general tramples palm fronds symbolizing the South. We are at Grand Army Plaza, a tribute to the Union Army where the great general is "striding straight on into the traffic," wrote the poet Lawrence Ferlinghetti, "at 59th & Fifth." Had Sherman not died a decade before the figure was completed in 1903, he may have savored that Saint-Gaudens' model for the Nik leading the general's horse was Harriette Anderson, an African-American from South Carolina, the state that had fired the Civil War's first shot.

And because the boat, the outstretched arms, the tower and golden horses demand our attention when we enter the park at Columbus Circle, I noticed only after many visits the quiet greeting on the wall.

Once off the leash, Bo followed me this time along the southern perimeter heading east: over bare, hilly ground, then to a roadway where I held the chain around his neck as cars passed. When free again he scurried across the road, up rock-face and down to a walkway encircling a dark, dirty pond. Across ten yards of water, a leafless forest, and behind us the grand palaces and hotels of 59th Street.

Nearly every visitor once entered the park here because most of us lived crammed below 38th Street on the East Side; 60th Street and Fifth Avenue was the nearest entrance. Even a century ago "the tyrant city towers above the trees," wrote John Meyers O'Hara in his 1915 sonnet "Central Park." Here a vendor with his cart shaded by a striped umbrella sold not hot pretzels as today but oysters or clams, a penny each. And whether the car-horn blasts and piercing sirens we escape now or else the rattling clamor of wagon wheels on cobblestone that O'Hara heard, "The grind of wheels and noise of feet depart" as the raucous sounds from the city instantly dim after we descend a stone staircase. Then as now, the walkway curves along the shore where "the little lake, sequestered from the wind/ is white with swans that on its bosom sleep."

The "little lake" is known as the Pond, but sixty years after O'Hara's poem, beer bottles and newspapers, not white swans, float in sticky bubbles along the greasy shore. And I realized with a small jolt that this was Holden's "lagoon"; here the young narrator in Salinger's *The Catcher in the Rye* worried there were no ducks. "I thought maybe if there *were* any around," he told us, "they might be asleep or something near the edge of the water...but I couldn't find any." These missing ducks would trouble him during his three-day misadventure in New York.

Bo trailed along the shoreline as the walkway crossed the Pond on

a steep arch of thick, gray stone. That bleak forest across the Pond grew on a small peninsula behind a chain-link fence, but my dog found a gap upon uneven ground and slipped under.

"Bo," I called.

After a moment, through the bushes and over a ridge of rock, his head peered out, then he receded into the thick brush, absorbed into the forest like a leaping dolphin returns to the sea.

I would have kept walking, certain he'd follow, but that may be the chain-link's only gap. So I waited on the stone bridge, on Gapstow Bridge, and waited. The dark, fetid water beneath me seeped a little deeper in the park to the walls of a deserted skating rink. Beyond that, a one-story building in the same dull red brick as my tenement downtown.

Like the surrounding city, Central Park was most battered when Bo and I first wandered it. Yet despite the barren landscape and dusty meadows, the rusted bridges, the malodorous tunnels, the mad lines in black or white spray paint, after rampant vandalism and slow deterioration and disrepair, an alluring aura both peaceful and exciting hovered beneath the trees and along the walkways, all accompanied by frequent, often startling beauty, and something I don't know what else to call but magic. Not that of deception or sleight of hand but the mysterious, overpowering quality that leads to enchantment.

Finally satisfied, Bo slipped back under the fence.

"Bad dog," but he didn't believe me. "So how was it in there?"

And as we moved deeper into the park and a light snow fell as a gray horizon stretched behind the wide, darkening buildings to the west, there in the freezing dusk—alert, motionless— an Indian and his dog. One hand holds a bow and arrow close to his bare chest, his other hand restrains his dog as I sometimes do with Bo. Both he and his dog gaze intently a bit to the right for prey or threat as the New York snow settled lightly upon Bo's back and my dark coat sleeves, and across the Indian and his dog who had quietly confirmed upon me the assurance that I was meant to be a part of this, that I belonged.

CHAPTER TWO

A Walk in the Park

Of Central Park's many winding walkways only one was designed to be straight. Bench-lined, wide as a street and nearly a half mile long, it is the park's grand promenade. On both sides of the walkway are groves of the finest rows of American elm trees in the nation. Almost half of the elms from Central Park to California were lost after Dutch elm disease first appeared in the park in 1930, but these along the promenade survived.

Elms are thick-trunked and rough-barked, their branches muscularly twisting. Growing tall, they stretch above the grove and across the promenade like entwined fingers forming a lofty canopy. Leaves are green or yellow and red depending on the season, a high tunnel of white after a snowfall or else nothing but the bare branches tangled overhead to "form one broad nave," wrote Annie Nathan Meyer of its beauty "beyond that of the most exquisite mediæval carving."

She was born in New York City in 1867, in the first glittering of the Gilded Age, to one of the city's oldest Jewish families, cousin to Emma Lazarus, lovely as a young woman and stately when aged. A fierce promoter of women's equality and founder of Barnard College (New York City's first liberal arts college for women), she loved bicycling through Central Park, a pleasure enhanced at "doing something in the face of society's frown." She wrote prolifically: novels, plays, and essays concerning the conflicts women encounter with both a career and a marriage, and one hundred fanciful pages about Central Park in her lyrical 1898 memoir *My Park Book*. In the park, "but a stone's throw from me the omnibuses rattle, the beer wagons rumble, the carts clatter, and the raucous cry of the newsboy rises above it all." And it is here, along the promenade, that she "withdraws from the crowded streets and is refreshed and strengthened by the solemn twilight of the cathedral, and sits there at peace with one's self, for one brief moment attuned to God... It is here that I worship."

Others have worshipped here also. On the first Easter of World War II, Mayor Fiorello LaGuardia, his wife Marie, and several thousand others gathered at a sunrise service not inside an ornate cathedral but along the promenade in Central Park. Their prayers of gratefulness at the Resurrection rose through the budding branches along with hopes for victory over an evil impossible to imagine that spring of 1942.

Also known as the Mall, the promenade begins just north of the Center Drive: 66th Street in the city. There is an oval patch of earth perhaps ten yards wide, blooming and tended, flanked by two dull statues on pedestals: Shakespeare (though he looked nothing like that), and Columbus again (who invaded a thousand miles south). Neither seems remotely part of the park.

Only one statue was intended for display in Central Park—one meant to portray the gift of love at a place known as the Water Terrace—but in a compromise to convention and financial pressure, the park's designers relented to have other statues placed along the Mall. However intrusive, the works would at least be isolated though other poor ones would appear at places besides the Mall. *The New York Times* art critic Grace Glueck spread the rumor "neither confirmed nor denied by city officials," she concedes, "that some pigeons from out of town, seeking a spot for their annual convention, have turned down Central Park because they find the statues dull."

Still, the Mall could have been worse. The family of Ulysses S. Grant feared that if Saint-Gaudens' golden equestrian of Sherman were mounted permanently outside his dear friend's tomb at 122nd Street and Riverside Drive as initially planned, it would diminish Grant's solemn dignity. Instead, the sacker of Atlanta should march triumphantly along the Mall in the city's new park where trees that might detract from his grandeur would be eliminated.

Along the first steps of the promenade, also called Literary Walk, three more statues, clumsy and overbearing, press upon the walkway. On bulky pedestals are larger-than-life-size renditions of Scotsmen Robert Burns (whose neck apparently had been wrenched before the bronze hardened) and Sir Walter Scott overburdened by a colossal robe. Nearby, Fitz-Greene Halleck, and though the literary reputations of Burns and Scott endure, few remember Halleck, once the favorite poet of New York before the Civil War. Peppy and wide-eyed with pen and notebook in hand, he seems more surprised than any of us that he's on the Mall.

"Sir Walter Scott look[s] as if he had eaten too much haggis," wrote Rupert Hughes in his 1904 novel *The Real New York*, "and Robbie Burns as if he had eaten too little." Hughes's novel is a stylistically awkward tour of the city given by Mr. Gerald DePeyster to a lovely young woman from Chicago, and though dazzled by Central Park, "in the broad light of day [she] could now see the ghastly population of ill-made statuary that disgraces this otherwise ideal pleasure paradise."

"Even were they all adequate as works of art," wrote Annie Nathan Meyer, "how strange to have only one American among them all."

As they did in Ms. Meyer's day fences now keep us from trampling the grove though none were there when Bo and I first roamed it, dusty and ragged, but the early spring day was warm, with soft sunlight reaching like golden fingers through the abundant entanglement of emerging leaves overhead. What first appeared as a thousand black stars descend beneath the elms before Bo scattered them and they rose to the treetops with an audible "whoosh" of their wings. Above us they whistled and squeaked.

Bo had lost a few steps since racing across the college Quadrangle at the sound of my voice. In his seventies now in dog years, he was content to stroll beside me through the meadows and valleys and up the black rock face. Beneath the elms he stalked a squirrel, slowly placing one paw carefully before another, the coiled predator ready to attack. And when the squirrel scampered for a tree Bo gave chase as best he could, barking up at the little creature perched on a branch with taunting chatter.

"Your dog should be on a leash," a woman said to me.

She wore a red coat and a red wool cap over her white hair, her gray-bearded Scottie beside her wearing an identical red wool coat in miniature. She glanced at *her* dog on a leash, then added, "It's the rules."

"Oh, just a little freedom in the park," I replied apologetically.

"He could run away," she declared with certainty.

"Not him," I comforted her. "He'll wander off some but he won't run away."

She considered this a moment, then shook her head, mildly flustered; "Well, it's the rules," and moved on, adding just loud enough for me to hear, "you little prick."

She was right, of course (about the rules); a dog must be "led by a chain or proper dog-string, not exceeding five feet in length," declared "Park Ordinances" of 1866. Nor could we bathe or fish or wade in any of the waters of the park or use "insulting or indecent language" (I should have told her this) or perform "any obscene or indecent act." Rules were once posted everywhere, and a cartoon from those times depicts two bewildered children amid the grove where a sign on every tree and along each footpath forbids something: Keep Off the Grass, No Dogs Allowed, Don't Pick the Flowers.

Frank Leslie's Illustrated Newspaper June 19, 1869

Suddenly a young man zipped along the promenade on a unicycle. He was all in black wearing a top hat and a rectangular black bag over his shoulder. Peddling with steady, graceful ease and leaning slightly forward, he rode quickly far ahead to where the promenade widens. He wound several large figure eights, head lowered and his intense eyes focused a few feet ahead of him. By then he had caught the curiosity of other visitors, yet he still looked at no one. In a quick slip backward off the unicycle he dismounted before a pedestaled bust, leaned the bike against a bench and placed his black bag beside it, bent the knee of his back leg and bowed to the statue—the somber countenance of Beethoven— as the top hat tumbled the length of his outstretched arm into his hand. He straightened up and, with a quick flip of his wrist, the top hat somersaulted back on his head.

From the black bag he withdrew in a dozen arm-lengths a thick rope. He appeared to be in his mid-twenties, fair-skinned and slender with mischievous eyes and reddish-blonde hair trailing from beneath his top hat. One end of the rope he tied to the lamppost near Beethoven, the other end to a tree twenty feet away. By now a crowd had gathered to watch his silent preparations. After securing both ends of the taut rope he took from his black bag a thick piece of white chalk and began drawing a large circle beneath the rope. This would be his performance space, his stage, and the circle meant that we were to remain outside of it. But he needed more room; with both arms extended he smiled politely and gestured for his growing audience to back up a few paces. To one pretty girl in a flowered dress he lowered his hands and wiggled his fingers like Chaplin; to a large fellow the young man mimed pushing a tremendous weight, leaning into it, grimacing. Everyone laughed, even the large fellow.

With white chalk the silent performer encircled the large area beneath the rope from pole to tree. Bo lay at my feet in front of me, his body extended part way into that space the young man was drawing on the pavement. When he came to Bo he abruptly stopped and, still bent over, turned his head; they were nearly nose to snout. He straightened up, glared at my dog and gestured for him to move back. Bo simply watched him. After a moment the young man pointed a finger at Bo and, more emphatically but still silent, gestured for Bo to move from the unfinished chalk circle. Again Bo simply gazed at the young man, one ear perked. With exasperation, the young man stamped his foot, but this triggered Bo's own defenses; he rose quickly and barked as I grabbed his collar and, mimicking fear, the young man took one light, quick step back. After a moment he shrugged his shoulders and continued drawing his circle only now with a small bulge in the line behind which Bo comfortably remained.

And so one winter afternoon in Central Park, my old dog became part of the act of the extraordinary young man who a few years before had given New York City its most captivating forty-five minutes.

Early one August morning in 1974 Philippe Petit performed on a steel cable less than an inch thick strung the night before between the towers of the World Trade Center. The entire city, then the world, was dazzled by his dream that at last came true, a dream conceived once the towers began to rise over lower Manhattan six years before.

"One day New York will be mine," he had written in his exuberant narrative *To Reach the Clouds* (renamed *Man on Wire* after the 2008 Academy Award-winning documentary film of his book). "I'll string a wire somewhere between the tallest buildings and I will become the king of the American sky!"

After that astonishing performance, Philippe finally relented to police demands —or, more accurately, the puzzled, perturbed red eye of a bird hovering above him as he lay on a thin cable invisible a quarter mile below. Once back on the roof of the South Tower he was arrested and charged with every violation the cops could devise: breaking and entering, criminal trespass, reckless endangerment, disobeying police orders (that was the one that really irritated them), even performing without a permit. His fingerprints were taken though Philippe suggested they should be his toe prints.

In the end, Guy Tozzoli, president of the World Trade Center, intervened with the judge to drop all charges. After all, "The Coup," as Philippe called the wondrous event, had occurred during a severe economic downturn in New York in which the city still suffered, and the performance had provided much unintended publicity for the World Trade Center badly needing tenants—but there was one condition: Philippe must perform a juggling act for children in Central Park.

Only days before he had walked a wire across the tallest structures ever created by man; a juggling act was no encore. Philippe declared (again without "permission") at a press conference that he would walk on a wire across Central Park's Lake Belvedere (aka Turtle Pond) to the Castle. People were thrilled, and both the city and park succumbed to his charming, mad, and holy aura.

Five thousand people gathered on the shores of Lake Belvedere that summer night. From anchorage on the eastern side to a castle window eighty feet above the water and the rocks, the wire stretched for six hundred feet (the distance between the Towers, he informed us, was a mere 135 feet) and made all the more dangerous after Philippe announced that he couldn't swim.

Wearing a silver satin shirt and white bell-bottoms, he was lit by a spotlight like a shining apparition in the darkness as a band played "The Daring Young Man on the Flying Trapeze." And though having danced a quarter mile above Manhattan, he nearly fell that night when someone yanked the wire near its anchorage along the shore. He caught himself, struggled to gain his balance, righted himself (all the while holding a thirty-five-pound balancing pole), then continued on his way before bowing with a flourish of his arm. *The Daily News* pointed out that, despite his close call, he had walked in Central Park and "wasn't mugged."

Keeping his walks closer to the ground and, along with Bo, his performance space within his chalk circle, Philippe Petit gave us a charming, daring show. He danced upon the sagging rope, juggled three clubs while standing on one foot, then swooped through the crowd with his upturned top hat into which we dropped dollar bills and all our loose change. We watched him untie the rope, toss it in the black bag, bow to us as he had earlier to Beethoven, then mount his unicycle and sped away; circling once, he raised his top hat before vanishing down the promenade.

"Bo!" I yelled as my dog chased after the unicycle. "Bo!"

To Make an Eden

Retreating glaciers as high as the Empire State Building molded the northern half of this continent 12,000 years ago, gouging trenches for a great river and forming land masses the Dutch would name Brooklyn and Staten Island. These gave natural protection from violent ocean weather to a slender island its first inhabitants called "Mannahatta."

From winter caves far at the island's northern tip, the Lenape – meaning "The People"— of the Algonquin tribe wound their careful, unobtrusive way south through thick forests of poplar and pines and oaks and chestnuts which they shared with wolves, bears, mountain lions, deer, fox, bobcats, beaver, and fifty million birds. Three thousand years before Europe invaded they crossed pure streams and circled ponds and skirted hills on a winding trail called Wichquasgeck until they reached their fishing coves at the island's southern end. Here lay enormous lobsters and bountiful beds of oysters and mussels and clams owing to Muhheakantuck, the "river that flows both ways." Like all rivers it seeks the ocean, but often a great tidal surge carries the Atlantic from the Upper Bay many miles upriver, and sometimes those surges mix with the river heading to the sea, and the river indeed flows both ways.

Late in the summer of 1609 the eighty-ton *Half Moon* sailed up Muhheakantuck, its three masts riding high on the water and, in the words of its captain, "proved clumsy in foul weather." A carrack with four cannon and carrying tons of supplies for its crew of twenty, *Half Moon* belonged to the Dutch East India Company and was under the command of Henry Hudson, an Englishman. Though Hudson never discovered the Northwest Passage as had been his lofty prediction, his Dutch patrons in Amsterdam soon realized he had dropped anchor in something more valuable than a quicker way to the Orient: the greatest natural harbor on the Atlantic Seaboard. As Hudson recalled, "God has never poured/ A stream more royal through a land more rich."

Nearly three centuries later, Norwegian explorer Roald Amundsen navigated his ship *Gjöa* through the elusive waterways from ocean to ocean just as Hudson had believed.

The Dutch quickly swindled the island from its aboriginal inhabitants by insisting the copper pots and axe handles and rope given them were not in gratitude for allowing the Dutch on their land but as full payment for it. The Dutch widened the Lenape's meandering trail and renamed it Brege Wege, the southern end soon blocked by wooden houses built from the cleared forest where could be heard snorting hogs, mournful dairy cows, a strange language (French, which some Natives would learn), and in 1625 the infant wails of Sarah, daughter of Catalina and Joris Trico, the first white child born in New Amsterdam.

Well the Dutch knew the natural resources and visual beauty of the New World's golden edge: "All the blessings man e'er knew," wrote the first poet of New Amsterdam, "does our Great Giver strew." Arriving in the colony from Holland perhaps in 1653 and serving as a clerk for the West India Company, Jacob Steendam wrote "The Complaint of New Amsterdam to Its Mother" where the town itself tells the reason for such gifts.

> Two streams my garden bind,
> From the East and North they wind,
> Rivers pouring in the sea
> Rich in fish beyond degree.

Despite several years of stumbling starts, the harbor town of New Amsterdam eventually flourished so profitably that the British claimed it; after all, Henry Hudson was an Englishman, so the island rightly belonged to England. In 1664 four ships aimed their deadly cannons at the small wooden town which surrendered without a shot fired. The town was renamed New York for the king's brother, the Duke of York, and the Dutch name for the Indian's old trail was translated into English; Broad Way remains the only street stretching the entire length of the island and still winding to avoid a vanished pond and leveled hill.

But those "two streams" that bind the Dutch garden are salt water, brackish at best; the island's freshwater rivulets and creeks—unspoiled by the Natives over several thousand years— gradually turned to sewers, the communal Collect Pond fowled with tanning and trash. In malodorous scenes Pete Hamill describes the consequence of this abuse in his magical *Forever*, one of New York's great panoramic novels. We follow Cormac O'Connor for over 250 years after he has received the gift— and curse— of eternal life on the condition he never leave the island of Manhattan, and we are with him in the 1830s when—

> The result [of so little water] was the stinking city....
> Many thousands of human beings were shitting and
> pissing in privies, emptying slops into the streets. Gar-
> bage was piled in the streets to be gathered later, and
> the mounds served as wormy meals for pigs and dogs
> and goats and rats....As the town filled up... the stench
> grew worse. Crowded Sunday churches used lots of in-
> cense to overwhelm the stench of the faithful, and when
> August broiled the city, sea captains claimed that they
> could smell New York six miles out to sea.

On June 27, 1842, a hundred and fifty million-gallon distributing reservoir constructed at York Hill in the middle of Manhattan opened with a thirty-eight gun salute, one shot for each mile of water carried along the Croton Aqueduct from the watershed to the north. This extraordinary creation–and the one most essential for this expanding city—piped water to a receiving reservoir 1,826 feet long and 836 feet wide between 79th and 86th streets, with Sixth and Seventh avenues its perimeter. The sloping stone walls extended deep into the earth, its base eighty feet thick tapering to eighteen feet at the top where a walkway provided stunning views from the center of the island. At higher sea level than downtown, water flowed by gravity to the smaller holding reservoir at 42nd Street, where the stately public library is today, on its restorative journey to the needy masses below 14th Street.

Now we could wash the filthy, garbage-filled streets of dead animals, human excrement, rotten vegetables, and hopefully yellow fever, cholera, and dysentery. After two centuries when so much had been lost to fire, here was a powerful weapon to fight it. Water had been so scarce most of us had warm beer for breakfast, not coffee and tea, and though we could find remedy for our thirsts, to bathe was divine. Nothing renewed and redeemed like a bath, and soon the first bathhouse opened on Mott Street.

But the extraordinary wave, year after year, of new arrivals into New York City during the middle of the nineteenth century soon exceeded the capacity of the reservoir. When it opened in 1842 there were 312,000 of us; within merely a decade, 515,000, and 850,000 in the next ten years, nearly tripling the city's population in a single generation; "Immigrants arriving, fifteen or twenty thousand in a week," wrote a rapturous Walt Whitman. More water was desperately needed, so another reservoir nearly seven times larger holding a billion gallons was, with practicality, planned a few steps north of the original reservoir, and this enormous, new supply of water—along with the insight of a brilliant, doomed young man—destined Central Park's eminent location in the center of Manhattan.

CHAPTER THREE

Garden of Sacred Gatherings

After Bo had chased the wire walker and I chased after Bo, we found where the promenade has been leading us all along: to a central plaza, an "open air hall of reception," the park's communal heart. Originally called the Water Terrace, it is where the efforts of four extraordinary artists blend: an English architect and landscape designer, an eccentric ornamentalist, a gifted sculptor with the right connections, and a writer living on Staten Island. Each part is dependent on the other three for the full effect, but even the artists were amazed by what their unified talents created.

We arrive by crossing the road ("Olmsted and Vaux Way" at what would be 72nd Street) or descending a grand staircase to pass beneath it. Before doing either, two squat balustrades stand at each side of the staircase. Carved into the balustrade to the east is a rooster, a sunrise, a thatched cottage; on the west balustrade, an owl, an oil lamp and book, a witch on her broomstick. We've entered a world of nature and imagination.

The wide staircase leads beneath the roadway through three Romanesque arches into the Arcade. We are enclosed on three sides, our steps reverberant, faded murals on the walls of nymphs entwined with branches. Here we find shade from the sun, shelter from rain, warmth in winter. But I did not take the stairs beneath the roadway. Instead, I followed Bo across the road to a balcony where two grand staircases, each with a landing halfway through the descent, leads to a large terrace of pink brick and stone. In the center, a basin nearly a hundred feet in circumference, and rising twenty feet from the basin is a column with a smaller basin atop it where stand four chubby cherubs. Hovering above it all, an angel.

Until now the park had been for us tall trees, rolling, barren meadows, bench-lined walkways, the polluted pond and, except for the Indian and his dog, uninspiring statues. But suddenly Central Park evolved into a palace under the sky or a temple to the sun, a sight regal, majestic, stunning, my eyes passing again and again over the terrace, the lake behind it and, beyond that, a forest. In my New York City dreams I never envisioned anything like this.

Though of bronze the angel hovering above the basin appears light and ethereal; after all, having descended from heaven she is buoyed by outstretched wings. Her expression is one of repose, a gown covers her to the ankles, and she steps lightly forward on her left foot. In her left hand she holds a long-stemmed lily, a symbol of purity. Her right hand extends before her as if she is about to touch something.

I descend one of the grand staircases. On the ramps along the first landing, intricate carvings of great, flowing scrolls of branches and entwined twigs abundant with buds and seeds, pine cones and flowers. In this land of plenty the nuts are big as baseballs, flowers the size of a sun hat; it's like Oz. Among this display are birds, also larger than truth, perched on branches snapping at a thick worm from a leaf or else in motionless flight that shifted with movement as the sun traveled through the day.

While perusing the scrolls I heard in the distance Bo's angry bark and the cackling from irritated geese. I ran down the staircase for a dusty embankment leading to the lake where three Canada geese had just

splashed into the water, rumple-feathered and squawking; Bo paced the shore barking demandingly even after the birds had quieted themselves and drifted further away.

"Leave those geese alone," I scolded. "And they're almost bigger than you."

He wanted to wade in after them but I pulled him back from the floating trash.

"Come on," and I pushed him ahead, then let go of his collar. "Now they know there's a new dog in the park."

As I was returning to the staircase Bo headed back for a last bark.

"Come on!" I yelled, kicking at him, and though he knew I'd always miss he scooted ahead anyway.

At the staircases again I tried picking up the pattern of the Terrace, but I would linger here many times before it came clear, like dots connected gradually. Those balustrades at the top of the staircases across the roadway were the first subtle indication: the rooster was to the east, the owl to the west, one is day, the other night. Each staircase ramp is a season: furthest east, spring on one scroll, summer the next, with autumn and then winter on the west staircase. And each season continues down the stairs with carvings of trillium and dogwood for the spring, roses and strawberries for summer; down the landing of the west staircase, autumn corn and peas, with thorns and pine cones for winter including a pair of strap-on ice skates. On the Terrace floor, each season's balustrade: a nest with baby birds for spring, a honeybee comb in summer, quail and dry tubers for autumn in the western balustrade, roosting birds in leafless winter branches. It was like discovering Homeric parallels in *Ulysses*.

"On no public building in America," wrote art critic Clarence Cook in 1869, "has there yet been placed any sculpture so rich in design as this or so exquisitely delicate in execution. All the sculpture on the walls of the new House of Parliament in London is not worth, either for design or execution, these four ramps of the great stairs of the Terrace alone."

But when I first saw the Terrace late that winter afternoon in 1977, no water sparkled in the basin clogged with wads of yellowed newspaper, beer cans, and discarded, filthy clothing. Black, mad lines marred the basin's blue stone rim, the balustrades and the Terrace floor. And every sandstone bird along the flowing scrolls of the grand staircases had been decapitated. Every one of them. Dozens.

Although Central Park is seen as the city's oasis, our lungs and backyard, it is also a victim of New York's brutality: busted lampposts, graffiti, splintered benches, the trash. But the violation of these tender birds was something different; this I could not shrug off with casual dismay as erosion, indifference, financial crises, and collapse. I brooded on the birds flying headless and still through the epic scrolls which seemed like the park itself, created with effort and desire but finally so fragile.

Suddenly I felt deep tenderness not only for these ravaged birds but the entire park; if my lover, I would kiss the scars. And despite the waterless, trash-filled basin, the bizarre, painted letters along the walls, even the brutalized birds, Central Park was beautiful, heartbreaking but beautiful, a glorious ruin, Babylon revisited or Apollo's oracle after the ravenous Huns. I am Ozymandias. Above it, unspoiled and serene, that angel.

The iconic image of Central Park and the only statue intended for it was created by a gifted and progressive sculptor from New York City. Born late in the summer of 1815 to a wealthy banking family, Emma Stebbins overcame the restrictions of antebellum New York by learning her craft despite the obstacles meant to inhibit female sculptors. Her drawings of an angel for the Terrace fountain intended for the city's new and glorious park found their way to the park designers because of the belief in her held by her brother Henry, head of the New York Stock Exchange, and chairman of the Committee on Statuary, Fountains, and Architectural Structures in Central Park. Her commission was the first in New York granted to a woman.

Her idea for the fountain was a variation of an earlier work. After reading Henry Wadsworth Longfellow's poem "Sandalphon" Ms. Stebbins completed a sculpture of the angel at the Gates of Heaven gathering people's prayers that turn to red and purple flowers.

> And he gathers the prayers as he stands,
> And they change into flowers in his hands,
> Into garlands of purple and red;
> And beneath the great arch to the portal,
> Through the streets of the City Immortal
> Is wafted the fragrance they shed.

Her angel that the poem inspired is a quiet, gentle creature, fe-male despite the traditional belief that angels were male, like the one in Longfellow's poem. She holds flowers, her short, wavy hair is pulled off her face, and her chin is lowered as if gazing at something beneath her to the right.

The designers of Central Park hoped "the idea of that central spirit of 'Love' " would emanate from the figure meant for the fountain with-out knowing of the deep, committed bond between the sculptor and her model Charlotte Cushman, the first native-born star of the American theater. Despite society's scorn and the wedge it drove between Stebbins and her family, the two women remained dedicated to each other for the rest of their lives.

They met in Rome in 1854, Stebbins studying under the sculptor John Gibson, and Charlotte Cushman recently separated after a ten-year relationship with Matilda Hays, translator of the works of George Sand, pen name for Amantine-Lucile-Aurore Dupin. But before Central Park's angel was complete, Charlotte Cushman was diagnosed with breast cancer. She underwent a lumpectomy where the tumor, not the breast, is removed, but the years that followed were arduous and emotionally draining on her as well as on those who loved her. "I pray to God to take me quickly," she wrote, "so that I may not torture those I love by let-ting them see my pain." Surely her greatest concern was Emma Stebbins, who, forsaking sculpture, devoted the remainder of her life to caring for her companion.

The angel was unveiled on a mild afternoon late in the spring of 1873 at a place forever afterward known as Bethesda Terrace. Though created with deep love, the piece was dedicated not to its spirit that the park creators had hoped but rather "to the blessed gift of pure, whole-some water" brought to New York by the first reservoir completed nearly three decades before. The inestimable value of fresh water "to all count-less homes of this great city," Stebbins wrote, "comes like an angel visi-tant." She alludes to the Gospel story in John and the pool of water in Jerusalem named Bethesda where an angel descended and 'moved' the waters that then healed the sick, the blind, the withered, and with Ms. Cushman's condition predominant in their minds, both women surely hoped for such powers at the angel's unveiling.

Angel of the Waters received mixed reviews. *The New York Evening Post* reported that "spectators [were] at once filled...with emotions of delight and admiration" that the angel was "soft and tender...a being of all light and love." But *The New York Times* thought the fountain first of all badly misplaced so near the lake, "like adding sugar to sweetmeats," and as for the angel, "from a rear view...resembled a servant girl executing a polka . . . in the privacy of the back kitchen" while "the head is distinctly a male head....and infinitely inferior" to John Quincy Adams Ward's *Shakespeare* placed along the Mall the year before. Ward also sculpted my beloved Indian and his dog.

The criticism wounded Emma Stebbins, eroding what little self-confidence she had. Despite her independent nature and unconventional lifestyle, she was a modest woman who "desired domestic contentment," wrote Elizabeth Milroy in "The Public Career of Emma Stebbins," along with "spiritual happiness, and quiet self-expression." But her primary concern now was not public reaction to her statue but the care of her companion and her final New York performance. On November 7, 1874, Charlotte Cushman played Lady Macbeth at Booth's Theatre on East 23rd Street and Sixth Avenue. After repeated curtain calls, accolades, a tribute given along with a wreath of oak leaves by William

Cullen Bryant, Ms. Cushman returned to her hotel in a carriage drawn by four white horses and flanked by 150 police. They did not have far to travel, for she stayed at the Fifth-Avenue Hotel, the city's most fashionable only a block east. Grateful for the lavish tribute, she must have been immensely pleased that her dear companion accompanied her, for we always want those we love most to share with us in our happiness. As America's first lady of the theater appeared on the hotel balcony, fifteen thousand people greeted her with applause and the Ninth Regiment Band serenaded as Roman candles and fireworks illuminated Madison Square across the street.

Charlotte Cushman died of pneumonia less than two years later, and Emma Stebbins spent the rest of her life writing *Charlotte Cushman: Her Letters and Memories of Her Life* published in 1879. Her other sculptures for the park's new reservoir—*Receiving Gates* and *Dispensing Gates* that resembled Greek goddesses enthroned with tritons—were cast only in plaster and never fully realized. Suffering for years with pulmonary diseases caused by marble dust inhaled as she worked, Emma Stebbins died in 1882 of an illness referred to then as phthisis, a "gradual wasting away." Rather than buried beside Charlotte Cushman in Mount Auburn Cemetery, Cambridge, Massachusetts, Emma Stebbins lies with her family in Brooklyn's Green-Wood Cemetery, and one early October afternoon in 1991, the first 5K "Race for the Cure" for breast cancer ended with 2,500 women beneath the Angel's healing fingertip.

CHAPTER FOUR

City at the Edge of the Trees

Reading over what I've written so far, it appears as if my new life in New York occurred only in Central Park, yet it had been the city that lured me, not in bewitching whispers but with a Siren's beckoning song. I had come to Manhattan in my seething, young manhood to partake in the fall of civilization; at the time New York was the capital of that too. Central Park was an unexpected bonus.

At the warm edge of a Midwestern summer six months before a pillar of my life had crumbled and I watched it happen: her interest in feminist literature courses (which I supported), wanting her maiden name again (I could understand), a curiosity about lesbianism (that aroused me), her annoyance each time I put grapes in my mouth and talked like the Godfather.

"I've met someone else," she said, her chin uplifted, "and I want no restrictions on this relationship."

There were only two choices but one was impossible: "Then we shouldn't live together anymore."

She nodded once affirmatively and moved out that afternoon, but her fragrance lingered in her emptied closet long weeks after she freed herself, and a ghostly outline of her vanished Vasarely poster remained on the bedroom wall.

Once the fall term began I abandoned any work in graduate school and instead drove with Bo too fast along the back roads of central Illinois, the dust raised by my spinning tires settling on the cornstalks, tall and dry and green. At night I prowled the sleeping campus after stumbling desperate and unsatisfied from the next woman's bed until one chilly November night when from the sky came a long, soft wail with tiny breaks in it. The sound grew closer until, like an endless, swaying rope, a flock of Canada geese flew across the white disk of the full moon, their necks outstretched like spoons. "Out! Out!" they cried to me far below, "Out! Out!" in a long and broken chant. Where to flee was easy; always New York's innumerable streets and dark, surrounding water had pandered with arrogance and anonymity, decadence and decay, renegades and romantics, promises, pain, the predatory taxi, and with the end of one world I no longer resisted the other.

When not in the park and with ever widening gyres, I began at my front stoop to find nestled amid a Puerto Rican neighborhood, diminished but enduring in this city of immigrants and grandparents, my Jewish heritage. My maternal grandfather as a boy had passed through Ellis Island, then lived on Willett off Delancey Street only a few blocks from here. His parents arranged a marriage to my Brooklyn-born grandmother, and together they journeyed across half America bearing seven daughters along the way. It was Grandma Gussie with her white hair and jolly laughter who had stitched in me the first threads of New York's wonder as she told how Grandpa always fed the "boyds" before going to "woyk" in the garment industry on "Toyty-toyd" Street.

Outside my own kitchen windows, traffic on Houston ran across town through lower Manhattan, and like a true New Yorker I pronounce correctly the name of this wide, two-way street: "house-ton" for the Continental Congress delegate, not the Texas hero who was a boy when the street was named. Nearby, in a small storefront of a dilapidated walk-up, Yonah Schimmel Knish Bakery, "Original Since 1910" (their knishes are so delicious). What's a knish? A kind of bun, thin dough stuffed with mashed potatoes and meats and onions, boiled or fried or baked, square or round, the size of a fist.

Each Sunday, Orchard Street (once James Delancey's orchard) is closed to traffic from Houston a half-mile downtown to Canal Street (once a canal, the young city's open sewer). On wooden platforms along the sidewalks, merchants closed for yesterday's Sabbath now sell underwear and socks, sheets and bed pads, linens and towels and spools of thread all at a discount beneath the aroma of fresh breads and butter cookies on delicious waves from small, battered Moishe's bakery. West of Orchard Street, Russ and Daughters for borscht and bagels, lox and halvah, cashews and jellied fruit candy. Further east at the corner of Ludlow, Katz's Deli where schmoozers behind the counter slice tender corned beef or pastrami on soft rye bread with pickles and coleslaw and we sip

Dr. Brown sodas. Above our heads, a greasy sign rotating on a string: "Send a Salami to Your Boy in the Army." With three sons in uniform during World War II killing the Nazi bastards, the owners themselves sent plenty.

Streit's Matzo still rose on Rivington Street, and on Essex a green booth where in large wooden barrels pickles and tomatoes bob in spicy brine. A few blocks uptown, the remains of the tyrannical, peg-leg Director-Governor Peter Stuyvesant at St. Mark's Church on Second Avenue; had he his way, none of us would have ever landed on this island.

The summer feasts in Little Italy were more vibrant and crowded than those I watched again and again in *Mean Streets* and *The Godfather II*. Chinatown still humbly remained below Canal Street, pandering with mysterious, narrow, congested streets. Open markets of fresh fish in icy tin trays crowded beside baskets of vegetables and fruits in exotic colors and shapes and bins of crabs still alive, their pinchers grasping, at air, for escape. Each Sunday morning south of Delancey, in a narrow park between Chrystie and Forsyth streets, Chinese men gather to chat and puff on cigarettes; exhaled gray smoke rises to their birds chirping in bamboo cages hung in the branches above their heads. Nearby on Eldridge Street, a bearded man dressed in purple pants and a purple tie-dyed shirt with a purple ski cap, purple sunglasses and purple Converse All Stars tended a flourishing garden of flowers and tomatoes and even stalks of corn six-feet high in an empty lot between two battered tenements. It was the first promise I saw for a better city.

In my East Village were Polish butcher shops, small Indian restaurants on East 6th Street where the sitar twanged through speakers, and the scary East 3rd Street headquarters of the Hells Angels (who'll toss you off the roof, ran one erroneous rumor, just for photographing their motorcycles). Above the doorway of the dim Ottendorfer Library on Second Avenue at St. Mark's (the first branch of the New York Public Library), a ghost lingered– spelled in stone– when this part of town was Kleindeutschland (Little Germany): FREIE BIBLIOTHEK u LESEHALLE. The German community that fled their fatherland's political terrors for New York in the middle of the 19th century once flourished on these streets, but in hopes of escaping a terrible memory moved four miles uptown. Because what began as a church excursion along the East River on the mild Sunday morning of June 15, 1904, ended with the death, by flames or drowning, of 1,021 souls when their steamboat *General Slocum* caught fire. There is a plaque of remembrance along the fence of St. Mark's Church, and in the center of Tompkins Square nearby is a memorial fountain of pink marble where two children gaze toward flowers beside the inscription, "They Were Earth's Purest Children Young and Fair." During his odyssey through Dublin the day after the tragedy, Leopold Bloom "passed Gorgan's the tobacconist against which newsboards leaned and told of the dreadful catastrophe in New York."

In a soft snowfall I stood beneath what had been Allen Ginsberg's fire escape at 206 East 7th Street where Kerouac had smoked a cigarette. I sipped ale down the block at McSorley's which appeared exactly like John Sloan's dim paintings of it, had mushroom-barely soup and lavishly buttered challah at the counter of B&H Dairy on Second Avenue, wandered Strand's stocked bookshelves on East 12th. To the west, Greenwich Village with bookstores, cozy restaurants, over-lit pizza stands, shops selling tobacco and rolling papers, and dark, intimate, tin-ceiling Café Reggio for cappuccino and almond cookies. On summer nights Washington Square filled with music, Rastafarians, NYU students, and us locals as marijuana smoke rose to the black, starless sky, starless because Manhattan burned so bright until the evening of July 13th when the lights blew out after several scorching days that without fans or air conditioners turned even hotter.

Candles sparkled from windows in the Blackout of 1977 as bodegas and restaurants gave away melting ice cream. People roamed the broiling streets with laughter and flashlights while kerosene lanterns lit stoops where we tried finding a breath of relief from the stifling apartments above. Only later did we learn of vandalism and looting, injuries and mass arrests, but East First Street partied with Latin music blasting from a battery-powered boom box and headlights harsh and luminous from Cisco's Firebird casting long, thin shadows down the street.

During those decaying, vibrant years each part of the city listened to its own music. Downtown around the corner at CBGB's, thin, edgy, pale kids smoked cigarettes and resembled Sid Vicious and Patti Smith; in the Bronx Bambaataa hot-wired the street lights to power his hip-hop parties. On my turntable I listened to a 45 of "Up on the Roof" by the Drifters but mostly played again and again *Darkness on the Edge of Town* ("life's on the line where dreams are found and lost" on these "streets of fire"). And while Bianca discoed on cocaine and 54th Street the real song of the city was "Shattered" by the Rolling Stones where "Life's just a cocktail party on the street…Laughter, joy, and loneliness/ And sex and sex and sex and sex."

And there was Times Square.

42nd Street west of Seventh Avenue was a teeming row of small movie theaters showing kung-fu or porn even if titled *The Swedish Marriage Manual.* Narrow storefronts of twenty-five-cent peep shows in video booths reeked of bleach while a mournful guy lingered in the rear with a bucket and mop. The huge arcade of "Girls Girls Girls" in private booths behind plexi-glass, that was Show World lewdly splayed across the entire northwest corner at 42nd and Eighth Avenue.

"Pride and joy and greed and sex," wrote Jagger in the back seat of a New York taxi, "that's what makes our town the best."

Tall, exotic black women and some black men dressed like exotic women pranced W. 42nd Street in towering platform shoes and short-shorts as colorful as their wigs. In winter they wore the same thing only with fake fur coats. Stooped men in cheap suits either approached them, settled terms, and headed for barren, battered Bryant Park or else scored quickly a packet of heroin from a young runner before taking *it* to the park. It was decadent and erotic and uninhibited, and we didn't know AIDS lurked in the shadows, mysterious and lethal.

In Times Square, West 43rd between Broadway and Seventh Avenue is named Adolph S. Ochs Street for the publisher of *The New York Times* who had the entire area renamed after his paper leapt here from Park Row in 1904; he celebrated the event with a New Year's Eve fireworks display from atop his new tower. Fireworks being illegal, Ochs lowered a lighted ball the year after that and we've done so off the same building ever since. But no street honored him when I first walked it, and where the police precinct is today was at that time a sex shop flaunting XXX and dildos in the Times Tower's front window.

"I've been shattered,/ My brain has been battered,/ Splattered all over Manhattan."

At the corner of Broadway and West 44th beating a snare drum, his shiny black hair greased back and twirling his drum sticks as he imitated different drummers' styles like he did on the big screen, that odd little man from *Taxi Driver.* He was the first movie star I saw. Nearby, loud with the clatter of strength tests, skee-ball, banging bells, and shooting galleries, Playland smelled of burnt popcorn and sweat. And there, between a circus and the seashore, a pinball machine of Central Park: lovers, the lawn, children skipping rope, a hurdy-gurdy man, tall buildings in the distance, and a monkey who tapped a bell for each one thousand points I rung up with all my quarters, feeling lucky.

And a desperate month after first arriving, I found that job I needed. Not what New York dangles as temptation, the pandering promise; no editor or publisher or magazine in the literary capital of the world returned my calls. But in the middle of East First Street, in a green storefront that became for an early hour each workday morning the center of a whirlwind of voices and air-brakes and the rattle of tail-gates thrown open, was the office of Spartacus Trucking. It was a small operation with three trucks, two step-vans, and a van, yet none of the vehicles carried the company's name nor was it written on the store-front window. So after twenty years of schooling I was as close as I could get to what Jack

London would have done.

Inside the store-front, a man wearing a Yankees ball cap and a Fu-Man Choo moustache was on the phone sitting at a desk with another man half-way through the room behind him. The narrow office was over-lit and cluttered with pieces of a sofa wrapped in gray blankets, dollies, a hand-truck, and open boxes of packing tape.

Still on the phone, the man at the front desk asked, "Yeah?"

"You hiring?"

"Talk to Neil," then jerked a thumb to the man behind him and returned to his call.

Neil was compact, sweet-faced, shaggy, also on the phone asking emphatically, "You're kidding, right?" but then, in a softer voice, asked me, "Got a driver's license?"

"Yes."

"CDL?"

"What's a CDL?"

"Not for that neither," he declared back into the phone. "Do better or it stays in Michigan," then quietly to me, "So you want to be a helper."

"Yes."

"Work early, late?"

"Anytime."

"Good," he cried into phone. "We'll be there in the morning," then hung up.

"Overnight?"

I hesitated, then, "No. I've got a grandfather to care for."

He sat back and smiled: "I've seen you with that dog," and he nodded a few times. "You're new on the block. Where from?"

"Illinois. Where *you* from?"

"Why you want to work the trucks?"

"You wake me every morning so I may as well get paid for it."

His smile faded as the phone rang; he sat forward and said, "Okay" while reaching for the phone. "Seven tomorrow. The pay's shit and the health insurance policy is don't get hurt."

That night I celebrated with bags of groceries from Met Food and a nickel bag of herb from the Rastafarian music and tee-shirt store on First Avenue; even a newcomer like me could spot it. Bo and I walked up Bowery where the top few floors of the Empire State Building uptown gleamed like a white castle floating above the city beneath it. We turned right on St. Marks, past a used clothing store and Grassroots Tavern a few steps down and a shop selling Bamboo and pipes of all sorts and where a young woman with short purple hair sat on the sidewalk with a wooden tray before her. Among leather lanterns where seashells dangled beside bracelets of colorful twine were the snipped, slender handles of filigree spoons bent to form a ring. "And they're so easily adjustable," she assured me.

I widened one, then slipped over my ring finger the first ring I had worn since removing a gold band last summer that seemed far more distant than just a few months ago. Because I had changed the look of my world, the past had receded quickly until it almost seemed as if it never happened, that I've always lived in New York, my life back there and then like recollections of a novel I can barely recall. And as we headed home down Second Avenue, among two dozen other 'a buck a book' spread along the sidewalk on a bedsheet, I bought my first book about the park simply titled *The Central Park Book*. Inside the tall, slender, paperback, battered and green like the park, were essays about the men who designed it, the forests and animals, the statues and bridges, even what's edible. Back in my apartment, after Bo had turned several slow circles on his rug in a distant link to the wolf flattening the leaves and twigs of its bed, he settled down with a grunt and was soon snoring like a grandpa as I read late into the night.

That was when I first saw the names Frederick Law Olmsted and Calvert Vaux and learned with mild astonishment that the park hadn't always appeared as it does, that these wooded acres and rolling landscapes once had few trees and no valleys or ponds until the winning entry of a contest held in 1858 set in motion a most remarkable transformation; it was called the "Greensward Plan." For the next fifteen years men with horse-drawn carts, explosives, pix-ax and shovels molded the land into the park it would become: across two pages, a detailed map of the park. With a finger I trailed along all that we had explored and how much more we hadn't. In the center of the map, a rectangle –'Croton Water Works—Old Reservoir'—and beyond that a much larger 'Croton Water Works—New Receiving Reservoir' shaped like a genuine lake. Then more park all the way to 110th Street.

"Tomorrow we'll head north," I whispered to Bo. As weariness spread upward through my body and First Street grew quiet, I clicked off the light, placed the open book across my chest, closed my eyes and imagined flying above the park, over the treetops and the pond, the meadows and walkways, rising until I could see the entire breath of Central Park, then I fell asleep.

To Make an Eden *continued*

New York is "more scantily furnished with breathing places…than any city in the world," scolded William Cullen Bryant in his1844 *New York Evening Post* editorial "A New Public Park." He demanded that city authorities "give our vast population an extensive pleasure ground for shade and recreation" before all the woodlands were devoured by Manhattan's relentless march uptown. A park "commensurate with our magnificent expectation," he added, "is a physical necessity and cannot be postponed without detriment to the true interests of the city." Meanwhile across the river in Brooklyn, a young Walt Whitman, writing newspaper articles and the poems that would change literature forever, pleaded that New York have "a dash of nature; greenness, a patch of sward, a tree, a grassy knoll."

Heeding Bryant's widely read and influential words, Mayor Caleb Smith Woodhull called for a park to serve as "the great breathing spaces of the toiling masses." His successor Ambrose Kingsland also pressed the urgency of a park that "would be the favorite resort of all" but essential "to the health, happiness, and comfort of…the poorer classes."

All agreed a park was needed, but why so large a park on such a slender island being rapidly devoured by rapacious and unprecedented urban spread was destined by a visionary, practical, short-sighted, controversial project commonly known as The Grid.

In 1796, so as to discontinue laying narrow, untidy streets randomly first planned out by the Dutch and later the English, the city council hired Polish-born surveyor Casimir Goerck to refine what he and several surveyors had created a few years before: a Jeffersonian-style grid to make small parcels of land more practical to sell on acres in the middle of the island referred to as the Common Lands. Selling the parcels proved so efficient that a similar grid was requested of the entire island, from the East River (also appearing as "the Sound" on the map) to the Hudson (referred to as both "North River" and "Hudson's River"), and from North Street (later renamed Houston Street) one hundred and fifty-five blocks uptown. It was a bold belief in the city's future as neighborhoods were drawn that would have no residents for another century.

Before designing the larger grid, Goerck died in 1798 during New York's third deadly yellow fever outbreak, this one killing more than two thousand. Many of the dead whose families could not afford the four dollar coffin were buried in a potter's field where Washington Square is today. Creating the enormous grid was assigned to a young man from Albany, John Randel, Jr., and though only twenty years old he had apprenticed the past eight years for Simeon DeWitt, Surveyor General of New York State. Four years later Randel completed the penciled, unadorned survey map; it is "simple but astonishing," wrote Hilary Ballon in *The Great Grid: The Master Plan of Manhattan 1811-2011*, "structured but flexible, and embodies the forward thinking that prepared Manhattan for its unimaginably great future."

All new streets would now be sixty feet wide and running parallel across the island: every half-mile or so, streets with two-way traffic one hundred feet wide. Twelve avenues, also one hundred feet wide, would run perpendicular to the streets, and all were to be numbered rather than named. This would speed up business and diminish by one the challenges for the city's vast immigrant population who struggled with an unfamiliar language but easily recognized numbers. Broadway was left to its meanderings created centuries before the Dutch invasion, and though the grid begins at North Street/Houston Street, Greenwich Villagers kept their own unconventional ways; the commissioner must have tossed the grid plan helplessly in the air had he stood at the corner where West 10th Street crosses West 4th. And the first street drawn on the grid, from Avenue A west to Bowery, were all three blocks of my East First Street.

The Commissioners' Plan of 1811 (as the grid was known) drained the island's ponds and streams and chopped down nearly every tree, including the last living remnant of New Amsterdam –the pear tree planted in 1667 by Peter Stuyvesant at what is now East 13th Street and Third Avenue. Remarkably, the plan leveled mid-town hills on an island whose aboriginal name Mannahatta means "Island of the Hills." Every foot above North Street was surveyed, the iron spikes driven into the ground eventually transformed into streets and avenues. What the map omitted was noticed immediately: no open spaces.

Few New Yorkers took carriages to their estates several miles up the island nor could afford a ferry boat to luxurious Coney Island resorts. For fresh air and distance from the city we walked to the rivers found at the end of nearly every Manhattan street; though the *Pequot* sailed from Nantucket on its fateful encounter with Moby-Dick, the epic story begins with Ishmael gazing across the waters off Battery Park "washed by waves, and cooled by breezes...." But in the city's energetic commercial expansion, the docks lining the thriving seaport soon made the rivers accessible only to the boldest boys skinny dipping among the pier posts beneath Walt Whitman's wistful eye. For pastoral scenes and open spaces there was Brooklyn's Green-Wood Cemetery.

Here among vistas and sepulchers was a "panorama hardly equaled on the Continent," wrote Junius Henri Browne in his massive 1868 *The Great Metropolis: A Mirror of New York*. Green-Wood's "walks and drives, and lakes and groves" give a "distant view of the Island City [Manhattan], the beautiful Bay, and the ocean stretching away into the clouds and sky." But for many New Yorkers, journeying to distant Brooklyn before the subway took us there was long and costly, and the green "squares" several blocks long and wide that the Grid Plan provided were soon inadequate for the city's rapidly growing population; when the plan was first drawn up there were 120,000 New Yorkers, forty-thousand more than a decade before, and several hundred thousand more would soon arrive. The bold solution would be to create a large park.

The Commissioners' Plan of 1811 is preserved in the New York Public Library at Fifth Avenue and 42nd Street, in the I.N. Phelps Stokes Collection, which may have amused surveyor John Randel, Jr. The renowned architect Isaac Newton Phelps Stokes, author of the six volume *The Iconography of Manhattan Island*, believed that the grid "destroyed most of the natural beauty and interest of the island." Many New Yorkers agree. To some, the rigid pattern of right angles and straight lines is conformist, unimaginative, predictable, repetitive, confining, oppressive, and "certainly the last things in the world consistent with beauty," wrote Walt Whitman. Others like the broad, two-way cross streets every half mile or so, offering light and a vision of the surrounding rivers, and how on the wide avenues we see vast reaches uptown and downtown through canyons of mighty structures. But straight streets and wide avenues never intruded on the acres that would be reserved forty years later for the physical health and spiritual renewal of the city's people, and had more open spaces been included on the grid plan, we wouldn't have needed Central Park at all.

An iron spike from the grid still in Central Park

In his June 13, 1851, editorial for the *New-York Tribune*, Bryant wrote "with so hearty an approval" that the city has agreed to create a new public park, and he praised its location: 160-acres extending from Third Avenue to the East River between 68th and 77th streets. Known as Jones' Wood, half the ground is "covered with a fine growth of forest trees," and "the East River side is bold and steep, with charming views up and down the River ...to the Long Island shore."

Almost immediately a young man from Newburgh sixty miles up the Hudson River tried dissuading the city from creating the new park there. For a city with such promise, he declared, the land was "merely a child's playground," then proposed a "People's Park" where "*five hundred acres* is the smallest area that should be reserved for the future wants" of New York.

Renown among New York upper classes for his artful landscaping of their estates, thirty-six year old writer and designer Andrew Jackson Downing had recently persuaded a stout, bearded young Londoner named Calvert Vaux (pronounced Vawks) to assist in his landscape enterprises. Shortly after arriving in the United States, Vaux married Mary McEntee from Rondout, a little town upriver from Newburgh. One afternoon at Downing's home, he met a sensitive, enigmatic young man from Staten Island, a farmer and writer who had recently toured Europe and published *Walks and Talks of an American Farmer in England*. His name was Frederick Law Olmsted.

Aware that funds had been allocated for a large city park and with the ear of influential New Yorkers, Andrew Downing argued that the land around the larger, newly planned reservoir several steps north of the present one was unappealing for residential and commercial development: too sloped, too swampy, and covered with massive outcroppings of immoveable schist, the island's half-billion-year-old bedrock. This black, iron-hard, furrowed rock was once molten lava squeezed and twisted, cooled and crystalized, baked in Earth's fiery depths, the hardened blood of the planet strong enough even when hollowed to an eggshell of a crust to support our steel and concrete towers.

Downing maintained that if the new reservoir's retaining walls, rather than the traditional rectangle, were constructed with curves and contours to resemble a lake, then the proposed park could be built *around* it. Despite Bryant's elation and the flourishing forest of Jones' Wood, the city agreed with Downing. As park lover and art critic Clarence Cook lyrically expressed, the city "took this sheet of white paper to write the future Park poem on that."

In 1853, Herman Melville added to his own deepening obscurity by publishing "Bartleby the Scrivener: A Story of Wall Street," one of the most enduring pieces of fiction ever written about New York City. That year Stanford White was born. Together with William Mead and Charles McKim, he would design some of New York's most striking structures before murdered in 1906 while watching *Mam'zelle Champagne* in the old Madison Square Garden by a jealous husband during the musical number "I Could Have Loved a Million Girls."

That same year real estate developer George Higgins began constructing a row of mansions along Fifth Avenue between 41st and 42nd streets. Unable to find buyers with the property so far uptown, Higgins sold off the buildings to a women's college. And across Fifth Avenue where Bryant Park is today, "The Exhibition of the Industry of All Nations"— America's first world's fair— opened on July 17 after a magnificent banquet for its promoters at the Metropolitan Hotel on Broadway and Prince Street the night before. On display were raw materials and produce, machinery and fine arts from around the world enclosed in the Crystal Palace, an enormous structure of cast-iron, steel, and glass, a building "loftier/ fairer, ampler than any yet," wrote Walt Whitman, "Earth's modern wonder." Here Elisha Otis first demonstrated his 'safety hoist,' his 'elevated railway' that foretold a fundamental element in New York's future; cities could expand not only horizontally but now vertically as well. And four days after the exhibition's opening ceremonies, New York enacted the Central Park Act, declaring that the ragged ground from Fifth Avenue west to Eighth Avenue, from 59th to 106th Street "to be a public place." At $5,169,369.90, the approximately one square mile in the island's center cost New York more than the 663,268 square miles of Alaska purchased by the United States a decade later.

Many wondered why the new park intended for the city's poor was built so far from so many who were. Expand Battery Park with its dramatic esplanade and sparkling views across the Upper Bay, suggested Dr. John Griscom, a leading advocate of his day for healthier urban living conditions. Or create not one vast park half-way up the island but eight smaller parks of one hundred acres closer to the people who need them. But eventually New Yorkers would visit the new park, and when they arrived they were astonished by what they saw. First, the city had to find someone to design it.

CHAPTER FIVE

The Wild Garden

After strolling beneath the lofty, splendid canopy of elms along the promenade, after viewing the grand terrace and the violated scrolls down the wide staircases and seeing the trash-filled, waterless basin as the angel descends with her blessings even upon this fallen paradise, what beckoned was the rugged forest across the dark lake. We walked west on a walkway as Bo flushed from the shoreline a pair of mallards that rose upward with flapping fury until, over a narrow part of the lake, a graceful bridge curved like an archer's bow or one used with a violin, and again the park changed by what we found on the other side.

Known as the Ramble, its borders are the East and West Drives, and from the shores of the Boating Lake across the bridge –Bow Bridge—north to a sunken transverse road cutting through the park at 81st Street. Within these perimeters is a forest with hills and meadows, cliffs and ravines, the remnants of a mysterious cave, two water cascades, and a tall, narrow stone archway emerging from the surrounding rock like a Wagner stage set or Maxfield Parrish painting, a passageway into magic. Winding walkways dip and rise, turning back on themselves in "intricate paths, crossing themselves and twisting/ Mazy configurations," wrote John Hollander in his poem "Visions From the Ramble" until the Ramble feels far larger than less than forty acres. We may pass the same landscape only above it on rock-face or else down through a gorge, and here are no food carts, no bathrooms, no drinking fountains or statues, no one selling something. We're completely surrounded by many tall trees, the city is hidden, with "none of the heights of buildings ringing the park is visible." To Hollander, as to many of us, the Ramble is "the heart of the park…the final garden…the garden regained."

The lake beneath Bow Bridge is fed by a small stream—at least on some days it fed the lake, and when there was no stream I assumed the park needed rain, not that somewhere a faucet did all that. Sometimes the stream, known as The Gill, flows at the base of great shafts of Manhattan schist, spilling over rocks and winding through the Ramble before disappearing beneath a cracked sidewalk and emptying into a small pond. At times the pond was merely a puddle, crumbled cigarette packs and beer cans stuck in the mud, but after a hard rain (or when someone opened the faucet), water clear and cold gushed from a rocky grotto into a pool that fed the muddy pond and flowed under a small wooden bridge to another pond that disappeared beneath a walkway before flowing downhill into the lake. Bo liked wading in the pool formed by the gushing water that rinsed him of mud from traipsing near Indian Cave.

The Ramble was designed for mystery and enchantment, so from their romantic imagination the park designers had a cave chiseled out beneath a great over-hang of rock. The lake flows towards it but had dried out long ago into a muddy ravine that Bo slopped through anyway and I followed him to a cave. For a moment I thought I had discovered what no one else knew, but a crude staircase had been chiseled into the rock leading up to the walkway, and from the cave came a rank smell of piss where wet newspapers and twisted clothes inside lay in the mud; twenty feet in, a brick wall.

But in his 1864 pamphlet *The Central Park*, Fred B. Perkins saw the cave before the wall, before the magic tarnished. At that time the muddy ravine was a lovely inlet of the Boating Lake flowing through the cave deeper into the park: "The cavern below is full of deep shadow," Perkins had written, "and the sullen and opaque water lies…motionless, as if unkindly water spirits shrouded themselves in its tawny depths…" His narrative takes the reader on a park tour with accompanying photographs by W.H. Guild, Jr. A series of these stereoscopic images –viewed through a stereopticon, an early version of the View-Master—was sent to President Lincoln with hopes they may give pleasure during his and the nation's nightmare of the Civil War.

Unfinished as the park was eight years before the officially opening, Perkins wrote, Central Park "is by far the greatest public work on the American continent, for grandeur, beauty, purity, and success." As for the water-spirits in the cave's tawny depths, "suddenly a gay group of youths and maidens appears in the…the cave; passing over as phantoms glide across a sorcerer's mirror, they disappear at the other side."

The Ramble instantly became the most enticing part of the park. Here the city seems furthest away, birds and squirrels and raccoons and bats at night alive and struggling like me in the center of this powerful, congested cosmopolis. And early on a summer morning we entered the Ramble just as dark clouds hovered over the park and that remarkable fragrance before a rain fresh and thick filled the air. When the soft shower turned into a warm, hard rain, Bo and I remained almost perfectly dry beneath the thick canopy of the trees' sheltering limbs. The sweet, humid scent of rain overtook the musky aroma of wet earth as Bo folded himself on the forest floor and we simply watched the rain on the Boating Lake and leaves fluttering from the droplets with New York City seeming very distant.

Then something occurred that forever altered my vision of Central Park. Until then these artful, abused acres had provided discovery, adventure, and beauty however tarnished, but in a single, merciless moment the park revealed itself as part of the most fundamental principles of the natural world. A few feet away, a bird perched on a branch extending over and several inches above the Boating Lake. The size of a football needing to be inflated, it had a black, hunched body, a white-feathered underbelly, legs neither long nor short, and a black beak, a wide, long, black sword of a beak, and it remained impossibly motionless. I was close enough to see its red eye. In an instant the bird jabbed that black sword into the water and snapped back with a little yellow fish. The fish too had struggled to survive even in this silt and garbage-strewn lake; as the eminent biologist William Beebe wrote in his *Unseen Life in New York*, within every drop of that algae-filled water imperceptible creatures also battle for life; to see them, "you need only scoop up a few drops of green scum from the Central Park cattail swamp."

These struggles are as real and consequential as those beneath the dark Hudson River or in Yellowstone's forests or between the lion and the wildebeest on the hot savannah. Though created by mind and muscle, this park is in miniature, in microcosm, the entire natural world.

"It's difficult to believe," Charles Darwin wrote in an 1839 journal entry, "in the dreadful but quiet war of organic beings going on in the peaceful woods and smiling fields."

Along with Fred Perkins's 1864 pamphlet about the park, in a flurry of journalist wonder and enthusiasm, many other pamphlets and articles about the park appeared years before its completion. Julian K. Larke's 1866 *Davega's Handbook to Central Park* was among them, a forty-four page pamphlet with ink illustrations describing "a Park unsurpassed for beauty, outline and design by any in the civilized world—where the masses, high and low, rich and poor, can breathe in their recreative hours, the fresh, pure air of Heaven." But the finest, most lyrical, and, at more than 200 pages, the longest of any previous park book was written by Clarence Cook.

His *A Description of the New York Central Park* appeared in 1869 and enhanced with detailed wood-cuts by the Hudson River School painter Albert Fitch Bellows. Art critic, author and architect, Cook was awed by the astonishing accomplishment of the park's designers, the divine spirit of Nature so artfully captured and preserved in the city, descriptions all the more disheartening after acres of textured landscape would later be lost or sacrificed for "amusements" like a zoo, a museum, lawns for sports. Cook too believed that "Nowhere in the Park has the result achieved been more worthy of the money, labor, and thought expended to produce it, than in the Ramble."

Central Park was created to have a civilizing influence on New Yorkers: Nature, it was thought, will curb our baser elements and cultivate harmony among the populous. But the park, and especially the Ramble, released in me something unrestricted, primitive, the statue of the Indian and his noble dog coming to life. At PayLess I bought a pair of moccasins and dressed in greens and browns to blend into the forest through which I tried passing silently as uncooperative twigs cracked beneath my steps, thorns and sharp-tipped leaves rasping across my arms as we wandered the Ramble, "a memory of the land," wrote William Dean Howells in his 1909 "Glimpses of New York," "as it was before the havoc of the city began." And then we sighted the mountain lion.

Hunched on a rock overlooking the East Drive, haunches coiled, ready to pounce on its prey below, it is life-size, with a thick neck, powerful jowls, deep-set eyes focused and alert. Like the Indian and his dog, like the angel with her blessings, the mountain lion entwined with the park though it too was victim of the abusive city. Someone had broken off its tail, leaving only a jagged stump. Despite this, the lion remained focused, undaunted, magnificent. In the base, as if written with a finger before the bronze hardened, the name of the artist above the imprint of a wolf's face.

For a misguided publicity stunt in 1927 Central Park hired So-Tslen-O-Wa-Ne, an Iroquois (from Brooklyn) renamed Great Fire; in a red canoe and wearing "buckskin clothes and plenty of feathers," the *Times* reported, he was intended to add local color ten hours a day with each stroke of his paddle on the Boating Lake. A tee pee was planned but never appeared, but nothing could ever give us even a hint of the fear "The People" must have experienced four centuries ago at the sight of an unfamiliar plant suddenly growing on their homeland.

Near the conclusion of Longfellow's mysterious poem *The Song of Hiawatha* set along Lake Superior in the upper Midwest –Gitche Gumee in whose cold depths the *Edmund Fitzgerald* sank— the old sachem Iagoo returns "from his wanderings far to the eastward." He tells the tribe what he's seen: a water "Broader than the Gitche Gumee"—

> O'er it, said he, o'er this water
> Came a great canoe with pinions,
> A canoe with wings came flying,
> Bigger than a grove of tree-tops

Perhaps he described Henry Hudson's *Half Moon*, and in the great canoe "came, he said, a hundred warriors,"

> Painted white were all their faces.
> And with hair their chins were covered.

The tribe laughs at these tales but Iagoo's words are confirmed by Hiawatha, the tribal leader who received the sacred gifts of the Great Spirit; "in a vision" he had "beheld our nations scattered...sweeping westward, wild and woeful...Like the withered leaves of Autumn." This foreshadowing of American Indian genocide was first ominously seen in a plant with spade-shaped leaves, as unfamiliar as Hudson's great, billowed sail carrying the white invaders;

> Wheresoe'er they tread, beneath them
> Springs a flower unknown among us,
> Springs the White-Man's Foot in blossom.

Along with small pox and the certainty that, from sea to shining sea, God had destined this new world for the white race, Europeans also brought in the mud of their boots, in horse hoofs and burlap wrappings, the seeds of plantain, *Plantago major.* For the Lenape, the first baffling sight of it must have gripped their hearts with the fear that the invaders would spread like the plant that today grows vigorously throughout Central Park.

Despite the meager pay, working long hours on the trucks sustained me with even a few dollars left over, and in New York there's much to do with little. Before writing *Low Life,* Luc Sante lived nearby, and for $10 he "bought three slices of pizza, a can of Welch's Strawberry Soda, a pack of Viceroys, six joints, two quarts of orange juice, two containers of yogurt, and a pint of milk."

I liked riding shot gun in the big furniture trucks high above the narrow, clogged streets and seeing so much of the city, and I liked the men I worked with. Tom was a top-shelf driver who did the Florida runs —six days on the road and back—and Pete had a family, fine weed, and knew the best places for sandwiches: fish fillet in City Island or a Carroll Gardens' Italian deli. Charlie was a Vietnam vet who smoked constantly, but if needing both hands while handling a piece of furniture he'd jam the cigarette in the gap where a tooth was missing.

One morning Tom drove us deep into Brooklyn to a quiet, shabby street lined with modest homes. Checking the paperwork, I said, "This one," and he pulled in front, then hit the air-brakes which sent a loud, sharp "whoosh" through the cab. We went round to a small yard in the back, white powder floating from two metal doors open to the basement where the powder floated far thicker and covered tabletops, the ceiling and floor, and on three men, their mouths covered with paper masks, their slouchy hats, shirts and dungarees, all covered with white dust but their eyes when they removed their goggles. We were here for a marble fireplace mantle which they had carved, white as porcelain, with birds flying through branches, sanded so smooth that once wiped clean it appeared damp. One of the artisans helped us with the heavy piece up the few stairs to the backyard. He was very strong and spoke no English, removed his mask, took a breath with his eyes closed, and lit a cigarette. I blanket-wrapped the mantle while Tom handled the paperwork, then we secured the piece to a wall inside the truck and headed back to the city on the Manhattan Bridge running parallel to the gentle-arching roadway of mighty Brooklyn Bridge.

We exited the FDR at East 96th for delivery to a multi-million dollar apartment high above Fifth Avenue, and here I first saw the full breath of Central Park, green and thick that afternoon. After we unwrapped the mantle and as Tom settled the paperwork with the customer's maid, I went to the windows looking to my left, then to my right, and all of it park. A lake flowed directly across nearly to the park's western edge—the Receiving Reservoir that I read about in *The Central Park Book*—and I thought how wonderful and mad of this city that a huge park grew in the center of it, a clean, deep breath from all the smoke, a sanctuary amid the brick and steel pressing along every edge of it. How could this happen?

"No tip," Tom grumbled back in the truck. "Maid musta kept it."

There were many long days on the trucks, and so after a quick walk in the morning Bo was alone until I came home sometimes late at night. Even his walks before bed were brief because I was so tired. But it meant that on a day off we go to the park, and we always headed first to the Ramble. We rode the B local to 72nd and Central Park West, Bo enjoying the subway ride as he led the way, alert, protective, and eager, knowing that our destination was the park. But I was drifting. Even though blind I watched pretty women walk past on the platform and once even bent to pick up a dollar bill. Worse, I looked to see if anyone saw. That people stared no longer bothered me though I laughed while imagining how I might turn to someone and ask, "What the fuck youz lookin' at?" And in the many times on the subway we had only one incident.

We were riding home in character when Bo lunged for the door just as a cop and *his* dog boarded the train at 42nd Street/Bryant Park Station. Now, what most angers Bo is a dog he doesn't recognize getting too close to me, especially one outweighing him by twenty-five pounds. Strays who find homes tend to be like this. As he's pulling on the leash a ridge of fur rose along his back and I'm saying, "Stop" or "Heel" or some command any real guide dog should know. Only after I snapped hard on the leash did he ease up though he kept shifting his weight on his front paws; if a dude he would have pulled up his pants ready to fight.

The police dog didn't move. He was a handsome black German shepherd with brown fur down his legs and tail. In his prime, with teeth not yellowed and chipped like old Bo's, he just stared at him, relaxed, undaunted, while the cop focused on me. I knew he knew I wasn't blind and I wouldn't look at him, so I stared at his shoes, my mind racing through all my crimes: an unregistered dog, defrauding the MTA, a knife in my coat pocket, and now with a little left from a toke or two in the park. Is it illegal to impersonate the blind? But when the train stopped at 34th Street the doors opened and the cop with his dog got off. That kind of lucky.

At 72nd Street we tapped upstairs to the Dakota, mysterious and dark, built so far west of town it seemed like Dakota Territory. Before the creation of Central Park, this two-way avenue from West 59th to West 110th Street was Eighth Avenue, but with such an exquisite park it was renamed the more glamorous 'Central Park West.' Wanting glamour too, Ninth Avenue soon became Columbus Avenue; Tenth Avenue, not to be without glamour of its own, is now Amsterdam Avenue, and Eleventh became West End Avenue. Both 59th Street and 110th along the park were bound for glamor as well: the very stylish Central Park South and Central Park North.

A generation before, to distance themselves from the notorious Bowery, residents above East Sixth Street had it renamed Third Avenue; in New York City, sometimes a rose by another name smells sweeter.

After tapping my way upstairs at 72nd I released Bo and broke down the cane as soon as we entered a bare, battered landscape. Just after we crossed the West Drive stands an enormous pedestal with a large statue high atop it of Daniel Webster in an expressionless, Napoleon-like stance. But in 1873 the park's Committee on Statues declared that only "works designed to represent objects of beauty, of dramatic and poetic interest, may be placed at any points in the park where they shall not dominate a landscape." This obtrusive object is neither beautiful, dramatic, nor poetic, and it certainly dominates the landscape. This is no disparagement to the noble statesman though most people seeing the statue think he's "the dictionary guy."

"Some of the worst of all the bad statues in the world," declared William Dean Howells who believed the "only one thoroughly good piece of sculpture in the Park [is] an American Indian hunting with his dog, as the Indians must have hunted through the wilds here before the white man came."

We walked the Boating Lake's trash-strew shore and crossed Bow

Bridge into the Ramble. Besides an imaginary Indian and his very real dog, the Ramble was regularly frequented by two very different groups. There were bird watchers—"birders" they were called; though everywhere in Central Park, birds too loved the Ramble most. So did gay men.

"I discovered the jungle of Central Park," wrote John Rechy in his provocative 1963 novel *City of Night*. "In the afternoons, Sunday especially, a parade of hunters prowled that area—or they would sit or lie on the grass waiting for that day's contact. Even in the brilliant white blaze of newyork sun, it was possible to make it, right there, in the tree-secluded areas."

Gay men had been meeting for sex in the park long before Rechy's novel, the sloping lawn at the Ramble's northwest edge where men displayed themselves in the 1920s called "the fruited plains." Though the city had become more tolerant of homosexuality by the time Rechy's novel appeared and the outrage after Stonewall in 1969 empowered gay men for the first time, some men found the cloak of bushes, darkness, and anonymity the Ramble provides far more alluring and discreet than loud, expensive bars and discoes. Besides, some men were too young to enter gay bars anyway. As Doug Ireland wrote in his article "Rendezvous in the Ramble" for *New York* magazine, "For the poor, working-class gays who can't afford the bars or the baths, the park is not just free, it is necessary." Then too, some men –straight in the daylight—needed to hide their occasional preferences. "The openness of the park encourages openness among people," Ireland writes, then quotes Chuck Orleb, editor of *Christopher Street*; "It's one of the few places in which this society allows us to meet each other."

Much of Ireland's article concerned "gay bashings" that occurred in the Ramble that summer of '78, a brutality that had been going on for years but attracted public attention only after the attack on former ice skating champion and sportscaster Dick Button. Gay sex in the Ramble also appeared in the movies; in 1980, William Friedkin's *Cruising* has Al Pacino as a New York undercover cop investigating a series of murders in the gay community. Night scenes set in the Ramble have men cruise, connect, and either seek seclusion or have sex among a gathered, seething group. John Rechy served as a consultant on the film.

"Central Park has always been a sexual playground," wrote Edward

Field in his poem "The Rambles" where "guys posed…fetchingly, against trees." Field recalls how, after picking up someone and before the other man "went home to his wife and children, we'd plunge into the dusk of the park" and—

> celebrating our polymorphous perversity in a city
> that has always meant freedom,
> especially for us sexual outlaws.

The Ramble is still a meeting place for gay men though it was hoped the AIDS epidemic might curtail, if not end, such random sexual encounters and by doing so save the lives of many men and women. Instead condoms are used; these, along with lubricant, soiled tissues, the condom's wrapper, plus cigarettes, empty packs, disposable lighters, bottles and cans of whatever they were drinking, all of it unsightly and some of it dangerous, left deep in the most secluded parts of the Ramble where Bo and I wandered. At dusk in the Ramble, the sexual hunters claim their benches in wait, and I knew better how women suffer annoying advances they must everywhere endure though, unlike women, I never felt threatened.

In the Ramble is a place called The Oven. Black cliffs of schist taper to form a gorge thick with vegetation extending twenty yards to the edges of the Boating Lake. On some days a small stream flows through the gorge that even in winter is warmed by the sun for most of its travels across this part of the park; that's how the Oven got its name. On sunny days turtles crawl from the water to the rocks, and in late summer hummingbirds gather nectar from long-stemmed flowers growing where the stream trickles into the Lake. The stream through the gorge provides a place for birds to bathe and, from the rock outcropping above on the western side, to watch them. Often in our wanderings Bo and I would see birdwatchers, in pairs and small groups, most of them dressed in outdoor gear with good hiking boots, backpacks, vests with many pockets, cameras (some colossal), and all of them with binoculars held to their eyes, necks strained back or, at the Oven, down into the gorge.

"Fine dog," one of the birders said to me, her eyes following Bo as he slipped into a clump of thin bamboo shoots along the shore.

"Yes, he is," I replied. "I'll tell him when he returns."

She was tall, with red hair and a kind face, her lively eyes shaded by a bright blue visor. Her companion, a short, round fellow, glanced approvingly at Bo, then —indifferent to me— returned his magnified gaze to the bathing birds beneath us. His name was Lambert Pohner, and in the band of his hat was a blue feather. She was Sarah Elliott.

After their explorations and discoveries, Sarah and Lambert head to the Boathouse nearby for coffee or hot chocolate on winter days and lemonade in the summer, then record in a loose-leaf notebook kept there all the sightings of the day. Other birders passing through will consult the book to see what is where—a thrasher near the Cave, a yellow chat on the Ramble's side of Bow Bridge.

"If it is possible to fall in love with a thing," Marie Winn wrote of it in her *Central Park in the Dark*, "I believe I fell in love with the Bird Register that day I first opened it."

The notebook, which also reports robberies and muggings in the Ramble, had been Sarah's idea; it is there today.

Late one morning I sat with her outside the Boathouse as she gave me lessons in birding and Bo lay near her chair catching the muffin crumbs she tossed to him.

"In the winter we have hawks and owls, kestrels and falcons, and just last week Lambert found a bluebird high in a tree. Oh, we were all very excited about that."

Sarah's eyes danced at the recollection while Lambert sipped his coffee with feigned indifference though a small smile curled in one corner of his bearded, elfish face.

"Is that the bluebird's feather in your hat?" I asked him.

His turned a disappointed glance in my direction: "Blue jay."

"I know blue jays," I replied. "Very handsome."

"Yes, very handsome," Sarah replied, "but very loud and cranky. Park bullies," she added with conviction. But if the blue jay were a mugger, wrote Donald Knowler in his birding memoir *The Falconer of Central Park,* it will take "your wallet but leave you with enough money to take a taxi home."

In *The Central Park Book* I read Chapter 8, "An Oasis for Birds," amazed by what was happening in the park and the refuge it gives to birds along the Atlantic Flyway during migrations. I bought a small pair of binoculars and Tory Peterson's *A Field Guide to the Birds* determined to spot some of the more than 250 species sighted in Central Park.

"More than the Florida Everglades!" Sarah declared, her green eyes widening.

Winter meant easier sightings since all but the pines and evergreens were bare though many birds had flown south months before. Summer's lusty leaves made birds harder to spot, but spring and fall migration brought many birds and birders to the park, especially the Ramble. Bo and I found a quicker way into the Ramble by riding the B train to 79th where the American Museum of Natural History spreads like a great brown fortress all the way to 81st Street. Once we pass through NATURALISTS' GATE, we followed a walkway on our left down to a wooden bridge that crossed a little steam. The roadway above is supported by a stone tower, round and formidable, known as Eaglevale, with a bridle path passing underneath. The stream flows east deeper into the park under Balcony Bridge that fed the Boating Lake.

Though as yet unable to tell a house sparrow from a purple finch or between a chickadee and a nut hatch, I was quick to spot them with my binoculars but nearly helpless with the guidebook. I'd see a bird, leaf through the *Guide,* but often the bird vanished when I looked again, and if one obligingly remained I couldn't tell what it was; one had or had not an eye-ring or a barely detectable tab of yellow above its beak, sparrows all seemed to look alike, while a downy woodpecker and a hairy woodpecker differed only slightly in size. Why, Nature, did you create both? There's a mystery.

If I stayed still, birds perched and hopped very close but scattered when Bo returned to check on me before wandering off again. Soon I recognized the sweetly chirping cardinal (the male is red while the female, though a dull brown, wears lipstick on her beak). That somber Night-crowned Heron I had seen pluck that little fish from the Boating Lake resembles a greaser in high school with his collar up, and the Great Blue Heron peacefully stood in the Gill on thin legs a yard long, in the middle of Manhattan. One little bird was bright yellow, one deep red with black wings (a Scarlet Tanager the *Guide* showed me), grackles sound like their names, a chickadee and a tufted titmouse sound similar.

Birds called back and forth in the treetops, squawked in chases through the branches, sang simply because they could and did for no reason but to celebrate being on Earth. Early on a summer morning as Bo waded and lapped the cold water from the gorge, a bird smaller than a robin perched on a branch nearby, its body reddish-orange, its head blue or purple or purplish-blue depending where the sun touched its luminous feathers, with wings and a tail like Monet's palette. I was dazzled as much by its beauty as that we were together here in New York City at least for that moment.

"We talk of peace," wrote Marianne Moore about Central Park. "This is it."

One cold winter afternoon we exited the subway at Central Park West and were crossing Bow Bridge into the Ramble just as John and Yoko came from the other side. They were enwrapped in furs and each other, he with an oversized newsboy cap and she shrouded by her thick, black hair. 'Say nothing,' I told myself but couldn't look elsewhere. John was speaking closely to Yoko, having eyes for nothing else, but her gaze— more searching and wary— met mine. Privy to my silent pledge or simply gracious, she smiled slightly and nodded as we passed.

But that day also had an ominous sign; after only an hour in the Ramble, Bo seemed to be limping on his left hind leg. Perhaps a pebble or thorn had lodged between the pads of his paw but I found nothing. A hitch had developed in his backside, the left hind leg catching; he moved slowly as in some pain, and the stairs down to the subway were difficult for him.

"Degenerative hip displacement," the veterinarian told me, typical for Bo's breed. "There's really little that can be done," he continued while rubbing Bo behind his droopy left ear. "Cold weather's the hardest. How old is he?"

"Only around twelve."

The vet nodded with a resigned smile: "How good will we walk when we're over eighty? Give him aspirin for the pain," he added as I lifted Bo from the cold examination table and placed him on the floor, "and be sure he sleeps on something soft."

We did not visit the park again until the weather warmed. By then Bo had improved slightly but stairs were still hard for him and we abandoned the blind act. On a leash he'd hobble to the corner where one taxi after another passed us, and the one that did stop I tipped graciously. A quiet grove lay just inside the park at Fifth Avenue and 76th Street and we sat beneath a tree. Though no longer able to prowl the forest or chase squirrels or wade through the chilly stream, Bo seemed content lying beside me, sometimes hobbling off but soon returning. He'd settle down so close that his back pressed against my leg, then sniff the air and at times close his eyes, partaking of the park's supreme purpose: to be quietly restored by Nature.

Still, ever my protector, he barked if anyone approached except for Sarah Elliott whom he somehow recognized from a distance. Perhaps her red hair or flamboyant coat or else just the goodness she emanated as Bo struggled to his feet as she neared. She said nothing of his deepening aliment but her eyes told me she knew.

After only our first taxi ride Bo could tell the park was near when we crossed Madison Avenue as he sat up to sniff at the opening in the window. Along the encircling walkway an elderly man was assisted by an attentive companion; I suppose we were like them too as I tended to my grandfather of a dog.

One February night after a walk around the neighborhood, after I carried Bo up the stairs and he settled on his rug to clean himself, my heart pounded; he could not get up again, his back legs unable to bear any weight at all. I brought him his water bowl, sat beside him on his rug through the night and fell asleep on the floor, his head on my leg. It was our last night together.

In the morning I carried him downstairs to the backyard which he used for what he needed, then I cleaned his fur underneath. We took a taxi back to the veterinarian who kept him overnight for tests but his condition was irreversible; he would only continue deteriorating, his pain increasing, and he couldn't raise himself up on his hind legs. We spent a few hours together in the kennel, his cage door open so I could pet him. That evening I went down to the basement of the building for a shovel, then returned to the park to find a place to bury my dog.

The night was very cold and clear with no wind. A few stars were in the black sky, a rarity to see in Manhattan. I had been thinking of where to bury him; beside our Indian and his dog were too exposed for me to dig a grave, and not in the Ramble amid all the tissues and lubricants left on the forest floor. Then I remembered Eaglevale just inside and down the walkway at NATURALISTS' GATE and 77th Street where birds bathe in the stream that flows beneath a wooden bridge. Few ever pass by, and the place is shaded and quiet. Here that late winter night I found a spot beneath a tree with a few protecting shrubs, then slammed the edge of the shovel into the ground an instant before a metallic twang ran up the handle, through my hands and into my arms; instantly I knew I could never break this frozen ground. Bo could not wait for spring thaw, so there was only one other way for him to remain in the park.

I visited him the next day with pieces of fried chicken, still his favorite. He was carried into the examination room and I asked for him to be placed on the floor, not the examination table. He pressed his head against my body as I sat beside him. We were alone for a while and I stroked him gently. Too soon the vet entered. I kissed the side of his head and inhaled the warm scent of him, then held him in my lap as the vet knelt down to give the injection. "There now," I said quietly and rubbed his head, "it's okay, my dear buddy." As always he trusted me completely. He took two deep breaths while turning his head towards me ("I love you, Bo,"), settled against my heart, and died.

The next morning I left the veterinarian's with a grapefruit-size porcelain bowl. Inside, light brown powder and little nuggets, bone and teeth perhaps. My wonderful dog, a far better companion to me than I was to him. I gave food and shelter; he stuck around, and in return I received loyalty and unconditional love. It was the best deal I ever made.

I'm sorry I lost my temper when you didn't obey, for my impatience when tired at night and kept your walks so short, for getting angry at the diarrhea you had all over the rug even though I gave you the large ham bone. Sorry for moving to New York; surely the increased inactivity brought on the condition sooner. One overcast February day I spread Bo's ashes through Central Park: inside MERCHANTS' GATE where our journeys began, upon the Ramble's forest floor, beneath the leafless elms along the promenade, and at the dusty base of the Indian and his dog. What remained I scattered like seed in that barren oval of earth where the promenade begins, hoping that in another form he'll appear again next spring.

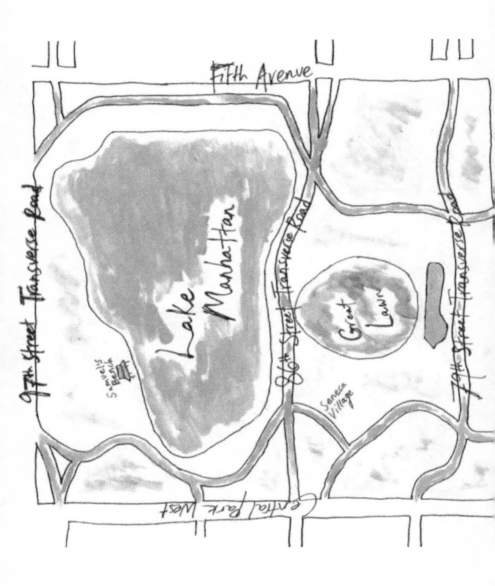

Part Two

"I know each lane, and every alley green,
Dingle, or bushy dell, of this wild wood,
And every bosky bourn from side to side."

John Milton, *Comus*

For a while I could not visit Central Park without my dog. I missed his moping eyes whenever I left the apartment without him, his sleepy joy at my return. With him I was never lonely, even those first months in New York. For years I'd still wake in the night hearing him snore or else running in his sleep, claws scraping along the floorboards. His rug beside my bed remained.

I missed the park too, and though I'd be closer to him amid his ashes than anywhere else except my recollections, I did not want to walk the Ramble without him. But then something happened which showed me how I might visit the park in ways Bo and I together never could. On April 1, 1980, New York City transit workers went on strike. News footage showed Mayor Koch walking the Brooklyn Bridge with a million others and encouraging us to have a martini after work to decrease the homeward-bound congestion. I needed a bicycle.

A storefront bike shop on East 12th Street just east of First Avenue had old bikes chained together on each side of the open door. Bicycles hung in the picture windows, all of them used. The inside was overwhelmed with bikes lined up together, and a wooden platform above them had more bikes. It was a cavern of bikes from floor to ceiling, even *from* the ceiling where hung shiny rims and graceful, curving handlebars until it seemed that three bike shops were pressed into this one.

Despite the seeming disordered entanglement, the shop was peaceful. Not even a radio. Incense burned somewhere, its scented smoke spiraling through the spokes and the smell of oil. Along a path open in the center a black air hose snaked its finger-thick way outside; deep in the shop a man repaired a bike. He was tall, dark, slender, patient, and he smiled quietly as I entered.

"I need a bike," I pleaded, "with gears and handlebars that drop down. And a skinny seat. And no basket."

He calmly considered this as he continued working, then put down his wrench, wiped his hands on a rag and carefully untangled a used white Peugeot 10-speed from the heaps. He oiled the chain, the hubs and levers, pumped up the tires, then stuck a yellow sticker on the down-tube: "Bikes, By George!" I liked the grammatical emphasis.

Before diving into city traffic for the park, I practiced some; years had passed since last I rode a bicycle and never one with gears and hand-brakes and drop handlebars, toe-clips and a skinny seat (saddle). For a few days on First Street I coasted, I glided, I swerved and sprinted, moving to balance and balancing to move. Never did I lock it to a lamppost but always carried it upstairs to my apartment where I gazed at its circles and symmetry, its lightness and strength.

I took my first bike ride to Central Park on a cool April morning after rush hour, the sky still misty from an early rain. Up wet, wide First Avenue to East 60th Street, cut left and simply glide west across Fifth Avenue into the park. Nothing to it.

But Manhattan traffic is thick and wild, and I flung myself into it on a thin machine as cars blasted past, taxis frantic with hunger; beneath me, the merciless pavement sparkling with shattered glass (and the width of my tires more narrow than my thumb). There were car-devouring pot holes and people popping from between parked cars like cardboard figures on a target range; in this city of speed, crosswalks are optional. I considered riding to the park on narrow sidewalks but that would look foolish, so I peddled on.

Slower traffic scurried in the right lane, but here buses bore down on me and stopped every two blocks; if I passed one, angry cars sped inches from my front-bumper-of-a-left knee. Suddenly one wild man on a bike with a large blue bag across his back raced passed me in the center lane, slipping between moving cars, vanishing in traffic, appearing again far ahead. Embarrassed, determined, I continued churning on with cautious cranks until, relieved, turned left on sluggish, narrow East 60th Street. After crossing Fifth Avenue I took a deep breath and again felt the park's most important purpose: refuge from the turbulent city.

And it's always been this way. In 1873 a novel appeared by Francis Forrester, Esq.— pen-name for Daniel Wise. *Little Peachblossom: Rambles in Central Park* follows a once prosperous family that has lost its fortune and must move to New York City. All are horrified except for

Peachblossom: " 'I know one thing that isn't horrid…Why, the Central Park!' " For the next 230 pages, with illustrations, we visit much of the Park, all of it enchanting but to no one more than Peachblossom.

Trees that April morning were bare of leaves but fresh, green life budded from bushes. I followed a roadway uphill, waited for the traffic and crossed the Drive to the oval of dirt where some of Bo's ashes lay. This morning, tiny stems pushed through the dark, tattered soil; I rubbed between my fingers a pinch of it, of him, remounted my bike and took my first ride through Central Park.

CHAPTER SIX

Garden of Champagne and Despair

I nside Central Park along its perimeter, a six-mile roadway gently winds through dips and rises with only a straight stretch of it running for a half-mile beside Fifth Avenue. Though later widened for automobile traffic, it was made for carriages: phaetons and hackneys, a surry seating four, a graceful Victoria for two, and hansom cabs where the driver sits behind and above the cab. "Ten thousand vehicles careening through the park this perfect afternoon," wrote Walt Whitman.

A brilliant aspect of the park's design largely lost today established separate paths for visitors on foot, on horseback, or in carriages. Never would someone strolling need cross a bridle path or roadway; rather, we pass *beneath* the carriages through artful tunnels, cross *above* those on horseback over elegant, cast-iron bridges. Each tunnel and bridge blends into the landscape, and each is unique and always opening to a carefully created vista though in time several of these graceful structures were lost, among them the lovely Marble Arch.

So we needn't cross the Center Drive amid all its trotting traffic of carriages and automobiles today to reach the promenade on the other side, a graceful staircase led us down to a white passageway where, on benches along the walls, we might sit, find shelter from the sun or rain. Another staircase led us up to the other side to the promenade. When the Marble Arch impeded the flow of automobile traffic choking the park in the 1930s, the Marble Arch was leveled. But only leveled; the rest remains beneath the concrete road, and a piece of the Marble Arch may have pushed upward, a square yard just between the Dairy and the roadway yearning to be uncovered and used again to safely guide us beneath the traffic.

To bike the entire six-mile roadway is "doing the loop," but for a while my rides were only along the curving rises and dips of the walkways. I climbed a gentle, rusting, iron-lace bridge, glided down the other side to a slight bend in the walkway, peddled up a small hill, then wheeled passed playgrounds and the dusty Sheep Meadow, gliding beneath the elms along the promenade and through another tunnel and over another bridge, wheels for wings.

During one rolling ride, I saw a large open space through a grove of trees, an oval two football fields long and one as wide. Today the Great Lawn in the center of the park is lush and healthy, with six baseball fields with real backstops, soft outfield grass, and infield dirt raked for pebbles. Trees grow only along the perimeter. An oval walkway encircles the Lawn where above mighty oak trees are visible tall apartments, immense and impossibly distant in the morning haze. "Buildings above the leafless trees/ Loom high as castles in a dream" wrote delicate, reclusive Sara Teasdale in "Central Park at Dusk." Looking downtown over the trees were the tops of the hotels and high-rises along Central Park South, so tall, level, plum, angular, remote.

The Great Lawn is Manhattan's largest open space, our Red Square or San Pietra Grand Piazza in Rome. A quarter million people trampled it on September 19, 1981, for a Simon and Garfunkel concert after Parks Commissioner Gordon Davis's deal for a cut of the sales from an album taped that night. The two singers performed on a set resembling a New York rooftop with a real water tank behind them. I wound my slip-sliding way through the dense crowd for forty-five minutes before I got near the stage when the two quickly beat it from the park once they had enough tracks.

Perhaps a million people jammed the Great Lawn June 12, 1982, for the largest anti-nuke demonstration in history, and one summer night in 1995 the Great Lawn held the premiere screening of Disney's *Pocahontas*. Despite150 audio-speakers blasting that "every rock and tree and creature has a life, a spirit, a name," fireworks terrified the park's animals for an additional fifteen minutes. A few months later Pope John Paul II celebrated a morning mass on the Great Lawn, the papers reporting the beloved pontiff more enthralled with Central Park than with St. Patrick's Cathedral; like Emily Dickinson had, he found true beauty "with a bobolink for a chorister/ And an orchard for a dome."

But beneath our trampling feet is earth and grass, not cobblestone or pavement, and that misty April morning of my first bike ride there was no great lawn at all but an oval dust bowl; had the wind blew and if no morning drizzle I'd have needed to cover my eyes from the dry topsoil carried through the air. At the northern end of the barren field a chain-link fence separates us from the 86th Street transverse road crossing back and forth from Fifth Avenue to Central Park West. Anchoring the fence is a stone wall, moss and fern struggling in the cracks; it's the foundation of the old reservoir from 1842 wherein lies why the park grows in the middle of town.

The old reservoir, rendered unnecessary by the immense new one, was finally drained, a portion of its southern end preserved as Lake Belvedere, Turtle Pond today. In time the great mud-caked pit in the center of the park would be filled in with dirt excavated from the site of what became Rockefeller Center. Until then, it was an attractive target for proposed "improvements": a sports stadium with pole-vaulting and cinder race track; a landing strip for airplanes; sunken gardens with a music pavilion; trenches like what our doughboys experienced "over there" in the Great War; apartments or a cemetery for New York's most dignified; at least a trolley track connecting the Metropolitan Museum of Art on the east side to the American Museum of Natural History on the west. Real estate tycoon Edward Browning offered the park $1million—at the time the largest sum ever offered to the park—if the site were made into a swimming pool/playground where, no doubt, he could ogle young girls. What Olmsted fervently did not want were baseball fields, for "nothing is more certain," he believed, "than that the beauty of these lawns would soon be lost…if these games were to be constantly played upon them." Perhaps he would have felt otherwise had his young son turned to him with irrepressible joy and uttered on the way to the park, "I'm dying of baseball happiness."

But before anything else a section of the reservoir wall supported a ramshackle structure called The Rockside Inn. This shelter and others made from materials salvaged by desperate men were built inside the great pit soon after the collapse of New York's most giddy and irresponsible decade.

If possible to return anywhere in New York's story, I would want first to see the island before Henry Hudson dropped anchor, to roam Mannahatta with Bo as the Indian and *his* dog wading through clear rivulets when the land was abundant with bears and wolves and mountain lions, when dolphins swam and whales breached in Muhheakantuck— the "river that flows both ways"— and the land cherished not for real estate profit but because it was a gift to "The People".

Surely the end of the 19th century was the city at its most progressive and boundless. In one astonishing leap into the future, John Roebling's masterpiece bridged the East River and connected Manhattan to Brooklyn with steel cables, granite, and grandeur. Our centennial birthday gift from France stood at last on her pedestal because of poets and Joseph Pulitzer and impoverished New Yorkers sending nickels and dimes which they badly needed but understood what 'The Statue of Liberty Enlightening the World' truly meant.

In the first years of the 20th century, New York had become the most exciting and innovative city on earth; now we must appear equal to London, Paris, even imperial Rome. Ornate Carnegie Hall rose at Seventh Avenue and 57th Street, and the towering Gothic echoes of the Cathedral of St. John the Divine gave the illusion of a long past. Cass Gilbert's Woolworth Building on lower Broadway reached the dizzying height of fifty-seven stories, its pinnacled dome like a medieval cathedral though for business. Stately Grand Central Terminal was completed on the East Side, muscular Pennsylvania Station on the West: between them, white and magnificent, the New York Public Library, a palace for the people, opened at Fifth Avenue and 42nd Street. It was during this age of grandeur that the park's two entrances immortalizing Hearst and Pulitzer appeared.

And in East Side neighborhoods far downtown lived a million uprooted people, my own family among them, where they forged in tenements and sweatshops a character of modern New York as enduring as the excess and splendor. They struggled at sewing machines or behind push-carts and with a new, baffling, often inconsistent language. They had no country estates nor vacations by the sea; for them, as for me, as for many of us today, Central Park gave relief from the crowded tenements, raucous streets, brick and concrete. "Unhouse/ Your head of human walls," wrote James Oppenheim in the city's first poetry anthology *A Book of New York Verse*. Appearing in 1917, his "Morning in Central Park" pleads for New Yorkers to "get from beneath/Shut ceilings" and find, even in the city, Nature's spiritual blessing in Central Park:

let the skies take off the roof
Of your small room— and into the Park at seven
Go with tremendous stride—
Earth there is open wide
To the sun and the wind and the amplitude of heaven!

I would have waved along the docks that June day in 1945 when the Queen Mary sailed into the harbor with 14,526 of her precious cargo of valiant and victorious men and women as the first large boatload of troops returned from liberating Europe. In Times Square after Japan surrendered less than two months later, I too would kiss a swooning nurse as New York rose up to be the capital of the world.

But if I could go back only once, I'll take Manhattan in the 1920s.

This was the Jazz Age, the radiant gathering in Harlem tenements, the rise of the shimmering Chrysler Building and its battle for supremacy of the sky. The city threw its most jubilant parade for Charles Lindbergh, that shy, young pilot who, Scott Fitzgerald wrote, had seemingly nothing to do with his generation except allowing it to dream once more of their greatest possibilities.

In the new Yankee Stadium Babe Ruth circled the bases again and again with those odd little steps of his. Helium balloons in the Macy's Thanksgiving Parade first bobbed above Broadway in '28 while Gershwin's "Rhapsody in Blue" wound its tantalizing chords like blue smoke through Harlem and Greenwich Village. Everyone was making money, or at least making the illusion of it until someone inconsiderately asked for the check and the whole flimsy structure crashed down like a crumbling plaster ceiling. Gangsters made millions supplying what most of us wanted anyway, and our mayor, as if hand-picked by a Hollywood casting director, was trim, charming, dapper, and his favorite nightspot was the elegant and lavishly renovated Casino in Central Park.

When running for mayor in 1925 James J. Walker pledged city funds to repair the park, and after winning the election he promptly kept his word though nearly all the money went to improving what he was determined would be the swankiest restaurant in town. Where the SummerStage is now —inside and a little southwest of INVENTORS' GATE at Fifth Avenue and 72nd Street— the Casino in the Roaring Twenties had expensive cars parked three deep in a lot built to accommodate three hundred. Bewitching cocktail music and the fragrance of rich foods drifted toward the entwined branches of the elm trees along the promenade before dissipating in the night sky where even the stars seemed a specialty ordered by the maître d'.

Designed by Calvert Vaux in 1864, the once modest restaurant was originally the Ladies' Refreshment Salon where women visiting the park could dine without male escorts. The building resembled the simple, stately country homes Vaux had created upstate for his private patrons: a "domestic-looking little cottage" as Clarence Cook described it in his park book, tucked deep into the trees with peacocks wandering the grounds and called 'casino' for 'little house' in Italian.

"The interior decorations...are neat in the extreme," wrote Julian K. Larke in his 1866 *Handbook to Central Park*, "the color being soft and refined, combining beauty with elegance, and each room having a different tint." At night "the building is brilliantly illuminated with gas from handsome pendants" and a "carriage step has been cut in the rock for the accommodation of the occupant of vehicles."

Often after cocktails or dinner, Casino guests strolled beneath the redolent Wisteria Pergola nearby; we still can. On Wednesday and Saturday afternoons, concerts were performed on a graceful, ornate, cast-iron bandstand set in the center of the promenade. Originally intended to be set on a platform floating on the Boating Lake, the music stand had a golden dome, a royal blue roof, and pillars and stairs in crimson, the hub around which we danced on summer evenings in the stunned, restorative years after the Civil War as dusk fell on the park and the gas lampposts brightened.

Eventually the Casino was renovated and expanded until the once-modest restaurant resembled a grand clubhouse for a Westchester country club. Soon the Casino catered only to a wealthy clientele arriving in the handsomest of carriages; on the restaurant's "Bill of Fare" were eggs and omelets, soups of all sorts, vegetables and relishes, fish and chicken, partridge and duck, lamb, mutton, and steaks (a porterhouse cost a dollar, an extra twenty-five cents with mushrooms). There was lobster plain or deviled, scallops stewed or fried, oysters raw, stewed, fried or boiled, and the establishment's signature dish, Clams Casino (forty cents). Russian Caviar, Spanish olives, and Vichy bottled water could be had, along with pastries, fruit in season, and a wine list with champagnes and clarets, cherry wine and cordials, including Paris's lickerish licorice absinthe.

By the early 1920s the Casino had deteriorated into what *Variety* described as "a somewhat dumpy nite-club style." Then on New Year's Day of 1926, the city's new mayor took office, a mayor perfect for an age of such excess and excitement. With affectionate monikers such as "Gentleman Jimmy" and "Beau James," Walker was once an aspiring songwriter with a popular little hit "Will You Love Me in December (as You Do in May)?" Pressured by his Irish-born, Greenwich Village alderman father, he attended law school, then won a seat in the State Assembly. Dashing in his gray spats and double-breasted suits, tall, handsome, fit as a dancer, and with a seemingly perpetual smirk, he was loved by the average citizen for passing a bill that allowed Sunday ball games, kept subway rides a nickel, and led the 100,000 member "We Want Beer" march up Fifth Avenue. Mobsters liked his penchant for speakeasies.

When city lawyers evicted the Casino's proprietor, Walker appointed his own— a hotel businessman named Sidney Solomon to whom the mayor owed a debt; Solomon had introduced Walker to his own personal tailor. Solomon quickly assembled a board made up of such powerful New Yorkers as William K. Vanderbilt, banker Robert Lehman, and show business tycoons Adolph Zukor and Florenz Ziegfeld. Rumor had it that one financier was Arnold Rothstein, the man who fixed the 1919 World Series and model for sentimental, cold-hearted Meyer Wolfsheim in *The Great Gatsby*, Scott Fitzgerald's gorgeous novel of the age.

Once in control Solomon did little to alter the Casino's brownstone exterior, but the interior, the new manager promised, would display "new standards of elegance and beauty." The Metropolitan Opera's renowned theatrical designer Joseph Urban was hired to modernize the inside and did so, he declared, "with the joyousness of a wind among new leaves." In the main dining hall that comfortably accommodated six hundred guests hung two glass chandeliers, their lights sparkling in black mirrors along the walls inlaid with a tulip design; dancers fox trotting on polished wood floors were dimly reflected in the black glass covering the ceiling.

"It's not just a renovation," Solomon told *The New York Times*. "It's something which has never before existed so perfectly in the world."

A dozen stars, each a yard wide, dangled above long tables and four-tops and those seating six which were perfectly set with maroon cloths and shining crystal glasses, gleaming cutlery and bright white napkins each pressed with deep creases beneath a waiter's persistent iron. Clusters of green and maroon balloons swayed to Emil Coleman's orchestra, and an unknown Eddie Duchin played one of the two grand pianos. René Black, the "Master of Forty Sauces," was the maître d'hôtel, and a special French menu was prepared by banker Louis Rothschild's former chef. Twenty-four hundred applications were submitted for opening night of June 4, 1929. With Walker's plump, matronly wife and their children packed off on a long vacation in Florida, holding the mayor's arm for the night of these special festivities was his mistress from the Ziegfeld Follies. Her name was Betty Compton. She was young, slender, dark-haired, alluring, with the adorable face of a kewpie-doll and just off a successful Broadway run of *Funny Face* starring Fred Astaire.

"The Casino will be our place," Walker promised her, but on opening night five hundred of New York's rich and powerful joined them at what was called "the high hat hut."

Perhaps on that night I'd linger near Bethesda Terrace and toss a coin into the Angel's basin wishing that I too were at the party dancing with a pretty girl beneath the artificial stars. It seemed that the mayor spent more time at the Casino than he ever did at City Hall, and when his chauffeur-driven, two-tone green Duesenberg equipped with a siren approached the Casino's long canvas awning that led from the parking lot, the doorman notified the orchestra leader moments before the band played "Will You Love Me in December?" as Walker swaggered in with his admiring entourage. Festivities lasted well past midnight. In John Dos Passos's novel *Manhattan Transfer*, the tingling of champagne glasses mixed with a "hot gust of foodsmell and the rhythm of a band" drift towards Harry and Elaine strolling near the Casino.

After the restaurant closed for the night owing to an old cabaret law requiring that the party ends at 3 a.m., chorus girls from the Ziegfeld Follies arrived by police motorcycle escort to entertain the most select clients in private rooms upstairs as dazzling light spilling from the windows shimmered off the leaves of encircling trees and blazed on the luxuriant exteriors of Fifth Avenue.

Running for re-election against a fiery Fiorello LaGuardia in 1929, Walker won overwhelmingly as New Yorkers kept their "promise on voting day" went a popular, timely song that "we will love you in November as we do in May."

But Walker's political journey paralleled the age in which he lived. While ominous signs of an impending stock market crash appeared as early as the spring of '29, stocks peaked by the end of summer, then gradually dropped before a massive plummet on October 24, forever known as Black Thursday. Bankers pooled their money and invested in the market; selling stabilized and people were again buying stocks at a bargain. Then on October 29, the bottom fell out. Soon steel production slowed, auto sales and the construction industry because of it. The Great Depression had begun.

Throughout the city hundreds of evictions occurred, the entire belongings of a family bundled and boxed on the sidewalk where stretched dismal breadlines of despairing, defeated men. Many New Yorkers forced from their homes found shelter in Bowery flophouses if they could pay or the lodging house on East 25th Street. When that and its annex grew too crowded, shelters were made in a converted ferry terminal downtown on Whitehall Street.

But others chose the uncertain, unconfined life in the vast, drained pit in the middle of Central Park. Referred to as Hoover Valley for the president unfairly blamed for the catastrophe in which the country found itself, the shacks were a startling contrast to the grandeur of apartment buildings encircling the park. Nearly two hundred shacks were constructed in the enormous pit of wood and tin and fruit crates pulled from the rivers as refuse floating to the sea.

One sturdy structure of brick with several rooms and a tiled roof built by out-of-work bricklayers was known as "The Manor." Trash can fires gave some warmth on cold nights and long days as desperate men scoured the park for food while a preposterous film of the day prejudiced public opinion. In the 1933 *Hallelujah, I'm a Bum,* Al Jolson played Bumper, a member of a merry band of homeless men living in Central Park, drinking excessively and without a worry. Jolson happily sings "Hallelujah, I'm a bum again" where "the moon is your chandelier, your ceiling is the sky." His love interest, the adorable Madge Evans, is the mayor's amnesiac girlfriend who, in a suicide attempt, jumps off Bow Bridge. Since the Boating Lake isn't deep at worst she'd break an ankle; the real damage would have been to Bumper who dived in headfirst after her.

Hoover Valley (the Great Lawn) with the Beresford in background left
Image via Skyscraper City

In the real world men gathered at night in a shack called "Radio City" because someone there had a radio. They heard the hopeless news of more bank closings, homes turning to dust in Oklahoma, and music: Ethel Waters singing "Stormy Weather" ("Can't go on, everything I had is gone") and Duke Ellington's "Wall Street Shuffle" ("Hear the money rustle/ Watch the greenbacks tumble/ Feel the sterling crumble"). But the Chrysler Building had opened, and in one double-header Lou Gehrig homered three times in the first game and Babe belted three in the second, and while "whole sections of the city had grown rather poisonous," wrote Scott Fitzgerald in his remorseful, reminiscent essay "My Lost City," he had "found a moment of utter peace riding south through Central Park at dusk....There again was my lost city, wrapped cool in its mystery and promise."

A narrow tunnel 150 feet long ran beneath the pit where some men found shelter and warmth; lit with red bulbs, it was called ungrudgingly "The Little Casino." Despite the mayor's glamorous playpen nearby, only in the deepening years of the Depression did New Yorkers turn against their beloved Jimmy Walker. He had resisted demands by Fifth Avenue residents to evict these "hoboes and bums" encamped in Central Park just outside their doors; although referred to as drifters and derelicts, they were in truth shopkeepers, salesmen, teachers, actors, and veterans of the Great War. Among them were skilled laborers who once had "built a tower up to the sun/ Brick and rivet and lime," ran a song of those days, "Buddy, can you spare a dime?" Jolson did a popular version of it.

In Robert Nathan's 1933 novel *One More Spring,* Mr. Rosenberg, an unemployed violinist, and Mr. Otkar, a bankrupt antiques dealer, live in a Central Park tool shed. The characters are sympathetic, unembittered, desperate, and each day search the park for something to eat or useful materials; sometimes Mr. Rosenberg collects a few coins from playing violin. "Only the Casino remained open, glowing like a lamp in the dark and rain-soaked night, it gave out a sound of laughter and music, the clink of dishes, and the warm odor of food."

Eventually public sentiment turned against the mayor. An investigation into his corrupt administration led to him resigning from office in September of '32. Vowing to clear his name, he fled for Paris where Betty waited and, wrote Sinclair Lewis in his novel *It Can't Happen Here,* we would find "Jimmy Walker and a few ex-presidents from South American and Cuba."

LaGuardia was now in power, a reform mayor with a special hatred for the Casino, its annual rent of $8,500 less than "that whoopee joint" made in one night. His henchman and master builder Robert Moses claimed that the Casino only "catered to a wealthy clientele with menu prices greater than the bill of fare of the Plaza Hotel." Since the general public could not afford to eat there, he declared that "such a restaurant does not belong in a public park." Despite a pledge from the Casino's manager to lower the prices, Moses was determined to raze an irritating symbol of the corrupt and decadent Walker administration which he despised.

On a mild evening after a splendid dinner at the Plaza Hotel, Parks Commissioner Robert Moses and former New York police chief Grover Whalen (who believed that "there is plenty of law at the end of a nightstick") strolled through the park to watch the Casino's dismantling. Already the shelters in the pit had been destroyed, their occupants driven off to Hoovervilles along the Hudson River. Moses was delighted, even celebratory watching the once charming structure come down. But Whalen grew sentimental; in a 1941 *New Yorker* article "Central Park: A Nasty Place" by Eugene Kinkead and Russell Maloney, "Here had been the entrance, here the bar," he sighed, "and here the dining room." Pointing with his walking stick to where the second floor had been, Whalen—

perhaps unknowingly— recalled the Casino's distant, forgotten origins: "And right up there…was the ladies' room."

Everything from the Casino was destroyed except a few stained-glass windows later installed in the park's 86th Street police station, but it seems that even those vanished years ago. In 1935 Moses had Rumsey playground erected on the once riotous site, it too lost in time to the SummerStage.

But there's an enchanting belief that any sound ever emitted reso-nates for eternity, that in some infinite, extraordinary way everything is still here. Late some summer nights along the promenade, after the park empties, the sky takes on a haunting iridescence. The faintest cocktail music rises softly like the clear, thin notes from a music box; the rhythm of the orchestra varies with the slightest motion of a white baton, and as a jeweled arm of a lovely girl pulls me closer to her lips the mayor lifts his glass of champagne and Betty's laughter, carrying upward through the park, forever fastens to the treetops like a loosed, snagged party balloon.

CHAPTER SEVEN

Kindred Spirits

For years much of the park had entered my apartment: brittle autumn leaves yellow and red on the desk, a twig of pointy pin oak leaves with acorns still attached, holly berries on a sprig of evergreen in winter, and a pine cone the size of an ear of corn. There were pebbles by the toaster, dark brown peapods that rattled like a primitive musical instrument, and a piece of wood with a remarkable similarity to a fish even down to its dorsal fin.

I saved a fragment of a blue, broken eggshell with dried liquid and tiny feathers inside. And a dead monarch butterfly with wings of the finest tissue paper, and a completely hollowed beetle, crisp, flaky snakeskin, and a squirrel's skull still with its two front teeth. Lots of bark, and feathers, many feathers: a red one from a cardinal, fluffy down from ducks, and one from a swan's wing, long and white, slipped in the beveled mirror. When enough of the park had come home with me, the time had arrived to spend all night in the park. Before air conditioning, hundreds of New Yorkers fled their unbearable apartments for the park to do the same.

My next visit focused on finding shelter for that night. There was the Ramble, but so many gay men rendezvous there, hidden places strewn with the mess they leave. Then I remembered how Bo had slipped under that fence in a part of the park where no one ever ventured.

Originally called the Promontory, surrounded on three sides by the Pond and fenced off from the rest of the park is the Hallet Nature Sanctuary. No part of the park is more isolated, and I liked the word 'sanctuary'— a refuge, a temple, the park's supreme purpose.

I circled the Sanctuary's perimeter on my bicycle and scanned the peninsula with binoculars. Formations made of boulders, decaying stumps, thick brush, tall trees abundant with summer leaves; along the northern side, with the skating rink behind me, the opening Bo discovered still there.

On the walkway along the Pond's west side I saw a plateau: rock above and to each side, with an opening facing southeast and on the high ground. From *The Central Park Book* I learned one could eat well in the park. Elderberries and cranberries, raspberries and mulberries, June berries, red and black cherries, apples, gingko nuts and acorns after boiling, particularly those from the Turkey oak (whatever tree it was). Japanese knotweed tastes like asparagus after steaming, and pigweed has a flavor similar to spinach. Chickweed and bark from the sassafras tree make tasty tea, and after a rain, mushrooms grow overnight. There was peppergrass and leeks, autumn olives and field garlic, walnuts and hawthorn. Occasionally I could snare a turtle or squirrel, and the park's lakes and ponds abound with largemouth bass, bluegills, bullheads, goldfish, shiners, banded killifish, yellow perch, fathead minnows, and enormous carp and catfish whose favorite bait, Jose showed me one summer dusk, is cinnamon raisin bagels. Taught by his father, he's been fishing the park's lakes and ponds for over twenty years. Sometimes feeding fish in the Boating Lake lures the giant snapping turtle that slowly slides through the dark water like a stalking alligator, only its nose holes and the tip of its tail three feet later above the water. The turtle too savors the cinnamon-raisin bagels.

Late one summer afternoon I filled my bicycle's water bottle, packed figs and beef jerky, almonds and challah, a small flashlight, a joint, my Zippo and Buck knife. I left my valiant bicycle at home and rode the F train to 53rd and Fifth Avenue, entering the park at 59th Street across from the Plaza, then took the stairs down to the shore of the Pond towards Gapstow Bridge. After a few steps on the other side of it I found the opening in the fence, and when dusk wrapped its mysterious arms around the park as trees darkened in that time of each day where Indians believed the dog turns to wolf, I slipped my pack through, looked around, then slid in on my back feet first. The Sanctuary was mine.

I sought the rock plateau before darkness fully fell. The Sanctuary, thick with summer growth, was unfamiliar, unlit, and had no pathways like the Ramble. I walked low and hunched to avoid detection, and soon found my shelter which I checked with a flashlight for rat holes. After spreading several armfuls of fallen leaves to soften my bed, I laid out an Army green plastic poncho then cuddled in.

Though very excited, I lay quietly listening to the park, at first hearing only a car horn and the low, varying rhythm of Central Park South's traffic, and close by a woman laughing for a long time, her laughter rising and falling off again and then again, each time further away before finally fading along the street. Among the darkening trees, fireflies blinked off and on while floating in search of love; "they burn peepholes in the night," wrote poet Ernest Slyman, "and take snapshots of my house." The western shore of the Pond was twenty-feet below me, black except for smeared, shimmering reflections from the Plaza Hotel. A tree close by steadily filled with hundreds of starlings. They flew in singularly and in groups, descendants of the first of their species loosed in Central Park by Eugene Schieffelin in 1890 because he wanted flying in our nation all the birds mentioned in Shakespeare's plays. As the sky darkened they all squeaked and cheeped back and forth, checking on each other and telling what they saw in the park that day or complaining about their place on a branch and taking longer to say goodnight than the end of *The Waltons;* after a few lingering, softened peeps, the trees were silent.

And a few small insects flew around my face.

I had planned exploring once darkness fell but the Sanctuary was so dark and using a flashlight might blow my cover. A deep, rolling sound came from the shore of the Pond where a bullfrog bellowed: a bullfrog near the Plaza Hotel, and again I shook my head at the incongruous combination.

Damn bugs flying around me! I slap at ticklings on my arms.

The leaves were lit from streetlamps along Central Park South, with Fifth Avenue glowing softly two hundred yards east. Soon after nightfall something slipped through the underbrush –perhaps a feral cat hunting mice—and sometimes the soft chirps of disquieted birds. But I had planned badly and had brought no bug repellent. I was considering heading home to spend another night here one bug-free autumn when, to my astonishment, a man descended a tree not twenty yards away. He held onto a rope while he walked down the trunk, visible only because light along Fifth Avenue outlined his silhouette. As soon as he touched the ground he vanished amid the bushes. Leaves rustled with his movement; was he circling behind me, for no doubt from the trees he saw my entrance and hideaway. My heart was pounding and I breathed silently through my mouth, but the sound of the rustling leaves faded, and then silence again.

My first impulse was to gather my gear and slip back through the fence, likely the same gap he used and where he might wait in ambush: a mad Vietnam vet trained in survival skills. Perhaps he was out scavenging the park and would not return for a while, but he soon did. Instinctively I curled deeper into the rock ledge, my Buck knife at my side. Damn bugs get out of my face! Bushes rustled, twigs cracked, and the shuffling from scattered leaves drew closer. I imagined a handmade spear crafted from a branch sharpened with his Ka-Bar knife.

Then I saw him again in silhouette scamper up a shorter, thin tree several yards away from the one he had descended. Faintly visible through the leaves on those slender branches, he neared the top when the tree gently bent the way Robert Frost described in "Birches," the boy climbing "till the tree could bear no more, /But dipped its top" as the thin tree swayed towards the larger one. When the branches entwined, he reached out with one arm and one leg, and for an instant he was motionless, he and the trees all silhouettes from Fifth Avenue's lights behind them. In that luminous instant he straddled both trees before shifting to the larger one, its thick leaves hiding him again. Soon the rope he had used to climb down began to slowly rise up the trunk pulling what appeared to be wood boards several feet long before, like him, disappearing in the tree.

For a while I heard rustling leaves but didn't see him again, and despite the bugs, I stayed. The city surrounding us grew quieter with the deepening night, and while slapping at insects and even crushing one between my fingers that I nabbed on my neck I wondered how my neighbor endured: a screened-in treehouse, a can of bug repellent, or did he know a natural remedy mentioned in *The Central Park Book*?

Nearby, softly, "Who, who," silence, then again, "Who, who."

Of course he could do perfect bird calls.

"Woof, woof," I answered softly. It seemed a long time passed before the excitement of the night settled in me. The park was very quiet and after a while the city too. Before long I drifted to sleep surrounded by the park and New York on a summer's night, and watched over by the spirit in the trees.

I woke momentarily confused to the earliest birds singing to the sun as if to wake it. Soon the sky faintly, very faintly glowed in the east, a heavenly, pale blue at the straight edges of the buildings. I lay comfortably as the sun rose higher and darkness peeled slowly downward from the treetops. At first only the highest leaves on the top branches were lit, but as the sun rose higher, the last of the night slowly descended down the tree until all but the dark trunk of it glowed in the soft dawn. Now was my chance to explore. After munching some Challah and a fig I slipped from my shelter, rolled up the plastic tarp, threw my pack across my shoulder and wandered the Sanctuary where no one had left anything: no cigarette packs, beer cans, filthy paper bags, crusty clothes. Perhaps in my wanderings he was watching me from his perch but I could see nothing through the trees. At the gap in the fence I threw him another look and brief nod to the canopy, then slipped feet first from the Sanctuary into the awakening park.

For days I worked on the trucks while a heatwave wrapped hot, muggy arms around New York, the swollen, unrelenting sun poking through any crack of the window shade like burning spears. Everything sweats, even the pipes and faucets. Open hydrants pour a cooling gush of water over the streets as garbage flows down East First Street's gutters. Subway tunnels were the worst, like descending into another, hotter ring of Hell. Most subways had no air-conditioning then as some people rode between cars for any wind however steamy. Overnight the Statue of Liberty had removed her heavy gown, poised now on her pedestal in undergarments grandmothers wear. Still, a French girl, she looked good in anything.

Night gave relief from the merciless sun but not the humidity; it was hard to breathe. Latin men in damp undershirts played dominos and sipped cold beer in the fuzzy pools thrown by streetlamps throbbing like bruises as a steady tap-tap-tap of a dripping air-conditioner hit an ashcan lid. Tar on rooftops remained pasty through the night, and from up there I gazed across East Houston and the Bowery, over Chinatown and municipal buildings all the way to the Twin Towers, many of its lights on at four in the morning when the temperature dipped to a damp eighty-four degrees and a hot breath of stale air came from the south. Soon the unforgiving sun rose again out of Brooklyn.

Each day was hotter than the next because yesterday's heat remained, and a local TV news team demonstrated that an egg really *can* fry on the sidewalks. After a while it seemed that it's always been hot, that it never was cold and never would be, and that it's only getting hotter. On my day off I cycled to the park, uptown so steamy it smoldered. Cars and buses choke the streets and even themselves as hoods untouchably hot are flung open as more steam rises into the broiling air and sunlight hits high-rise windows like a rectangular fireball. At East 60th I head west just behind the statue of Sherman, his gold leaf melting, the park no forest now but a steaming jungle.

"And they says the sun's gettin' colder every year," said Sunflower, taking a break from blowing his alto saxophone into the hot air beneath Denesmouth Arch. With the few quarters tossed that day into his open case he buys a popsicle from Manny.

"Colder?" Manny cried with amazement.

"That's what they says."

Looking defiant, Manny moved his arm from the shade of the cart's umbrella into the slash of sunlight.

"Feel that?" he declared triumphantly. "That's hot!"

Dropping to the Pond's filthy eastern shore, I peddled hard to take the small rise up Gapstow Bridge, then coasted downhill with the Sanctuary to my left. But something was different; the Sanctuary was busy.

A cherry picker stretched its mechanical yellow arm high into the trees, lowering plank after green plank. With binoculars I scanned the magnified workers but saw no one unusual or disheartened, Tarzan free to build another. I put my specs away, slipped into my toe-clips, tightened the straps and, after stopping at the struggling flowerbed to roll a bit of Bo through my fingers, cycled deeper into the park.

Now is a good time to show how to find your bearings in Central Park. On every lamppost along the six-mile Drive are indicators of what side of the park we are on and its nearest cross street. The letter and numbers are large and white –"E" for the east side, "W" for the west side, and "C" for the center— followed by numbers: E83 means 83rd Street on the east side, W06 means we're on the west side near 106th. This will help in our journeys and enable you, if I'm somewhere else, to find your own way.

I had bought a pair of fingerless biking gloves, palms padded to soften the feel of the handlebars. But that spoon ring purchased along St. Mark's kept snagging on the glove, so it joined in a cigar box a high school athletic medal, my grandfather's pocket watch, a matchbox from my Bar Mitzvah with "Today I am a Man" on the cover, and a gold wedding band. By now I had learned to smoothly shift all ten gears and leg muscle groups from the quadriceps pulling up on the toe straps to the hamstrings pushing down on the pedals— pull with one leg and push with the other— how to feather my feet and decrease wind resistance by holding on to the lower drops of the handlebars; it was time to "do the loop."

from *Central Park* by Frederick Wiseman

I cycle the East Drive to the north—Fifth Avenue on my right—then a slow descent that turns a quick left to become a soaring downhill, a thrill of a ride with my hair blown back, eyes wide in terror and wonder, rolling past gravity and fear to what gets as close to flight as we can get still touching the earth by only the width of a thin rubber tire. The momentum carried me along the flat road for a while, a tremendous blue, incongruous concrete swimming pool to my right that had swallowed a large portion of the park. But soon the road curved west and began its uphill climb. I panted and peddled as the roadway kept ascending. A curve ahead hopefully meant that the road flattened, but it kept climbing. My legs ached, I gasped for air and felt as if loose shards of glass were poking in my left side, but the surroundings were beautiful; here was another forest to explore. After the roadway dipped and rose a few more times I dismounted at Sheep Meadow, took off my jersey, stretched my legs, did sets of push-ups, then sprawled bared-chested and pumped beneath the sun with my right leg protectively over my wheel for when I fell asleep those serene, summer afternoons.

And on some hot summer nights, I and a few other renegades found heavenly relief in the cold, black water of what some of us know as Lake Manhattan. I locked my bike to a busted lamppost along the great reservoir's western side near 90th Street, then slip through a nearly undetectable gash made by bolt cutters in the chain-link fence. Luxurious apartments diminished by the distance along Fifth Avenue reflect on the water like transient cubes of color. Only ever a few of us and silent to avoid detection, we slid down the rock foundation and with a hushed sigh of pleasure slip into Lake Manhattan so chilly after the hot day that we lose a breath. Some dipped naked in the night, their bodies glistening beneath the moon amid this midsummer night's dream when each of us bobbed inexpressibly happy to be young and alive in New York.

To Make an Eden *continued*

Desigining the city's new park would certainly be handed to Andrew Jackson Downing and Calvert Vaux who were already collaborating on a plan for it. But on a summer day in 1852, Downing and his family were on the steamboat *Henry Clay* along the Hudson River when the boiler exploded. Downing drowned attempting to save his mother-in-law. He was thirty-seven years old. Late in 1857 Vaux asked Frederick Law Olmsted to assist in designing the new park despite Olmsted having never before designed anything.

After he failed at farming an unrelenting piece of land near his Hartford, Connecticut, home, then losing interest in more promising acres on Staten Island, Olmsted created a publishing firm that quickly went bankrupt. Like many young idealists touched by the era's Romantic spirit (and with his father's financial and emotional support), he traveled England and the continent, writing of what he saw.

In England he roamed the 223 acres of Birkenhead Park, the first publicly funded English park. With its "winding paths...[and] constant varying surface... set in borders of greenest, closest turf," Olmsted wrote of it, "I cannot undertake to describe the effect of so much taste and skill." Perhaps it was then he had the first vague imaginings of his life's work, for in "America there was nothing to be thought of as comparable with this People's Garden."

Back in the United States and upon the recommendation of his father's friend Charles Elliot, Olmsted applied for the post of superintendent of labor for ragged, swampy, schist-covered acres in the center of the island where a future park would grow. On September 11, 1857, the thirty-five-year-old was hired for $1,500 a year and proved a reliable, hard-working employee soon in charge of hundreds, then thousands of day laborers. Most important, he repeatedly explored both on foot and horseback every acre of the designated land with a detailed typographical map created by Chief Engineer Egbert Ludovicus Viele known as "the Viele Map" and still used by contractors today.

Olmsted climbed mounds of iron-hard Manhattan schist to see great distances across the barren landscape. The only water on the site (excluding the 1842 Receiving Reservoir) were stagnant pools— one a putrid swamp—as well as two small streams: DeVoor's Mill Stream, which trickled in at the southeast corner from a part of the city known as Turtle Bay, and Montayne's Rivulet, beginning somewhere near what is today Columbus Avenue and 95th Street and still flowing beneath the park. For an island so well forested its center was oddly barren save for a few oak and willow trees, scrub grass and poison ivy. In his 850-page panoramic *Lights and Shadow of New York Life; Or The Sights and Sensation of the Great City* published in 1872, James D. McCabe wrote that "nature had done nothing for this part of the island" which he described as "bleak, dreary and sickly...."

There was a stone fort far to the north, a convent near it: to the west, several hundred struggling people as distant as they could get from the miasmic congestion downtown. And surely Olmsted detected uncertainty in their eyes; the city wanted the land upon which they lived, raised crops and families, built schools, churches, even a cemetery, and with the ruthless scythe of Eminent Domain, the city would take it.

"It would be difficult to find another body of land upon this island," Olmsted wrote with dismay, "which possessed less of ...the most desirable characteristic of a park." And though, as Clarence Cook stated, "a more unpromising locality has never been given to any Adam to make an Eden of," Olmsted accepted Vaux's offer.

An early task for Olmsted soon after his appointment as superintendent was to establish a perimeter around the area that would become Central Park. The commissioners expected a black iron fence ten feet high and locked at night like Gramercy Park downtown. The low stone wall that surrounds the park was a compromise; Olmsted wanted only a tree-line.

One day "the Park is to be surrounded by an artificial wall," he predicted, "twice as high as the Great Wall of China, composed of urban buildings." When this occurs, he continued, the "imagination would be checked abruptly." But a perimeter of tall trees would "leave an uncertainty" as if beyond the treetops is not the teeming city but the infinite expanse of Nature. What the young idealist could not foresee was how a single invention displayed only days before New York committed funds for a large park would greatly affect his design. Elisha Otis's 'safety hoist' doomed the illusion that the park extended beyond the treetops, and the changes brought by Otis's invention grieved the grand old man whose vehement editorials decades before had pressured the city for a large public park.

Strolling with his friend Minister Samuel Osgood through a park far larger and more beautiful than anything he had imagined in 1851, with his splendid bald pate, a beard full and white, "leaning on his cane, half in meditation, half to gain breath," William Cullen Bryant is deeply concerned about the city's encroachment on this remarkable creation. His distress would be captured in a charming memoir by Mabel Osgood Wright who, as a child, had accompanied her father and Bryant to the park soon after its official opening in 1873. Her *My New York* recalls a pleasant childhood in Greenwich Village during the second half of the nineteenth century, a world of manners and customs, buttons and books, her family's friends seen not for their notoriety and influence but simply through the eyes of a young, privileged girl for whom the park was "the most desirable end of all journeys. Sixth Avenue was always a very friendly way, for it ran by our street and straight up into the arms of Central Park."

In that visit long ago, with a solemn sigh and furrowed brow, Bryant fears that someday "this gift, blended of nature and art may be surrounded on all sides by buildings eight, nay possibly ten stories in height, until the spirit of the Park's loveliness will go from it."

Today the park is surrounded by towers many times higher than twice the height of the Great Wall in China and far higher than anything Bryant could imagine on that distant afternoon, but these did not accomplish what the great old man had feared; the spirit of loveliness remains in the park. Nor does the soaring skyline check our imagination as Olmsted had feared though it is redirected, and while there are only a few places in the park where the city is hidden by trees, nowhere is this intrusion more dramatic than along the great reservoir with buildings visible above the shore.

CHAPTER EIGHT

Garden of Earthly Delights

From its opening in the summer of 1862, the new, immense reservoir around which the city created its magnificent park was encircled by a four-foot-high cast-iron black fence, restricting but not intrusive, and comfortably allowing us to gaze across the great expanse of New York's fresh, life-sustaining water. But sometime around 1926 the Department of Water, Gas, and Electricity replaced the fence with one ten-foot high of chain link. This outraged some park people who demanded its immediate removal, but city officials insisted that the fence kept our water supply safe from sabotage (though how exactly the fence could do that remained far less clear than the reservoir's fine water), and would keep distraught New Yorkers from continually using Lake Manhattan as their final, soaking step into eternity.

The first suicide occurred in 1884; an unidentified man chose a watery death rather than the quicker one of blowing out his brains with the revolver in the pocket of his brown Prince Albert coat. A few years later Oliver Perry Lewis, in full evening dress, hopped over the low fence and did the same. And in May of 1897, identifying herself only as Titania, a woman left a note that read, "Never mind who I am, or why this is done. My house of love was builded on the sand."

She was Ethel Reiss, a young, pretty, brown-haired woman from Brooklyn who left, along with the note of heartache and farewell, a trunk of books and handwritten pages of her own poetry. The reason for her untimely death very likely was unrequited love for an elderly man known only as "The Professor" with whom she often shared breakfast at the Hotel St. George in Brooklyn Heights. On May 12, 1897, *The New York Times* ran a story with the headline "The Central Park Suicide" that "Unless she saw him at least once every day she became morose" and frequently "cried all night if he had not been with her that day."

Three suicides occurred there in 1924 and two more in '26, and so the "suicide fence" appeared and topped with barbed wire. A week later the *Times* published a letter to the editor from novelist Edna Ferber who cannot look across the reservoir anymore without getting seasick or dizzy. She wonders if next there will be fences along the Hudson River, the Atlantic Ocean, "and when is Chicago going to do something about that menace Lake Michigan?"

"Besides," she adds in Lake Manhattan's finest compliment, "I can't think of any nicer bit of water to drown one's self in than the park reservoir." Unless the fence is removed, she threatens to drown there herself though the fence remained for the next 77 years.

No longer is "the reservoir drying," songwriter Malvina Reynolds sang of it, "because it's supplying/ The faucets that drip in New York," for the reservoir hasn't piped water to the city since 1993. It still feeds the Boating Lake and the Conservatory Pond, the Gill and the Loch, the Pool, the Pond, the Meer, playground sprays and the streams at the Angel's feet, replenished by the Croton Reservoir else we'd soon have a 106-acre mud hole in the middle of the park.

And then in 1996, during a volunteer, underwater clean-up of the reservoir, scuba experts George Parry and his wife Catherine discovered – along with bass, eels, sunfish, trout, perch, turtles, an alligator (rubber), *many* plastic and glass bottles, knives, and guns (including the one Dustin Hoffman used in the thriller *Marathon Man*)—a piece of the original 1862 fence. When Donna Schwartz heard of this during a park nature walk, "Red lights went off," she said in a *Times* article. Donna and her portfolio-manager husband Marvin, who cherish the view of the reservoir from their Central Park West apartment, graciously bank-rolled the creation of a new fence based on the old one. And while providing some of us with adventure and sensual delights on summer nights, Lake Manhattan gives others a place for peace and contemplation.

Except for the last two years of his life and on as many pleasant days as possible, Samuel Menashe often made the arduous journey from the fifth-floor of his walk-up downtown to his favorite bench along the reservoir. Both the C and E subway lines close to his apartment took him to Central Park West and 96th Street where he found pleasure entering the park at the GATE OF ALL SAINTS: not that he thought himself one but here a saint might be encountered. He followed the walkway to his right that gently rose and then descended through a meadow, tennis courts to his left, eventually leading up to the graceful Gothic Bridge, one of the most beautiful and seemingly delicate bridges in the park, a bridle path passing beneath it.

He often wore khaki pants with rainbow suspenders over a white shirt and always took his time getting to his bench, not only because of age but he composed as he walked. Samuel did not "write" poems as much as compose them throughout the days and nights, the language of it never letting go of him as he trudged the streets or sat in the park, revising and refining. When he reached his bench and with the shimmering water before him, he had perhaps forged a poem that is compressed, crystallized, evocative, and lyrical.

Shaded by trees, Samuel's bench faces southeast, the North Gate House to his left, and one brisk September afternoon, just as he had written in "Sunset, Central Park," light from the setting sun blasted off the polished windows along Fifth Avenue before reflected in the reservoir.

> A wall of windows
> Ignited by the sun
> Burns in one column
> Of fire on the lake
> Night follows
> As embers break

Occasionally someone nodded to this frequent visitor with bright, lively eyes and most of his long white hair, and often he was greeted by an equally old man with a white mustache (who greeted nearly everyone along the path encircling the reservoir) walking clockwise rather than the customary counter-clockwise that runners take. His name was Alberto Arroyo and known as the Mayor of the Central Park Reservoir. "Central Park is my Riviera," the old man once said, "it is my wealth."

But camaraderie is not why Samuel frequented the park, nor was it for the unobstructed vista across the water though he cherished both of these. I believe that Samuel often returned, and to this bench in particular, because here he felt restored, just as Olmsted had hoped he would. As Samuel wrote in "Sheep Meadow," where "on the south side…towers of the city rise," we find in Central Park—

one of those hours
in early afternoon
when nothing happens
but time makes room

When nearly eighty years old Samuel received the first *Neglected Poets Award,* and in 2005 the Library of America published his *New and Selected Poems.* As much as anyone I know, Samuel loved the park; over his bowed and tottering bookshelves hung a dim painting of the *Angel of the Waters* he had bought off the street.

"Beauty makes me sad," Samuel wrote in his poem "At Cross Purposes," for it "makes me grieve /I see what I must leave."

As with all of us, the reservoir's future is uncertain: perhaps more ballfields like the Great Lawn or (to share with those few of us on sensual nights) a lake for swimming. But recently the common loon —a rare, endangered water bird—has used the reservoir for stopovers in its ancient migrations from Iceland to Mexico. A haunting Manhattan moment is to hear at dusk its mournful, tentative wail to its mate across the water that hopefully remains a bird sanctuary. For just as loons rendezvous in the park, many of us, especially the poor and the young, find only in Central Park what lovers need most and what we had those summer nights: quiet and seclusion.

To the outrage of some, the park has always provided this for many. Soon after its opening, Jan Vier wrote a letter to the *Tribune* concerning a sordid sight in Central Park: "horrible indecencies perpetuated after nightfall" were couples "caressing each other...in a way fit only for strict privacy." Not everyone was as outraged as Mr. Vier. "Whenever I go [to the Park]," wrote Edward S. Martin in an 1894 *Harper's Monthly,* "I see lovers in profusion."

D.W. Griffith's 1909 film *Politician's Love Story* has couple after bundled couple cuddling and kissing openly in Central Park where "the habit of meeting young men in sequestered spots was not unknown" to Undine Spragg, the heroine of Edith Wharton's 1913 novel of New York society *The Custom of the Country.* A lover croons how "In Central Park we'll stroll," from Rogers and Hart's "Manhattan" where "our first kiss we stole," and Billie Holliday sings seductively in "Autumn in New York" of "lovers that bless the dark/ On benches in Central Park." An April 12,

2010, *New Yorker* cover by Edward Sorel has naked nymphs and lusty satyrs frolicking in Central Park with Balcony Bridge in the background.

On summer days, bees and hummingbirds probe delicious flowers; at night ten million fireflies glow with yearning through the park while crickets rub legs in foreplay. When movies do a love scene in New York, often it happens in Central Park, the city's finest set with ideal places to woo. In the third and most elaborate version of *King Kong* released in 2005, a touching relationship develops between Kong and his former captive Ann Darrow, played by Naomi Watts, the most enchanting scene occurring on the ice of Central Park's Pond.

Vigorous young men rent rowboats with oars that accidently-on-purpose splash their shrieking girlfriends perched in front of them. Lovers riding noble, painted horses at the carousel laugh at their futile kisses while one rises as the other descends to a calliope's galloping rendition of "The Sidewalks of New York." On the park's swing-set in Lily Wolf's "Pinetum, Through the Seasons" daring teenage boys try out-soaring each other to the admiring cries of the girls, and young lovers "feel silly and cold and in love as they again ride on the swing as snow falls" before "they'll go home and have hot cocoa and hot soup, and later into the night he'll rub her feet and she'll kiss his nose and they'll go to bed."

More than a century ago, when "buildings aren't tall enough/ yet to contain the park," wrote James Doyle in his poem "Central Park, 1901," the "pale green benches that ring the park" soon "fill up before the dinner hour" with "girls in stockings of white lace" and "wearing on either side/parents…[whose] sole purpose is to set off/ the daughters" for young men strolling selectively passed. While "driving in a Victoria through Central Park" Nick and lovely Jordan Baker in *The Great Gatsby* pass a barrier of dark trees as "a block of delicate pale light beamed down into the Park," Nick tells us, "and so I drew up the girl beside me, tightening my arms. Her wan, scornful mouth smiled and so I drew her up again, closer, this time to my face."

Connie Rivera from Spanish Harlem "is young and beautiful, and all her thoughts are on the cloudless sky and the knowledge that on this June day Angel Santiago waits for her in Central Park." As described in Orde Coombs' 1982 *New York* magazine article "The Cherry Orchard," these teenagers are two of thousands "who will crowd Central Park this Sunday…the only piece of real estate they will ever love. For them, Central Park is a refuge from the slums."

While frolicking in "Central Park" one autumn "on a nervous amble/ in the chilly dusk," Martha Hollander and her lover stop, turn, then fall:

> The corresponding flurry of dry leaves
> sweeps over us, spreadeagled as we are,
> drenched in the early attitudes of lovers.

Sex in the park isn't always allure and whispers; in Dixie Salazar's bizarre "The Lost Underwear of Central Park" we watch a "trembling wool coat" and—

> a dress hitched up around her hips...
> under Midnight's
> churning hips and seed pearls
> scattered loose by tattooed hands
> that couldn't wait.

Even the Yiddish poet Moishe-Leib Halpern, visiting the park to see the trees, can't help but look instead at how "the woman strolling through you displays/ A bosom that rises and falls." His poem is one of only a few addressed directly to the park which he affectionately calls "my garden of snow," but he worries that the park will see—

> that I'm foreign to you
> When my funny shawl and my cap appear
> Like nothing that anyone else wears here,
> When I still have a beard that the wind picks through
> Like a woman through straw, for the egg below
> garden of snow, my garden of snow.

The poem appears in Halpern's 1919 collection *In New York* that tells in first person an uncommon story of immigrant disillusionment and loss of hope. But Halpern may have felt that he took other wrong turns; in a poem to his son he writes that the boy can "be a loan shark, a bagel lifter," even a murderer, but if he becomes a poet, "I'll chop up... all the ties that bind us now."

Sit on the soft green lawn of Sheep Meadow one sunny afternoon in summer and gaze at beautiful New Yorkers displaying themselves with the boldness of youthful immodesty. Here, barefoot and perspiring, her skin white and fragrant as her goat's milk soap, Barbara danced beneath the sun, then slipped into the perimeter's shade; muted light poking through the leaves formed patterns on her flesh as if even the sun could not resist touching her. A thin dress clung to her in damp wrinkles as she rinsed in the cold spray of a playground's fountain where she freed her black hair from a ponytail and bent back her head, eyes closed while water streamed down her face.

Slender, fragile Nina often asked, "If you could have only me or Central Park, which would you choose?" but found my evasive answer less satisfying than our amorous encounters.

In a white summer dress, her toenails painted as red as her lipstick, Karina perched in the stern of a boat as I rowed around the Lake. We slipped beneath Bow Bridge, sunlight reflected off the water shimmering on the arch above us where pigeons nested. In open water I removed my polyester Hawaiian shirt and gave masculine, competent pulls to the oars wearing a white undershirt and imitation Panama hat. She smiled, put both hands on one white, impossibly smooth knee, bit her lower lip and leaned back, her thigh rising off the seat. The more I rowed, the further she leaned back and the higher rose that juicy thigh, so I tied the boat to a rustic shelter's landing along the shore, led her to a secluded spot in the Ramble, turned her so she could hold a tree, and deftly lifted that white dress.

Women seemed to believe I possessed some pastoral power because squirrels snatched peanuts from my fingertips or, if she remained still long enough, a titmouse pecked seed from her open hand.

"Now I know why birds suddenly appear," whispered Irene enamored, "every time you are near."

A blue jay arrived, late and angry on a branch.

" 'cause I carry seed."

And I realized what the park was to me —unusual, incongruous, unconventional, romantic, a little untamed—was how I appeared to women, as if showing them those aspects of the park actually revealed these traits in me.

When Christina hadn't enough time to visit my apartment downtown (and since we could never meet uptown at hers), I'd wait for her some early evenings in summer at a rustic shelter on a rise just west of the Pond. It is an open-air room made of twisting tree limbs, the roof entwined with green, shading vines. Often she is late –her life, after all, with more commitments than my own—and when she at last appears on a walkway and her blue eyes turn from mine when our glances meet, I stroll toward her and we wander apart down to the shoreline of the Pond. We draw nearer while dusk slips quietly over the park, then she takes my hand and we leave the walkway to nestle near the wall under soft shrubs. On this secluded place we set free our desires, her quiet cries rising through the New York night before my seed spills from her into the park's soil. Here might grow now a new stalk, one not native to this area but, with luck, adapting well.

And though not the only woman I loved in Manhattan, my love for Audrey Munson endured while all the others turned to ruins.

Surely I had seen her many times before I fell in love. There were two of her whenever Bo and I entered the park at Columbus Circle; she stands immobile in the *Maine Monument* boat, arms outstretched, and she is also the golden figure driving a chariot atop the tower and probably the model for the figure at the back, her arms reaching for Central Park. But I'll always recall when I was struck by the blind bow-boy's arrow.

Beneath cooling drizzle on a warm August night I cycled home, stopping as always at the dirt oval of the promenade to roll a bit of Bo between my fingers. But something had changed; the oval had been tended, weeds removed, slender green stems emerging from the earth. For this was a summer in the middle of the 1980s and, like this oval, the first buddings of the new Central Park Conservancy. A slow, costly restoration was occurring which would restore the park in ways unimaginable that summer day.

I mounted by bike, tightened my toe-straps and glide downhill before crossing 59th Street, the wet pavement smeared with city lights. I slip between the Plaza Hotel on my right and the Pulitzer Fountain to my left where Central Park trees have broken the confines of the stone wall to enwrap the fountain's wide basin. Here a column rises and a woman is poised tentatively on top of it. Lamplight from Fifth Avenue glistens on her body, naked and damp. In her hands and braced by her left thigh turned coyly inward is a basket of fruit beneath which fabric flows between her legs. For she is Pomona, Roman goddess of abundance, but she's also my Galatea as I am her Pygmalion; if I could I'd scale that basin and kiss her into life.

Audrey Munson was the model most in demand during her era, sought by artists not for her physical beauty alone but also for her ability to understand the spirit of the piece, to possess its aura and serve as both model and muse. She's the reclining figure with the dreamy expression and toes nearly dipping into the small basin of the memorial to *Titanic* victims Isidor and Ida Straus at Broadway and 106th Street. Nearby at Riverside and 100th Street is the haunting, harrowing monument "To the Heroic Dead of the Fire Department," a seated woman on either side of the sarcophagus-like memorial. In the figure titled "Duty" she cradles a fireman's helmet in one arm, her other encircling the waist of a young boy. Her face is pensive, fearful. In the other seated figure, "Sacrifice," her expression is resolute, even strong: sprawled across her lap, a dead firefighter. Audrey modeled for both figures. Since September 11, 2002, this memorial has also become a place for our collective mourning and tribute. Bouquets are placed on the fountain's rim: a red carnation display with the number "343" in white carnations, the number of firemen killed that day, nearly half of the firemen killed in New York's long story lost in twenty minutes.

Audrey Munson is the draped figure over the pediment at the Frick Collection on Fifth Avenue and 71st Street, the reclining woman above the proscenium of the New Amsterdam Theatre on West 42nd Street, and she was a movie star. Released in 1915, *Inspiration* is the story of an artist finding the perfect model in a shabby, waif-like gutter girl who poses for him naked, the first in a feature-length film. The film shocked and outraged some people, but since Audrey didn't move while naked— re-enacting classic images from sculpture and painting— the film could not be censored any more than could a Botticelli or a Rubens.

She's "Memory" in the Metropolitan Museum of Art, a naked, reclining woman done in marble holding a mirror that reflects not herself but, thematically, what is behind her. Audrey was model for the stunning figure with an heroic, outstretched arm at the entrance of the Manhattan Bridge, "Peace" above the Appellate Court Building just off Madison Square, and for a shrouded, mournful figure that once stood outside glorious old Pennsylvania Station. The twenty-foot-tall gilded goddess "Civic Fame" high atop the Municipal Building downtown, the tallest statue in Manhattan, is also modeled after Audrey Munson. There are so many images of her throughout the city that she was known as "Miss

Manhattan."

In my dreams I wait for her early one warm spring evening outside Karl Bitter's studio on West 77th Street. She lives with her mother in a boardinghouse on West 65th, but before escorting her home I led her for a stroll through the park.

She walks unhurriedly with easy, perfect posture. She was five foot seven or eight with heels on her stockinged feet that I pictured beneath her long dress. Her black hair with a hint of blue in it when touched by the late afternoon sun trailed half-way down her back. Carriages trot past us on the West Drive, gentle rowboats floating on the Boating Lake to our left; even horses withheld their own needs so as not to spoil the scent of lilacs growing thick as grape vines on the pergola. In our stroll I hoped to encounter some acquaintance, one as dazzled by Audrey and envious that my hand lightly touched her bare elbow. But as the warning foretells, my wish unfortunately came true in the bold, brash continence of a literary fellow in expensive clothes stretched across a powerful body developed in years off-loading cargo on the South Street docks.

"Miss Audrey Munson," I reluctantly said, "Robert Stricker."

He removed his derby to reveal his shaved, sweaty head, kissed her fingertips which, for an instant, he appeared about to taste, then spoke to her as though I were not there at all. Aware of his charms, she in no way eased her attachment from me, yet I still feared that perhaps Stricker, not I, would be one of the seven lovers predicted for her by a fortune teller.

As we neared Mineral Springs I asked if she would care for a glass of mineral water. She smiled softly, lowered her chin, eyes in mine: "Thank you."

Mineral Water Pavilion on Sheep Meadow's north edge looked nothing then like the one there today. I escorted Audrey Munson to an enchanting one-story pavilion, part Moorish in design, its effervescent water bubbling like my blood.

She had large eyes, grayish-blue with long lashes, and she wore no makeup which is meant, she believed, only for theater performances or advertisement photographs. Surely she could feel desire in my eyes, so I turned away to join her gaze upon the green, rolling acres of Sheep Meadow where sheep ambled as if this weren't New York City at all but the English countryside. At dusk the woolly, white animals were herded by their shepherd across the West Drive to spend the night in the Sheepfold, a large, quaint structure resembling a sprawling country cottage; in the years ahead, after the sheep were deposed, the Sheepfold transformed into Tavern on the Green.

Sometimes live music played as it surely did on the day of my fantasy. After the first slow, familiar notes of "Waltzing Matilda" I felt confident enough to ask Audrey to dance; her right hand perched in my left like a white bird. "You have the only perfect hands and arms I have seen on a woman," Karl Bitter had declared. He used her hands and arms as models for a restored *Venus de Milo* commissioned by Queen Wilhelmina of the Netherlands.

She moved easily with my steps as if we've danced together before, a promise of how well we would make love if I have the chance. The faint aroma of almonds rose from her neck, her dark hair brushed my cheek, and I pulled her closer into me with my right hand that encircled her waist mere inches from the dimples above her derriere.

"They are the rarest and most attractive beauty spots," declared the sculptor Salvatore Scarpitta. "Guard those dimples, my girl," he warned her, "and if you ever see them going—cut out the apple pie!"

In Sergio Leone's operatic gangster film *Once Upon a Time in America*, on the heavy door of the mausoleum in "some fancy cemetery up in Riverdale" where Noodles' dear friends are entombed, Audrey is the grieving, half-shrouded figure –dimples visible. She later admitted the dimples "proved to be as valuable to me as government bonds."

"One day you'll be the most celebrated figure in town," I promise her. "Bigger than Shakespeare, bigger than Webster and Washington and Columbus."

She smiled modestly but perhaps already foresaw the unhappy fate that awaited her.

"What becomes of an artist's model?" she wrote in one from a series of articles entitled "Queen of the Artist's Studio" for the old newspaper the *New York American*. "She wonders if anyone standing before a masterpiece of lovely sculpture or a remarkable painting of a young girl... ever ask themselves, 'Where is she now, this model who was so beautiful?' "

For the last sixty-five years of her life we know exactly where Audrey Munson was: the St. Lawrence State Hospital for the Insane. The dark trail that ended here began February 27, 1919, when the owner of

Beauty by Frederick MacMonnies

the boardinghouse where she lived with her mother, the respected physician Dr. Walter Wilkins, murdered his wife who, he believed, prevented an intimate relationship he fantasized with Audrey. Convicted and sentenced to die in the electric chair, he hanged himself in his jail cell. The papers printed unsubstantiated rumors concerning Audrey's part in the tragedy, and in the ensuing scandal the American Film Company dropped her contract. She quickly became an object of ridicule to those who for years disapproved of her independence and inhibitions, her depression worsening when her impending marriage to a former aviator from Michigan collapsed. And then in May of 1922 she attempted suicide, her life saved because only one of four mercury bichloride tablets had dissolved in the cup of water. Audrey would later be committed to the asylum by her mother for "mental blight," today routinely treated with counseling and anti-depressants. Yet despite decades of confinement, her hair completely white, her complexion clear from milk rubbed daily on her face, she apparently had neither bitterness nor resentment and remained remarkably lucid. For her 100th birthday she requested an airplane ride and a bottle of wine though receiving neither. She died five years later, in February, 1996, and until 2015 lay in an unmarked grave in Oswego, New York's New Haven Cemetery, nor is 'Miss Manhattan' mentioned in Kenneth T. Jackson's revered, encompassing *The Encyclopedia of New York City.*

But her beauty and inspiration endure. Audrey Munson was the model for the white, other worldly nude in a portal outside the Public Library at Fifth Avenue and 42nd Street, eyes and right hand uplifted, cold and fragile in the winter, sensuous and pale each summer.

Just above her image are carved John Greenleaf Whittier's words "Beauty Old And Ever New," and when summer rains glisten on our statues and ghosts tap at the windows, I remember the sunlight lowering to the treetops and how the green lawn of Sheep Meadow darkened as I held Audrey in my arms that distant, golden afternoon in Central Park.

CHAPTER NINE

If Not in the Park

When the leaves of the trees were summer-thick I searched for Tarzan anywhere but the Ramble; he'd know that the MOB (many old birders) peered far beneath the canopy and wouldn't miss a thing. Never did I see him in the tall trees of the North Woods nor the grand row of elms along Fifth Avenue or the promenade. With my binoculars I scanned the treetops but still spotted nothing unusual until almost two years later. Late one summer afternoon a rainstorm brewed to the east as dark clouds lumbered in, gathering and piling up one on the other like great gray pillows. Soon the winds blew and a few drops fell, then the rain turned heavier as dark circles the size of a nickel hit the walkways with audible taps. The park quickly emptied though some hurried to the Angel Tunnel where someone always has a guitar and we sit amid the pastoral murals on the wall and gaze at the wet, peaceful Angel.

For this summer storm I took refuge in Winterdale Arch, about midway between the Delacorte Theater and Summit Rock near West 81st Street. The wind whipped the trees, their tops, heavy-leafed and green, bending beneath the torrents of the storm, ten thousand tree tops waving like women drying their washed hair from side to side. High in one tree, as if a curtain had been blown aside by the wind, a dark shape did not move as the branches did. With binoculars I focused on the inflexible form; it was a treehouse all right, and painted green. How high it was —nearly to the top of the great, leaf-thick elm— and its size; it seemed larger than my bedroom. Perhaps Tarzan was there right now, swaying with the tree and gazing down at the park thirty feet below.

After the storm I sought out the treehouse, so well-hidden I had difficulty finding it despite knowing which tree it was in. At the base it was impossible to spot, so high and well protected by the thick leaves. From another, more distant angle its shape against the sky behind it was faintly visible, though one day a maintenance crew with ropes and that cherry picker was at it again, disassembling the treehouse and lowering boards to the ground. But there was no loin-clothed man in handcuffs, so I rode closer.

"Found another one?" I asked a Ranger.

He smiled with mild surprise, then wiped his face with a green bandanna.

"That makes five," he said, holding up his gloved-hand spread wide.

"Have they caught him?"

"No, but I'd like to shake his hand."

He turned to me as the next load of boards descended.

"He never uses nails," he said, quietly amazed. "The trees are completely unharmed."

Shaking his head and with a small, pleased smile, the young worker reached for the dismantled treehouse as I tightened my toe-clips and glided deeper into the park.

In time and after many lopes I became strong and fast enough to circle the park three times under an hour; that's averaging more than eighteen miles an hour and even faster when several of us rode together, one in the lead breaking the headwind, then falling back and riding in the rear as another cyclist pulled the rest of us mere inches off his whirling rear wheel. Sometimes an extraordinary continuity occurred within me, muscles in a steady rhythm unalterable and persistent until I am both human and machine all silver and spinning down the Great Hill. And then, pulling with my quads and pushing with my hamstrings, up out of the saddle leaning over the handlebars attacking the long, thigh-burning climb.

We revitalized at tables outside the Boathouse with coffee and perfectly burned raisin bran muffins, all of us in black padded cycling pants, our Spandex jerseys color-coordinated with our bikes leaning against each other in metallic array. Sarah and Lambert were also at the tables outside; she waved and Lambert raised a skeptical, bemused eyebrow. Before remounting I'd check the Bird Register inside: a Great Blue Heron at Bank Rock Cove and a screech owl in a knothole high in a dead oak tree where the Gill trickles into the Lake. In May and September, pages of warbler sightings. Beside the register today is the park's supreme bird photography book, *Birds of Central Park* by Cal Vornberger published in 2005. Cal is a solitary bear of a man with a penetrating eye whose subjects are birds and the park: a sparrow living in a lamppost, a full moon rising over the Boathouse, and outside the Delacorte Theater a photo of a robin's nest upon swooning Juliet's upturned throat.

I slowly cycled the West Drive to Sheep Meadow for stretches and push-ups under the sun and there in the center of the Drive gathering with a shovel and rake the horse shit from the roadway into a cart attached to his bicycle, that bearded man dressed in purple whom I had seen tending the garden on Eldridge Street; so it was this fertile cargo that supplied nourishment for his garden flourishing far downtown with the goodness scooped from what he called Zentral Park.

My last day working for Spartacus Trucking was after we moved everything from the East First Street office to a warehouse in Queens as Neil again dodged the IRS. Overnight the office transformed into a bicycle messenger company, and after a word to the owner from Neil, I became a messenger.

A century and a half ago we were "runners" scuttling on foot along Wall Street and the city's municipal buildings. On the walls were cork bulletin boards covered with tattered maps of Brooklyn, Queens, and Manhattan: also, a 1940s pin-up girl on a bicycle with her dress blowing, a delicious thigh and panties displayed. Jimmy owned the company. His desk was in front, and two dispatchers sat deeper inside at tables with notepads and several telephones. When to start and quit is up to the rider, but there was always work early in the morning and often into night, so with need and stamina a messenger could make $100 in a ten-hour day with good weather. We're paid strictly on commission: how much is picked up, how much dropped. From the street we called the office on a special 1-800 number (no cell phones then), but many public pay phones in those battered days had receivers torn out, a dangling metal cable with exposed, colorful wires.

Besides a bike, a messenger's only equipment is a large, strong canvas bag with a thick strap thrown over his head on the opposite shoulder so he can swing it on his back when riding and swing it forward to get what's inside. Apart from letters and manila envelopes and packages we carried apples, candy bars, water, a street map, and a valuable photo-copied chart to find Manhattan addresses; if a drop is at 576 Third Avenue, the chart indicates the cross street is East 38th. A pickup at 1632 Broadway means we're aiming for 50th Street. We rode with disinfectant, bandages, a strong lock and cable often worn around the waist for quick access, and faith that we get home safe. Most messengers wore baggy jeans or sweatpants (with padded shorts underneath so our scrotums don't numb), a T-shirt, sweatshirt, windbreaker, all depending on the weather. One messenger resembled the guys from *Road Warrior* with shoulder pads, knee guards, and fingerless gloves all in black. Another covered in black bird feathers did a remarkable imitation of a crow. There was Pit Bull, the Flash, Geronimo (yelled each time he leapt a curb), and Achilles, unhurt after seven crashes. Dexter Benjamin had only one leg (he lost the other in a bike accident), his crutch strapped to his bike frame, and for a while on the streets of New York City rode Nelson Vails, gold medal winner for the individual sprint in the '83 Pan Am Games and silver medalist in the '84 Olympics. He was nicknamed Cheetah, fastest cat in the jungle; you saw Nelson only when he stopped for a delivery.

Sometimes we'd ride together jabbering along Fifth Avenue before one of us raises a clenched fist and cuts down a Midtown cross-street, but we always stopped if a messenger needed help with a breakdown or flat. For in ways we all shared something similar besides a love for the bike; we were young and struggling and fit but also renegades and outlaws, and though the work was hard and only the best made any real money, we worked outside in all weather and felt hardy and free because of it.

Reflecting the true business spirit of New York, time is money; we were all Mammon's Messengers no matter the company stenciled on our canvas bags. We rode on sidewalks, raced the wrong way on one-way streets, streaked through crossing lanes against the light just missing someone who'd shout profanities at our backs rapidly fading in traffic. All this was illegal, and a ticket cost a good day's pay. Stoner had a weed delivery service on the side, and we knew he was carrying when we blasted passed him stopped at a red light and, smiling, he gave us the finger.

At the bike shop George replaced worn brake pads and strung new cables, checked the crank, levers, and rims, then he trued my wheels. He worried about me doing messenger work but could only shake his head and whisper, "What a man must do."

"How much for all this?"

He turned uneasy, hesitated, and always charged too little.

Of all the seasons, messenger work in summer is best: wearing a Chicago Bears T-shirt, the heat rising off the street while singing "Ride Like the Wind" by Christopher Cross: "I'm on the run/ No time to sleep/ I've got to ride, Ride like the wind." Nearly a dozen messengers were killed each year in New York then and nearly all the same way: the deadly "right hook." A car in the right turning lane makes a turn but so does the car in the *center* lane just as we're riding through the intersection: chained to a lamppost near where the messenger fell, a bike spray-painted white, a "ghost bike,"

With rain the iron plates on the street became slippery and brake pads don't clamp well on wet rims. Winter was rough: icy streets or, worse, snow quickly turning to slush, and the brutal North Wind who the Greeks named Boreas, cheeks puffed, ice in his beard. All day I was cold and wet, the weather slowed me down and I worked longer for less money. But whenever I blasted through Midtown, the park always beckoned: up Sixth or Seventh avenues where the corridor of tall buildings ceased at the fuzzy trees on the horizon.

On a damp, chilly November day I had a pick-up on East 13th Street, the first dull door east of First Avenue. I buzzed the top name –Studio—then walked a long corridor, dim and dusty, where a large freight elevator waited with a young man inside. He was tall, lean, his black hair combed back as if with Brylcreem. Definitely an Elvis man. After tugging a rope that slammed together two iron plates, one rising, one descending, he pulled another rope and the elevator lurched up with a great mechanical racket as a huge counterweight along the wall lowered. Six flights later the elevator clamored to a stop and the two great plates parted again. I entered a kitchen to my left and a huge living room to the right stretching in the distance. Colorful paintings hung on the walls between dirty windows.

"Want some orange juice?" the young man asked.

In the kitchen on the glass table, amid coffee cups and bagels, several open jams, butter, cream cheese, a rubber dildo and a box of Cheerios were two large books each two inches thick. On the covers, a painting of Fred Astaire dancing, with LARRY RIVERS in red capital letters across the top.

"One goes to the Marlborough Gallery on 57th," the young man said, "the other to the Brookford at Central Park West."

From deep in the back end of the loft behind the kitchen an elderly man emerged, his gray hair rumpled, with a nose like a hawk's beak and eyes penetrating and curious. He nodded at me before signing something first in one book with a paint-spattered hand, then the other. The young man placed both in a heavy-duty paper bag as the older man handed me a twenty-dollar bill. It was the only tip I'd ever receive on the job.

"Thank you."

"Just be careful," he replied in a deep, raspy voice. "It's supposed to rain."

"The books will get there safe and dry."

He glowered at me as the young man and I entered the elevator and we rode down to the long, dim corridor. The two books were a heavy load in my pack.

"If you have any more deliveries," I said, "call me directly and cut out the middleman."

"Give us your number."

I wrote it down on a blank receipt.

"And any time. Even weekends. I live nearby."

"Stephen Wolf," he read energetically, then held out his hand. "John Dyke."

After blasting up First Avenue to 57th Street, I headed west almost to Sixth before dropping one book at the lobby's front desk. I smiled at the appropriateness from entering the park at ARTISTS' GATE (Central Park South/Sixth Avenue), sailed over broken walkways but stopping at the dirt oval to rub some of Bo between my fingers before swirling along the empty promenade, passed the stiff, clumsy poets, the trees beneath the gray sky thinned of their leaves and many having fallen already to the grove. I cycled passed the quiet angel, through the winding Ramble, along the Great Lawn and then to a walkway leading to 91st Street and Central Park West. Here I left the second book with the doorman just as the rain began.

"All the sadness in the city," Hemingway wrote in *A Moveable Feast*, "came suddenly with the first cold rains of winter." But that November afternoon Central Park was melancholy, wet, silent, empty, and I flew to the Boathouse, locked my work horse beneath an awning, then with a dollar from the twenty bought hot chocolate and an apricot Danish before spending an hour by a warm fire watching the lake in the rain.

For a time I worked for a juicy former hippie going gray who ran a home-clutter removal service clearing apartments of years' worth of magazines, newspapers, junk mail piled everywhere. Everywhere. Walking the rooms was like walking a shifting sea of tightly packed paper two feet thick, loose and shredded on top but walked on for years until pressed so hard that the last half-foot had to be loosened with a crowbar. Receipts from the grocery store kept in bags in a drawer stuffed with dozens of boxes of unopened note cards. All the bills for the phone, the power and gas, saved from the last twenty years, closets stuffed with paper until not one more folded paper bag could squeeze in. Even the discarded mail of other tenants, schedules to the Metropolitan Opera from a decade ago, every advertisement for Serta, Sealy, limousine services, real estate brokers, every bank and medical statement, every bill and insurance form, stacked two feet deep in boxes all made from trees.

Christmas season in New York City begins when ten thousand lights sparkle on the great pine tree above the ice rink at Rockefeller Center where a battered man in a wheelchair holds a soiled paper cup with an Acropolis on it.

"You don't have ta be a Rockafella ta help a fella," he says kindly without making eye contact.

A few weeks after New Year's the tree is cut up for junk mail.

All of that paper—the years of receipts in the desk drawers, the unopened magazines, the note cards and letters, the insurance forms and bank statements—made from trees. Nothing represents the park more than trees. The varied ground, the slopes and meadows, the Great Hill and the Ravine, and especially the tree-lined promenade are molded around the trees, more than 26,000 with diameters greater than six inches. There are 399 Hawthorns, three Camperdown Elms, including the small one enclosed by a fence just inside and south of INVENTORS' GATE (72nd/Fifth Avenue). There are 1,648 other elms (one partly hides Beethoven along the promenade), 3,839 black cherry trees, a fringe tree, two poplars, a Japanese umbrella tree, the Tanyosho Pine, thirty Carolina Silverbells, and a Royal Paulownia from China

Each spring, in long pink corridors along Lake Manhattan, Yoshino Cherry trees blossom when leaves of many trees are still buds. These were gifts from Japan in 1912, and during their achingly brief weeks of glory it is impossible to look at them hard enough.

Central Park has 1,138 Sycamores (known also as a London Plane), the one on a bridle path just beyond lamppost #9614 perhaps the oldest tree in the park and one of its tallest; its diameter is larger than four of my outstretched arms from fingertip to fingertip. West of ARTISANS' GATE (Seventh Avenue) at about where 61st Street would be, three Dawn Redwoods, and another along the Ravine to the north. Two elms miraculously grow from schist on the promenade's east side (lamppost E6818), and a thick-limbed elm extends its muscular arms outside the park's wall near the bust of Alexander von Humboldt at NATURALISTS' GATE (Central Park West/ 77th Street). Near the rock outcropping that overlooks Wollman Rink, one of 181 Ailanthus trees; known as the Tree of Heaven, an ailanthus grew in the backyard in Betty Smith's novel *A Tree Grows in Brooklyn*: "It grows in boarded-up lots and out of neglected rubbish heaps. It grows up out of cellar gratings. It is the only tree that grows out of cement."

A beech tree inside the park at 59th Street near the Pond is carved with initials, some with hearts with names inside, carved so long ago they are faded like names on old tombstones. An enormous beech just west of Bethesda Terrace appears like four trees growing from one. There are Tea Oaks, Red Oaks, Black Oaks, and Shingle Oaks, Turkey Oaks and Willow Oaks, 1,542 Pin Oaks, 120 Black Oaks, and three Burr Oaks, one over three hundred years old. And there's the spectacular Silver Linden on the Great Lawn, its branches reaching out far and bending gently back to earth.

There's a Turkish Filbert, seventy-nine willows (first to awaken each spring with pale green buds), the Golden Larch between the Boat Pond and Trefoil Arch (there are ten more) and the only American Chestnut near the Timothy Laupot Bridge in the Ramble. 353 Gingkoes are in the park, the pungent, fallen fruit gathered by Asians for its secret properties. Trees just south of the Model Boathouse remember lawyer Robert Skirving Pirie who made Nixon's enemies list. There's a magnificent Blue Spruce near Alice and her zany group, and elegant cedars grow along Cedar Hill. There are tulip trees, two Mimosas, one Franklinia, 221 torturous Hornbeams, twenty-one magnolias, the little evergreen in the Ramble decorated each holiday season with ornaments and photos of our beloved pets, and the tree dedicated to Joyce Kilmer

There was a time when his "Trees" was one of America's most

popular—and parodied—poems, memorized by schoolchildren though nearly forgotten today. Immediately after the United States entered World War I, Kilmer resigned his position as a staff writer for *The New York Times*, enlisted in the Army and assigned to New York's legendary Fighting 69th. Exceptionally brave in scouting patrols across deadly No Man's Land, Joyce Kilmer was killed at the Second Battle of Marne while in search of a German machine gun nest. On the western side of the promenade's elegant elms is a small bronze plaque on a concrete square raised several inches off the ground in memory of the "Poet of the Trees." And just as Audrey Munson is forgotten in *The Encyclopedia of New York City*, so Kilmer's tree is not found in *Central Park Entire: The Definitive Illustrated Folding Map*.

Immediately after a brutal Nor'easter hit town the night before, I rode to the park, its roadways blocked by fallen, dying giants, with one great stump sliced smooth by a chain saw, a table-top unsanded five feet across. These outer rings of it appeared when Bo and I arrived that winter night in '77; just a few inches deeper, a ring when I was born. These next few mark when Robert Moses leveled trees for skating ponds and shuffleboard, these as automobiles first puttered through the park and trees along the roadway took their first breaths of carbon monoxide. This ring grew when elms along the park's perimeter –Olmsted's living veil meant to close off the city from us—were cut down during "Boss" Tweed's power in the 1870s so park visitors might better see the new palaces along Fifth Avenue. And these smallest, tightest, oldest rings: this tree was alive during the Civil War, back when the park too was born.

Twenty trees were chopped down in the late 1980s by someone dubbed "The Mad Axeman." On Halloween of 2011, a freak snow storm –the only snow of the year— damaged more than a thousand trees, branches still abundant with autumn leaves holding the wet, heavy snow until limbs cracked. A year later, 800 trees were either ravaged or completely uprooted by Hurricane Sandy, the most devastation Nature ever wrought upon the city. But the park suffered its most terrible night on August 18, 2009. "It looks like someone opened up with artillery fire," Parks Commissioner Adrian Benepe told the *Daily News*, "something you'd see in a war zone."

In the Ramble, the whine of a chainsaw, the shriek from a tree being severed. Though a few autumn leaves had already begun to fall, the storm tore millions from their branches, covering the walkways with bright yellows and reds and greens. There were broken branches throughout the forest and along the walkways, one section cordoned off as workers gathered the larger, fallen limbs while someone high in the treetops dislodged others dangling on branches.

Shouldering my bike, I scaled a slab of rock-face that brought me closer to one worker moving easily from limb to limb, cutting, tugging, branches dropping to a mulcher below that devoured the limbs with a terrible, high-pitched grind. Some ripped limbs still clinging in shards to the tree had to be cut away with a saw, but there was one just out of his reach. Rather than descending and climbing up with ropes at a different angle, the worker held with one hand to a branch behind him, then stepped further out on the limb that soon sagged beneath his weight.

"Don't risk it, Bob," a worker called up to him. As the limb sagged, he reached out with one hand and one leg for the other tree and for an instant remained motionless, half his weight secure on each tree, then deftly transferred his weight just as he had done several years before on the night we shared the Sanctuary.

By a system of ropes and a harness he lowered himself quickly back to earth, so I shouldered my bike and descended the rock.

"You got to love this job," I said to him.

He was tall, fair-skinned, fit.

"Yeah, sure do," he replied, then glanced upward to the trees. "Just hate seeing the park so battered."

Nearby a mulcher chewed the branches into shards.

"You're him, aren't you?" I asked before he set back to work. "The one who lives in trees like a great ape."

He hesitated, turned with a quiet smile and replied, "Actually, I admire the squirrel."

"Did they ever catch you?"

"Yes," he said, eyebrows raised. "That's when they offered me this job."

"Careful up there," I said, and while shaking hands I told him my name.

"Bob Redman," he replied before lightly lifting himself back into the trees. I walked my bike along the battered Ramble as the whine of the mulcher faded, then I heard in the distance somewhere behind me, softly and clear, "Woof, woof."

To Make an Eden *continued*

Before the sublime imaginings by Olmsted and Vaux could be created, before swamps were drained and tons of poison ivy uprooted, before blasting through iron-hard schist and digging great pits and laying underground water pipes that would become lakes and ponds, before millions of cartloads of topsoil were brought in —enough to raise a football field to the top of the Empire State Building—and before planting the first tree in 1859, several thousand people living on the newly purchased acres had to be driven off.

Public support for evictions is often manipulated by casting those living on the desired land as social outcasts, in this case labeling them "squatters" despite the fact that some owned the land on which they lived and most others paid rent. But the victims were easy targets: freed slaves, American Indians, Irish and German immigrants who had fled either the poverty of one country or the totalitarianism of another. Awaiting in New York, along with a hatred similar to what they had fled, the filth and dangers of Lower Manhattan, especially the Five Points where 290,000 people lived in each square mile of the most densely populated place on Earth.

But on remote areas of the island to the north, what is today the West 80s, were communities referred to as Pigtown, Nigger Village, and Seneca Village. Two powerful Tammany bosses were born in an Irish area called Nanny Goat Hill. Although referred to as bone-boilers and rag-pickers, many residents had jobs. Women were laundresses and domestics, men unskilled laborers, and within their tattered little villages were churches, schools, and cemeteries. But the public's perception of them had been set; these villages, wrote James D. McCabe in *Lights and Shadows of New York Life,* were "more filthy, squalid, and disgusting can hardly be imagined" despite that McCabe most likely never saw them.

Perhaps a truer, certainly a more sympathetic, vision of these distant

New Yorkers appeared in Kevin Baker's novel *Paradise Alley* that follows the struggles of three women far different than the people histories depicted.

> [Ruth] was still living up in Pigtown with Johnny Dolan .... It was just a boil of a village then, a hollow of shanties made out of wood and bricks scavenged from demolitions, and caulked with mud and grease. The men went out to work in the morning on the construction sites, or in the fat houses and the bone boilers, the butchers and leather dressers a few blocks away.

Beneath the ruthless absolutism of Eminent Domain, in a scene reminiscent of Tevye and other Jews forced from their village of Anatevka in *Fiddler on the Roof*, Baker depicts—

> The whole village gathering up its few belongings, and walking away in still-unbelieving silence....All of their friends and neighbors, a whole village, simply drifting away, so that there would scarcely be a trace of them left by nightfall.

During the park's construction, a worker near 85th Street and Eighth Avenue unearthed barely a foot beneath the surface a black rosewood coffin with an inlaid plate that read "Margaret McIntay died 1851, aged sixteen years, three months and fourteen days." A century later, a gardener turning up topsoil found a human skull. Further diggings discovered a graveyard, referred to as "Gilhooley's Burial Plot" for the gardener. In a 1959 *New Yorker* article reporting the story titled "Paddy's Walk" the bones were still derogatorily those "of tramps and squatters." And in the summer of 2011, students from Columbia University and City College under the guidance of Nan Rothschild and Diana Wall excavated buttons and fragments of pottery, a tea kettle, a child's shoe, and the bones of New Yorkers buried before there was any idea of creating Central Park. Beneath this rolling landscape, fallen pine needles and acorns and crisp, browned leaves and our footsteps lie those who called this area home and who, as many of us have wished, remain in the park forever.

All the struggling, brittle villages on the park's acres disappeared, their inhabitants driven off like those many years later from Hoover Valley a few steps away. But there were other far sturdier structures on the land now meant for the new park. The Arsenal is a three-story fortress on Fifth Avenue at 64th Street completed in 1851 by the State of New York as a repository for the city's arms and ammunition. To the north, a squat, stone blockhouse built during our second war with England and meant to protect Harlem Heights, the Harlem River, and Long Island Sound, protection all the more urgent after the British attacked Stonington, Connecticut, in August of 1814. The blockhouse guards have been mustered from service decades before; more complicated was the Convent for the Sisters of Charity of St. Vincent de Paul with its graceful, gabled building, classrooms for two hundred girls, a recreation hall and a residence for the seventy Sisters.

Near the convent is a valley, at one time a Lenape trail that became the Old Post Road to Albany and Boston, also known as the Kingsbridge Road. Here in 1684 the English built a halfway house where travelers freshened up after the dusty, jostling journey before arriving in New York still several miles to the south. In the 1750s the Dyckman family built a tavern there, later sold to Mrs. Catherine McGowan though sometimes the name appears in New York records as 'McGown.' But in Viele's 1856 "Plan for the Improvement of the Central Park" the name is spelled "McGowan" and so we adhere to it still. The old tavern was leveled and replaced with a comfortable inn until 1847 when the building became the Convent for the Sisters of Charity of St. Vincent de Paul. Once the land on which the convent stood (around 104rd Street just east of center in the park) came under the control of the park commissioners, the Sisters were uncharitably moved to the Bronx so that Vaux and his family could reside in the convent, referred to then as Mount St. Vincent. Also moving in, Olmsted, his new wife and her children.

Grieved at the death of his brother John from tuberculosis, Olmsted had married his widowed sister-in-law and adopted her three children. Though previous heartache from love had led him to pursue other desires, Olmsted and his pretty wife Mary made a strong, tender relationship, eventually having three children of their own though one died in infancy. The marriage vows were exchanged in Central Park, the first of many exchanged there.

Clearing the 624 acres from 59th Street to 106th between Fifth and Eighth avenues began on a hot August morning in 1858. Over a year later the first tree was planted, but New Yorkers almost immediately began enjoying the altered landscape; our love for Central Park may have begun with ice skating on the few inches of water allowed to trickle and freeze into a vast, shallow pit that one day would become the Boating Lake.

With good ice a red ball on a white flag affixed to horse-drawn buses headed downtown and back uptown. Before global warming, when all this brick and glass and human heat of today were still far downtown, winters in the park were colder. Water on the ponds and Lake froze more frequently, and the visions of gliding ice skaters inspired paintings by Winslow Homer, Edward Hopper, Charles Parsons for Currier and Ives, William Glackens, and John O'Brien Inman's beautiful "Moonlight Skating—Central Park, The Terrace and Lake." In a 1900 article "Central Park Winter" for *Munsey's Magazine*, Raymond Spears recalled that "Illuminated by white and colored lights, the figures on the ice [are] a spectacle not easily forgotten, while the chinking music of the skates sings an unforgettable chant."

Only a year into work on the park George Templeton Strong wrote in his diary on June 11, 1859, that he "Improved the day by leaving Wall Street early and set off ... to explore the Central Park." Strong was a prominent, pompous, opinionated lawyer from a powerful and influential family, but his greatest pleasure and invaluable gift to the city was recording everything and everyone in his diaries, begun in 1835 when he was fifteen and continuing for 2,250 pages over the next forty years.

> Though now in most ragged condition...'lakes' without water, mounds of compost, piles of blasted stone, acres of what may be greensward hereafter but is now mere brown earth; ... Celts, caravans of dirt carts, derricks, steam engines, these are the elements out of which our future Pleasance is rapidly developing.

As the once-barren acres transformed into beautiful landscapes, writers praised with increasing wonder this "free and public resort," wrote Junius Henry Browne, "where no aristocratic law can interfere with the enjoyment of the masses, one of the best ideas that was ever conceived." Although "many of New-York's pretensions are absurd," he added, "it has a right to boast of the Central Park."

T. Addison Richards' twenty-six-page "The Central Park" with illustrations appeared in *Harper's Monthly Magazine* in 1861. "If the generous people of New York shall be remembered and blessed by their posterity for any good deed," he wrote, "above all others it will be for this inestimable gift." Known for his popular *Appleton's Illustrated Hand-book of American Travel*, Richards later published a far longer guide to the park which he believed "the first grand proof of our greatness."

That greatness would soon pass through a crucible after a predawn attack on a Federal fort off the coast of South Carolina.

CHAPTER TEN

Garden of Darkness and Light

Mistaken for an Irish Catholic by a gang of Irish Protestants, William Kane was the first person murdered in Central Park. That was 1870; two years later a park visitor was killed in a robbery "that has actually stained the turf of [our] green fairy land," wrote *The New York Times*. The *Police Gazette* published an article ominously titled "Perils of the Park" with frightening illustrations of muggers and sexual predators, of pistols and billy clubs; only a few years after its official opening, "our beautiful city resort is polluted by foul tidings in human form." A distraught Olmsted "recommend no woman to stroll in the Park after dark, and I answer for no man's safety in it from bullies, garroters, or highway robbery after dusk."

And so began the park's infamous but often exaggerated reputation for danger it still carries today.

"A man strolling in London's Hyde Park after nightfall might possibly find himself in a police court next morning," wrote Collinson Owen in his 1929 often disparaging *The American Illusion*, "but a man who strolled in Central Park after dark would almost certainly find himself in the morgue."

Radio commentator Barry Gray declared in 1959 that "the park is one great open-air cesspool. If you value your life, keep clear of Central Park, especially at night." Poet Ogden Nash wrote that "If you should happen after dark/ To find yourself in Central Park,"

> Ignore the paths that beckon you
> And hurry, hurry to the zoo,
> And creep into the tiger's lair.

In Robert Lowell's "Central Park" we "beg delinquents for our life,/ Behind each bush, perhaps a knife."

Though statistically Central Park has less crime than any other of the city's police precincts, when a terrible crime is committed there –rape or murder—it receives much media attention and outrages New Yorkers; as one New York police captain said, "Crime in Central Park…shocks people like crime in heaven."

Mick Jagger walks "in Central Park, singing after dark, people think I'm craaazy," while Octavio Paz warns us in his poem "Central Park" with the refrain "Don't cross Central Park at night." There, "light turns to doubt" and "there are two eyes the color of anger,/ a ring of cold, a belt of blood":

> a wind that scatters the reflection
> of Alice, dismembered in the pond.
> Don't cross Central Park at night.

From 1979 to 1986, thirty-five people were murdered in Central Park, ten alone in 1982, more than twice the number of the year before. "After dark, be smart," the red-bereted, self-appointed city protectors known as the Guardian Angels declared on handbills posted around the park, "Stay out of the park."

On a sweltering July 21, 1983, Diana Ross gave a free concert in the park. For days we'd suffered a brutal heat wave, but neither that nor a threatening sky kept us from the Great Lawn packed like Times Square on New Year's Eve; TV news said 400,000 were there, the papers, a million. Diana wore a sparkling orange bodysuit, but to me far at the northeast corner of the Great Lawn she was merely a tiny orange figure on a raised platform at the shore of Lake Belvedere singing, "Ain't no mountain high enough…." When the rains began, she put on an orange cape with a long train whipped by a wind that dragged in the impending storm.

Despite the soaking Diana sang until gusts of wind rattled the spotlights and lightening flashed in the east. She announced that for everyone's safety we should leave the park calmly. Most of us fled for shelter and subways though some people remained in the park ripping off purses and gold chains, attacking vendors and stealing their money, then "charged through the patio section of Tavern of the Green," the *Times* reported, "knock[ing] over tables and assaulting patrons who fled into the restaurant for safety." Eighty were arrested, and one who pulled a knife on a Transit Authority detective was shot. As compensation, Diana Ross donated money for a new playground, the Diana Ross Playground at West 81st Street and Central Park West, and she performed again the next night with neither incident nor stormy weather.

One summer afternoon in 1986 near the Harlem Meer, Officer Steven McDonald was questioning three teenagers suspected of stealing bicycles. A boy pulled a gun and shot McDonald three times, leaving him paralyzed; given only a few months to live, Officer McDonald died thirty-one years later.

Forty-three people were murdered *each week* in 1989, and that year 5,415 women were raped in the city, ten in the park. But no atrocity has terrified, angered, and divided more of us than did a single, brutal attack in the park one spring night.

Composed of tended gardens, sylvan forests, and quiet ponds, Central Park is entirely surrounded by Manhattan. Although an essential purpose for the park was to induce in each visitor a civilizing influence through art and Nature, perhaps some deep, incurable, innate flaw immune even to the park's magic lies in our character, a flaw that nothing can extricate. The viciousness of the city freely appears at any entrance, and in the park there are fewer eyes to witness and it's so easy to vanish in the night.

The moon was nearly full on Wednesday, April 19, 1989, when perhaps thirty teenage boys entered the northern end of the park and began a series of attacks which they called "wilding." Joggers and bicyclists were the main targets. Around 10:30 p.m. near the willow-lined Pool at 101st Street on the park's west side, five boys were grabbed by police. Three hours later, two construction workers walked through the park after a few beers. They took the "cut-through" —a passage at 103rd connecting the West Drive to the East Drive to avoid the Great Hill — and heard faint moans in the bushes leading down to the Ravine. Here they found a naked woman, badly beaten, her skull crushed, one eye hanging from its socket, and nearly eighty percent of her blood soaked into the park's soil.

The victim, forever after known as the Central Park Jogger, was twenty-eight, white, a Yale graduate and Wall Street bank investor living on the Upper East Side who often jogged in the park after work. She had been raped and nearly beaten to death, and the four black and one Hispanic teenagers were charged with the crime. In a city already deteriorating from severe economic problems and a devastating crack epidemic, this brutal crime was the most recent in a series motivated by race. Both local and national news, overwhelmingly white, never referred to the five arrested —known later as the Central Park Five—as suspects in the crime, in part because four of the five confessed to the beating and rape, implicating the fifth.

The crime intensified the racial tensions and distrust in the city then. Some equated the attack of a white woman that night as revenge for the fatal beating of Willie Turks by a white mob in the Gravesend section of Brooklyn in 1982, and for Bernard Goetz, a white man attacked by a group of black youths on the 2 train in December of 1984; Goetz opened fire, wounding all five, and —a Charles Bronson-like hero to white New Yorkers—was called the Subway Vigilante despite being a frail, balding man. In 1986, twenty-three year old Michael Griffith was struck by a car while fleeing a white mob in the Howard Beach section of Queens. An angry Mayor Koch compared his death to lynching parties in the Deep South. Several months later, Yusef Hawkins, a sixteen-year-old black man, was beaten and shot to death in Bensonhurst. Spike Lee's 1991 film *Jungle Fever* was dedicated to Yusef.

Constant, simmering friction on the streets between whites and blacks grew hotter during the media's extensive coverage of the rape of a white woman in Central Park; had she been black, a Harlem minister said, we wouldn't have heard a thing. A few summers before, little was reported of two homeless women gang-raped, one beaten with a tree branch, the other with a golf club. Now a bumped shoulder or the hundred daily, casual irritations among us made sparks like subway wheels on rails, quick and edgy. For weeks the park was nearly empty, even of cyclists and birders, and there were many cops, especially north of the reservoir, the spot of the young woman's horror cordoned off and guarded by two uniformed officers. News crews lined the cut-through, and a bouquet of carnations lay just off the pathway.

Twelve days after the attack of the jogger, she miraculously came out of her coma. The Central Park Five were placed on trial in 1990, found guilty, and sentenced to long prison terms despite Donald Trump's full-page ad in the *Daily News* demanding the death penalty. After the young defendants served the first twelve years of their sentences, another man's confession and DNA confirmed that none of the boys arrested, accused, and imprisoned had raped her. Convictions of all five were vacated, the case settled with the city owing the wronged men $40 million. In 2003, Trisha Meili's memoir *I Am the Central Park Jogger* was published. She continues helping people survive the horrors we inflict on each other.

Yet during these dark days, as the city— already staggered by the epidemic of heroin and cocaine—nearly collapsed entirely beneath a more sinister addiction to crack, something new was occurring in Central Park, something wonderful. It began gradually, as the deterioration once had, a little at a time, nearly unnoticed. One day the water in the Pond at the park's southeast corner –Holden's lagoon—seemed cleaner, there was less graffiti on statue pedestals and the black rock face, and the dirt oval where I had spread much of Bo's ashes, tended now and blooming hesitant and green. Soon the mountain lion coiled for attack above the East Drive had a tail again, and one day a special bird returned to Central Park.

I was still barely able to identify something besides cardinals and robins but knew I'd never seen this one before; I've passed this shelf of rock above the 72nd Street Drive many times and never saw a nine-foot man of bronze dressed as if from a Shakespeare play with an upraised arm from where a falcon was about to launch itself into the sky.

The falconer's pointed-toed slippers curve upward, on his belt hangs a sheathed dagger, and his face turned to the bird on his arm holds an expression of wonder for the bronzed creature at the instant just before its talons release its human perch, wings outstretched, primary feathers at the wing tips spread. Nearby is the hulking, unavoidable *Webster*, but like only a few other statues *The Falconer* seems part of the park and celebrating our connection to an animal, especially one embodying the supreme act of freedom.

Yet this bird is not the one sculpted by the falconer's creator George Blackwell Simonds. That falcon had not been as sleek, its feather-tips not separated, and despite its broad wings spread the bird was not about to leap into the air. In 1957 Simonds' falcon and some of the falconer's arm where it perched had been torn off. For his own safety, the maimed, falcon-less falconer left Central Park for storage. A decade later, Joel Rudnick, a young sculptor supporting himself as a park employee, cast a new gloved hand and the trimmer bird that stirs our anticipation an instant before launch; nearly twenty years would pass before the park could afford to display the piece again.

Wealthy New Yorkers who loved Central Park have always helped it; a century ago Olivia Slocum Sage, wife of robber baron Russell Sage (more customarily called a "financier" who left her $50 million to do with as she pleased), paid for $100,000 worth of evergreens planted along the east side of the reservoir. Recently, hedge-fund billionaire John Paulson donated $100 million to the park.

Persuasive, autocratic, indifferent to the fundamental principles of Central Park, Robert Moses raised private funds to drastically alter the park in whatever ways he chose. In 1949 he convinced Kate Wollman to donate a part of her inherited fortune to build the ice rink that devoured a lovely piece of the Pond north of Gapstow Bridge. Soon a huge skating rink and swimming pool marred the northern part of the park with contributions from Albert and Mary Lasker. In 1954 financier Carl Loeb provided money for a new boathouse along the east shore of the Boating Lake, and in 1961 Governor Herbert Lehman paid for a children's zoo a few steps north of the original zoo, its enchanting entrance gate of a playful Pan dancing with animals sculpted by Paul Manship whose golden Prometheus flies above the ice rink at Rockefeller Center. And there are gifts to the park from someone known only an 'an interested citizen.'

Between the back of the bulky band shell along the promenade and the SummerStage is a wisteria pergola. Vines thick as an arm and hard as the band shell's Indiana limestone are twisted and entwined, blooming each spring with purple flowers fragrant and lush as juicy grapes. Someone paid to repair the crumbling wooden trellises the vines need to climb to survive, but the boulder along "Wisteria Walk" simply reads "restored by an interested citizen." These same words are on a boulder in the Ramble near one of the park's three remaining rustic shelters, and at the Pinetum's southeast corner is a plaque set into a rock with modest anonymity: "This Pinetum is a gift to the city from an interested citizen."

But I have an idea who this might be.

"Big I'm not," Arthur Ross said in a *Times* interview, "but I'm interested."

Once a Macy's shirt salesman and eventually vice president of an investment company, Manhattan-born Arthur Ross financed in 1971 the Pinetum, seven hundred pine trees of twenty-five different species, some transplanted from Macedonia and the Himalayas, now flourishing at the

Great Lawn's northwest edge green even in January. Funding for research on a Chinese elm tree (there are six in the park) resistant to Dutch Elm Disease along with help financing restoration of our sacred Bethesda Terrace were given by this interested citizen.

Six days after John Lennon's murder outside his Dakota apartment, tens of thousands gathered for a silent vigil directly across the street in Central Park that cloudy Sunday afternoon. When the vigil concluded, the sun broke through and people started singing "here comes the sun" softly through tears. Many of us returned here ten months later for John's birthday. Always someone had a guitar.

> There are places I remember
> All my life, though some have changed
> Some forever not for better...

Two months later, another gathering a year to the day of his murder.

> I know I'll always stop and think about them,
> In my life, I loved you more.

Candles were lit and we shared joints and tears as our warm breath and exhaled smoke wound like ghosts to the leafless branches.

Yoko Ono's million-dollar donation —at the time the largest ever made to Central Park—enabled the creation of Strawberry Fields in that ragged edge where we had gathered to remember John. Dedicated on October 9, 1985—his 45th birthday—the tear drop-shaped garden was designed by Bruce Kelly although the lampposts are not as beautiful as the others in the park. When the memorial was conceived, Yoko invited the world to send gifts but quickly limited to only plants and flowering shrubs after an elaborate fountain, memorial benches, and a totem pole arrived. One artifact has become the garden's most noted symbol: a large mosaic set upon the ground where three walkways join at the single word IMAGINE. Some people treat the mosaic reverently and do not set one foot on its ten thousand white and gray and black tiles. Others kneel in the center for pictures. For several years the mosaic was adorned with flowers, Hershey kisses, pennies, leaves, crabapples or grapes, all arranged in a large peace sign by a shaggy, sometimes belligerent man about forty years old named Gary. He lectured each new group of tourists about

Strawberry Fields, about John (referred to as "the Brother"), the Dakota apartments and the night of murder. Informative, intimidating, he asked for donations which he called "contributions to peace."

Everyone knows what the word implies and what happened to John, and because of this Strawberry Fields has become something like a gathering place for our collective sorrow, Central Park's small-town church where we share our grief. Not only on John's birthday and the day he was murdered but also when George Harrison died, and September 11.

In 1980, to supercharge the process of collecting donations to restore and revitalize Central Park, Mayor Ed Koch appointed a brilliant, beautiful woman as head of the newly created Central Park Conservancy; for the first time since Olmsted one person would oversee managing the park. This non-profit organization would seek financial help from the city's corporations and foundations as well as wealthy New Yorkers, especially those living along the park's perimeter who she convinced would benefit daily with a renewed garden outside their front doors. Her name is Elizabeth Barlow and over the next two decades she became the park's second angel; providentially, Emma Stebbins' *Angel of the Waters* –bringing restorative, healing power in her outstretched hand—served as the Conservancy's icon, and then I remembered that Elizabeth Barlow had written and edited that first park book I picked up for a dollar along Second Avenue.

The Conservancy grew from efforts of the generation that had done much of the damage to the park. In the 1960s and '70s, amid be-ins and Schaeffer rock concerts, anti-war rallies and gay rights demonstrations all held in the park, there was growing concern for the damage caused. One May weekend in 1983, each of us entering the park gave a dollar for a fund-raiser called "You Gotta Have Park" that raised $50,000.

A single Barbra Streisand concert and decades of Sunday soccer had trampled Sheep Meadow to dust; today a fragrant carpet of healthy grass thrives beneath our bare feet where children toss awkward cartwheels while weary men lug coolers of ice-cold water and beer for sale to us sprawling happily upon it. The Great Lawn has transformed into a green field with baseball diamonds and smooth dirt infields, and Donald Trump restored the empty, battered Wollman Skating Rink in less than four months; the city had been trying for years. Nearby, the Dairy—a quaint cottage from a fairy tale— was scraped of graffiti, repaired, and, though not dispensing free milk as it once had done, now sells park clothes and books, calendars and cards. In the Gill's muddy ponds in the Ramble golden koi would swim in clean water with azaleas blooming along the shore. Beside the walkways logs knee-high served as barriers for mountain bikes streaking down rock-face before tearing dusty paths through the forest, and one night, after flickering with uncertainty, lampposts glowed softly as the park darkened, each globe held by a cast-iron tear drop of curling black vines so artful that its creator Henry Bacon later designed the Lincoln Memorial in Washington. And in 2016, more than thirty years after I snuggled one summer night in a cozy, rock-enclosed nook while Bob Redman swayed in his treehouse above, the Hallet Nature Sanctuary opened to visitors. We can all now stroll wood-chip pathways lined with logs to keep us from wandering off the trail, and Conservancy volunteers make sure we do not wander too far on the cliff overlooking the Pond: still along the bottom of the chain-link fence, the gap through which Bo slipped for his own exploration.

In the years ahead, the carousel, the bridges and gardens would display modest plaques baring names of those who donated to the restoration, as would several thousand benches each dedicated by someone often to someone else, and a few loving tributes to the park. Along a Ramble walkway is a bench to Ed Ruckle: "In a city of dreams, mine grew best here."

The bench for Russell Leavitt's sixty-fifth birthday reads, "Every Mensch Deserves a Bench," while north of the zoo is "A Bench for Book Lovers." There's one for fathers and daughters on Turtle Pond's eastern shore, and near CHILDREN'S GATE (Fifth Avenue between 76th and 77th) is a bench with Ulysses' words to Achilles from Shakespeare's *Troilus and Cressida*: "One Touch of Nature Makes the Whole World Kin." A sloping walkway in the Ramble is called Iphigene's Walk in memory of Iphigene Ochs Sulzberger, a founding member of the Central Park Conservancy. Facing the East Drive north of lamppost E9101, a bench with a passage from Walt Whitman, its donor anonymous:

I loafe and invite my soul
I lean and loafe at my ease

A boulder honors Elizabeth Barlow at the southern side approaching Summit Rock, near the Diana Ross Playground. At the top of the summit is a bench with a love-note to her from Theodore, another admirer no doubt. A bench at the western edge of Oak Bridge is in gratitude to Sarah Cedar Miller, author of the informative and richly photographed (by Sarah) *Central Park: An American Masterpiece*.

In the summer of 1989 a film was released about Central Park. More than three hundred have been made *in* Central Park since the first filmed version of *Romeo and Juliet* in 1908, but this documentary is *about* the park, "a record of New York's exuberance," wrote film critic David Denby, "a celebration of the city's surviving lyricism and idealistic impulses."

Central Park by Frederick Wiseman reveals how this urban space fulfills many needs: an oasis from the streets, a playground, stage, museum, wildlife sanctuary, a social and political platform, a place to once ride horses, a holding tank for those busted selling weed. As with all Wiseman films there is no narrative or voice-over as the camera simply records the park's thriving, infinite variety for nearly three hours.

Seeing the film today, we notice there were more homeless people in the park (I know it's where I'd head), that no one is lost in an I-phone, and how the park looks much healthier now. Wiseman cuts several times to the transverse roads, the two-way cross streets occurring four times in the scant two-and-a-half-mile length of Central Park though visitors barely notice them. That we barely notice is one reason the Greensward Plan won the design competition in 1858. Since crosstown traffic would not be rerouted around the new public park in the center of the island, these roads were a requirement for any plan submitted. So as not to sever the park into four interrupted parcels, the roads were placed unobtrusively *beneath* the park, and when Wiseman cuts to these roads we remember how the park is surrounded on all sides by churning, steel rivers of traffic fed by streams flowing through it.

Like a parent with young children, the Conservancy will always have plenty to do, but park lovers felt special joy and gratitude when at last Bethesda Terrace was cordoned off; strong machines lift sandstone balustrades or a large panel of the grand staircase. Months passed, seasons changed, the Angel remained behind scaffolding, and when the panels were reinstalled all the birds along the stairway scrolls had heads and beaks again though the new stone is a bit lighter and there is a thin ring around each neck as if from an operation. Before long, clear water once again flowed beneath the toes of the Angel, showering the chubby cherubs and filling her wide, shallow basin; once again we were renewed. Bo never had a chance to wade in this fountain's water; if he had, like the Bible story tells, he may have healed and walked well again.

Strolling amid these restored scrolls and the graceful Terrace, beside the Lake and a forested Ramble across the shore, New Yorkers again knew what they had a century ago when first ambling among such artistry and grace. This place belonged not to a king or an Astor but to us: a black man denied the opportunity to build the park, an immigrant from Frankfort picnicking with his family on Sunday, a teenager from Spanish Harlem eager to meet her boyfriend, a Sikh from Bay Ridge who does not work on Saturday and likes reading the newspaper beneath a certain willow while watching the rowboats. At a time when the terrible gorge separating the few enormously wealthy and millions of the city in need grew wider and ever more deadly, the park, and especially the Terrace, "would let the New Yorker feel that the richest man in New York," Calvert Vaux declared, "cannot spend as freely as is here spent just for his lounge."

The Terrace today looks much as it did a century before Bo and I ever visited. Few places in the park and far fewer in the city have remained as timeless and immutable. Here no one hurries for a bus or to work, dinner reservations or a curtain time. Instead, we stroll around the basin, we dawdle by the lake, pause for photographs beneath parasols and straw hats, Afros and fedoras, yarmulkes and Yankee ball caps and colorful babushkas, in tank-tops and shirtwaists, pushing wicker carriages or lean McLaren strollers. Coins now tossed each day into the Terrace fountain are retrieved at dusk by one old man, his frayed trousers rolled up as he wades into the water gathering all the wishes before the Central Park Conservancy tries doing the same.

Occasionally winding among the visitors was a young black man with thick eyeglasses and dressed as a sorcerer from the Middle Ages. Covering his left hand, a large hand puppet of a dragon, a sorcerer's staff in his other hand, his pointed hat held in place with a safety pin, and he wore a fake gray wig and beard and a heavy green robe even on hot afternoons. He is Blackwolf who will speak in what he believes a Scottish accent to anyone who accepts his eccentricity.

At the Terrace, with the Angel behind him, Kishan creates with bamboo sticks tied with soaking rope giant soap bubbles, transparent, waving tunnels that vanish with an inaudible pop; a portion of his profits, he assured me, goes to the cooperating wind. And Paul, unlike the rest of us who only visit, lives here, in the park, in all weather and every season. He is young, resembling what Jesus's disciples must have been like, sitting peacefully, his belongings in black, heavy-duty plastic bags on a problematic hand-truck. He takes no money though graciously accepts food, travel toothbrushes, socks, small cakes of soap, knit gloves in winter. If it rains and on very cold winter days he sits quietly in a corner on a bench along the wall in the Angel Tunnel listening to the music and greeting those of us who know him. For my birthday, he raided a dumpster and found vanilla cupcakes.

Drawn to the Tunnel for its reverberations, for the faded, haunting images of women along the walls and for the people who casually come and go, is a man who in summer appears as if transported from the Amazon. He wears a gold loincloth, his lean, muscular body sparkling with glitter, armbands, silver necklaces, ornamental bells laced around his ankles, and a long red feather like a crescent erect from his ebony cornrows, each artifact placed reverentially. In cooler weather, wearing a skirt and black leggings, he might have just descended from the Himalayas.

He is Thoth, named for the Egyptian god of the moon, of writing and magic, and when he performs ("prayforms" we learn), he chants an unknown language, at times high-pitched and airy, at other times deep and growling, all the while playing violin and often spinning like a dervish. Some people laugh at him, some are enthralled, and others are uncomfortable or confused with this mixture of black and white, male and female, tender and mad. "All/ (s)he wears," wrote the poet Dean Kostos,

> is a golden
> breechcloth, veiling more fore
> than aft, secret of the gender(s)
> untold.

With time and fate an equally ethereal creature accompanied Thoth only costumed in pink satin and lace, her face white as paper sprinkled with pearls and tiny stars. Lila Angelique too plays the violin and twirls while still playing as her voice like Siegfried's woodbird carries from the Angel Tunnel across the water to the Ramble's mysterious trees.

"To the park New Yorkers bring the images they propose of themselves," wrote Mireille Johnston in *Central Park Country: A Tune Within Us*. "All this deliberate new identity gives relevance and beauty to our existence. We do not seek total disguise: we simply assume the features of the person we want to be and in doing so gain delight and pride."

Nowhere else in the city have some people so comfortably adapted as in Central Park –especially along the Terrace— where they smoothly weave into the park's rich and varied tapestry. Often we pass gently through each other's paths to the lyrical, plucked strings from a harp and the quiet babel of the languages of the world; these are my city's most graceful steps, Central Park's perpetual waltz.

CHAPTER ELEVEN

Garden of Grandeur

O ften when visiting the magnificent New York Public Library on Fifth Avenue and 42nd Street, to use its vast resources or simply find oasis from energetic Midtown surrounding it, I would spend a while with a special painting in room 316, the Edna Barnes Salomon Room, on the third floor. Up the marble staircase, wide and regal, past the somber busts of its architects John Carrére in bronze on one landing and Thomas Hastings in marble on the other, I pause amid the McGraw Rotunda: its arched bays and Corinthian walnut pilasters beneath Prometheus painted in the center of a ceiling twenty-five feet above as he steals fire–enlightenment—from the gods to give to us. Along the walls of this stately hall, four large murals depict, appropriately for a library, the history of the written word. In the first panel Moses descends Mount Sinai with the Ten Commandants, written by the hand of God. In the second panel, a monk, dedicated and oblivious to any struggles, transcribes the Bible; after many years' work there will be another Bible in the world. In the third panel Johannes Gutenberg shows a page freshly pressed by his world-altering invention, while the fourth panel dramatizes the early version of the typewriter, heralding a new age for journalism. On a piece of paper randomly tossed on the floor in the panel's bottom right corner, the artist modestly signed his work: Edward Laning.

The painting I came to see—a yard wide and nearly four feet high— is *Kindred Spirits,* a dramatic forest landscape with slender, leafy trees filling the edges in the foreground, mountain ridges in the distance. Two men dressed as if strolling the city's fashionable street rather than exploring the wilderness stand comfortably in the middle distance on a shaft of rock above a gorge. White water from a distant waterfall winds through the rocky stream far beneath them.

The painter is Asher Durand, the work completed in 1849. The waterfall is the Kaaterskill Falls in the Catskill Mountains little more than one hundred miles up the Hudson River from New York City. One of the two kindred spirits in the painting is Thomas Cole, regarded as the founder of the Hudson River School, the first truly American art movement; he had painted the same falls more than twenty years before.

In *Kindred Spirits* Cole has a sketchbook in his left hand and a flute or recorder in his right. As for waterfalls, he saw each as an "incongruous idea of fixedness and motion...change and everlasting duration. The waterfall may be called the voice of the landscape." Beside him on the rock, his friend, a poet, newspaper editor, and an early, avid advocate for a great public park in New York City. He believed, as did Durand, that in Nature lay the spirit of God;

> Thou art here—thou fill'st the solitude
> Thou art in the soft winds
> That run along the summit of these trees.

Once again, this time in Durand's painting, we are with William Cullen Bryant for whom the lovely park behind the library, our Tuileries, is named.

Like all Hudson River School paintings this one presents a powerful, divine sense of Nature: its trees, its ridges of hill and rock, its clear water and majestic sky where amid all this splendor two men, even two as esteemed as Cole and Bryant, are minimal in the landscape. So as not to mistake them, their names are faintly carved into the tree on the far left.

Though most paintings from the Hudson River School are horizontal to display a wide expanse of a vast landscape, this painting is vertical; now we sense the towering trees and the depth of the gorge. The painting, an homage to Cole who, at forty-seven years old, had died of pleurisy the year before, was commissioned by New York merchant, philanthropist, and art collector Jonathan Sturges as a gift to Bryant who spoke so eloquently at Cole's funeral service: "It is as if we were to look over the heavens on a starlight evening, and find that one of the greater planets, Hesperus or Jupiter, had been blotted from the sky."

Bryant and Durant maintained a deep friendship until Bryant's death in 1878; while dedicating the expressionless bust of Italian patriot and revolutionary Giuseppe Mazzini that glares down at Central Park's

West Drive, Bryant was overcome with dizziness and fell, suffering a concussion. Twenty years later his daughter graciously donated *Kindred Spirits* to the library.

But one day the painting was gone. Perhaps it was on loan or the frame needed repair or else simply tucked safely away so we appreciate it that much more when again displayed. But the painting will never hang in the New York Public Library; needing funds for endowments despite its quarter billion dollar annual budget, the library sold Durand's painting at auction to Alice Walton, heiress of Wal-Mart, for $35 million. Exhibited briefly at the National Gallery, the work can now be seen only at the Museum of American Art in remote Bentonville, Arkansas.

What the painting and others like it inspired can be seen every day in Central Park.

The brilliant men who designed Central Park were greatly influenced by public parks and gardens in Paris and London designed by Jean-Pierre Barillet-Deschamps, Capability Brown, Édouard François André (designer of Buttes-Chaumont in Paris and a friend of Olmsted's), and Joseph Paxton's Birkenhead Park in England. The paintings of the Hudson River School also influenced Olmsted, and though our city's great museums did not exist before the 1858 Greensward Plan, it is easy to imagine Frederick, black-cloaked and melancholy, riding a ferry boat from his Staten Island farm across the windy Upper Bay to frequent the annual exhibit of the National Academy of Design on Leonard Street and Broadway. Each spring the paintings of Durand, Cole, and others were displayed, and here in 1849 the public first saw *Kindred Spirits*. A year later, he would gaze on Durand's masterpiece *In the Woods*.

Frederick Law Olmsted came of age when the seed of belief in the divinity found in Nature –planted by the first European settlers in this Eden-like, unspoiled New World—came into full flower. The supreme purpose of Central Park – more than a place for the city's varied social classes to mingle, not merely providing the rich a proper setting to display themselves in their carriages, more even than for the general population's physical good health and re-creation (rather than 'recreation')—was to give New Yorkers a "specimen of God's handiwork" in the glory and restorative qualities of Nature, wrote Emerson. Olmsted wanted to recreate and preserve in Central Park a portion of Henry Hudson's initial vision two and a half centuries before, what Scott Fitzgerald expressed in his greatest imaginary leap, "the old island here that flowered once for Dutch sailors' eyes— a fresh, green breast of the new world."

Today the paintings of the Hudson River School hang in our city's museums, and I'm at the Metropolitan Museum of Art at 9:30 in the morning. I like the museum the way I often like the park—nearly empty: just the artwork, the bored gallery guards, and me. In the American Wing hangs Asher Durand's *In the Woods*. As with *Kindred Spirits* this painting too is vertical, beginning with the forest floor in the foreground and filling the canvas with trees too tall for their canopies to be included in the frame. This gives great upward movement to the trees. A rotting tree trunk lays in the foreground with a squirrel on it; a stream winds through the forest, a bird flies between low branches. At the top a patch of sky is visible, and another at eye-level in the distance through the forest.

As in the Ramble I remain quiet and still, but as what often happens in Central Park, my seclusion is interrupted, this time by a group of well-dressed, middle-aged women with a chatty and surprisingly loud guide. They are here to view the Thomas Cole painting on the wall adjacent to my Durand. I wait patiently for them to pass but another Cole hangs near the first and the guide had plenty to say about that too. She laughed apologetically, but I finally gather my hat and pack and head for the North Woods where it seems Durand's painting has come to life. He hadn't visited the Catskills at all but simply set up his easel in Central Park. Here these boulders were placed with the same care as Durand took to capture on canvas what Nature had created, but in juxtaposition Durand used oil, while Olmsted used the real thing. Daniel Burnham— the genius behind the World's Columbian Exposition, Chicago's 'White City' in 1893, and architect of our Flatiron Building— said of his friend Olmsted that "he paints with lakes and wooded slopes, with lawns and banks and forest covered hills."

Life in our great city, Olmsted believed, causes "nervous irritation...depression" and a "loss of faith and lowness of spirit." This is truer today as we now endure blaring sirens and ferocious helicopters, the screaming airbrakes of city buses and the staggering number of us, which alone causes "nervous irritation." On the island of Manhattan live 70,000 people per square mile; Montana has six. For some New Yorkers, seeking Nature is "a self-preserving instinct," and the beauty and solitude of the Hudson Valley that inspired the painters who inspired Olmsted still remain in the park's remote North Woods.

I write this next section with some misgiving; despite my desire to tell you most of what I know about Central Park, I considered avoiding these places we approach in hope you never find them. If today were yesterday I would sit with you by the serene, tree-lined Pool, then wander the quiet Ravine along the Loch and tread our way through the solemn North Woods toward the melancholy of the Conservatory Garden. I would be silenced by the grandeur of the trees and not conjure up the old stories, for nowhere in the park lives more of old New York than here.

Today the park is healthy and groomed. Green meadows and fields are well tended, the trees, except when battered by natural forces far older than our caring for them, trimmed regularly and checked for disease. Graffiti is gone, statues repaired, ponds and fountains and streams run again with clean water. Even now in the remote Ravine that cuts through the North Woods – once the most unruly and unfrequented of all the park—walkways are smoothed, woodchip pathways lead to viewing stations, the bridges crossing the Loch overbuilt and flourishing with woodwork. But I often miss when the park wasn't so tidy, with less fences and no "Keep Out" signs as there were in the park a century and a half ago, when Bo could wander free and we could stay all night. Still, I'm thankful for the clean water, the tended trees, weeds pulled, and I understand the fences: forty-five million people visit Central Park each year, more than jam Times Square and twenty times the number recommended by the National Parks Administration. So I'm asking, can you keep a secret?

We are in the northern reaches of the park, on its west side, entering at BOYS' GATE (100th Street). One walkway cuts quickly left, down to a valley where again much of the city's noise miraculously remains behind the stone wall surrounding the park. On one side of the wall, traffic and streets, on the other, trees and swans; "Jay Gatsby meets Natty Bumppo," wrote Olmsted biographer Witold Rybczynski of this phenomenon.

We pass beneath an Osage tree bearing heavy, bumpy fruit like a green orange used in kitchens by some New Yorkers to keep away roaches. Indians liked its wood for bows. Another walkway to the right leads to a rocky gorge where gushes cold water piped from Lake Manhattan to the south. The water tumbles beneath the walkway and appears again on our left down a slab of black, wet, rippled rock where birds often bathe, wings aflutter and little heads dunking beneath the surface before flying off to preen with sparkling waterbeads dripping. The water empties into a pond known as the Pool, then flows east for nearly two acres and enwrapped with colorful, strong limbs of locust trees, maples, horse chestnuts, and a sycamore that can live five hundred years, back to when the Lenape worshipped it. The sight is incongruous; we are only one hundred yards from Eighth Avenue and a bodega is half a block away.

East along the Pool leads to a cascade, ever-changing yet constant (or at least when the waterfall's faucet is open). The stream is channeled through the formidable, stone Glen Span Arch (for it spans the glen); similar to the Rustic Arch in the Ramble, it seems to emerge from the surrounding rock and serves as a portal to another experience. The stream that cascaded from the Pool narrows to become the Loch flowing through the Ravine: above us, the towering North Woods as if we stepped into the canvas of Durand's *In the Woods*.

The North Woods and Ravine bear a similarity to the Ramble but are less textured, less precious. There are no tended bird feeders or rustic shelters, no schist to climb nor benches made from fallen tree limbs, and fewer winding walkways. Unlike the better-groomed Ramble, trees here torn from the earth by storms more often remain where they fell, their intricate root systems exposed in packed, pale earth. Before the recent renovations these walkways were too broken and dusty for my delicate racing bike, but "the best, most various, and most numerous views lay along the paths of the walkers," wrote historian Fred Perkins in 1864. "The rider must find in his exercise…what compensation [he] may for the loss of all the endless minor beauties of the Park, and many of its chiefest ones."

Occasionally during migration each May and September a group of a dozen birders ventured to the North Woods led by a slight, sprightly woman giving tours for as long as I'd been wandering the park. With her head wrapped in a light-blue scarf and holding binoculars in her left hand the way a tailback carries a football, Starr Saphir, like the best of birders, could name a bird merely by its song or call or the way it flies. I'd tag along on the edge with my binoculars –a sort of membership card for birders—and seeing no difference between the Louisiana and Northern water thrush but Starr could. And though I'd remain generally inept at identifying all but the park's most common birds, I soon needed private communion more than human camaraderie and wandered off again.

At the end of the Ravine, the Loch trickles beneath another stone arch, a counter to Glen Span, the other portal guiding us from the Ravine to a different part of the park. This is Huddlestone Arch, far lower and more narrow than Glen Span, with great boulders weighing many tons above us held together by gravity alone "under which we pass for the first time with not a little misgiving," wrote a cautious Clarence Cook. Eventually summoning his courage, Cook passed through the arch with an apprehension which "nothing but our confidence in the skill of the engineers enables us to overcome."

The Loch once wound swiftly beneath Huddlestone for another thirty yards before spilling into the Harlem Meer at the park's northeast corner, a waterbody similar to the Pond at the park's southeast. But just as the Pond was marred by a skating rink, Nature again has been lost to amusements when the northern acres were violated in the mid-1960s by the construction of an enormous concrete swimming pool resembling a blue 1950s drive-in and costing extra millions in miscalculations. In the winter it converts to a skating rink where constant music rises upward to the trees on the ridge of the North Woods. But Central Park tries "to be something for everybody," wrote Henry James long before this unalterable addition, "a cheerful, capable, bustling...overworked hostess... often at her wits' end... but who, none the less, for the honor of the house, never once failed of hospitality." And despite its clumsy intrusion, the Lasker Pool graciously gives us all cool, clear water in which to swim and bob on our brutal summer's hottest days. And it's free.

Creating Central Park proved more expensive than initially planned, so when work reached the northern acres dwindling funds destined the North Woods to remain nearer Nature's design rather than the Greensward's plan. On the Ravine's western side rises the Great Hill, the tallest trees at its summit towering above us where only a passing helicopter rattles the illusion that we're not in the Catskills. Here in this once ragged solitude I ate the sacred, magic mushroom and listened to the speaking of the trees. Soon the mushroom's hazy, drifting power settled throughout my body as sunlight softened by shade shifts along the knotholes and rutted, craggy contours of their trunks. Faces resolve before each whispers a name: Father May, Jack in Green, The Leaf Man, Green George, the Wood Wives, and Yggdrasil with roots to the waters of the world.

In the warm sunlight the Loch is cold on my feet. Birds bathe on its banks. *Cheek-a-dee-dee-dee* and an angry blue jay close by. Can one tree become really two? Yes, for here they share the root and first yard of trunk before parting. High above, the trees stretch for essential sunlight, redeeming rain, leaves gently touching with a sound like your hand across this page. When the breeze turns stronger the trees moan, they groan deep from within their trunks which hold all the rings of their years. Snap off a branch and the tree will bleed. Dangling on their stems like earrings, like ornaments, is the kernel, the seed, spark of new life, a giant waiting within an acorn.

I scatter birdseed on the ground and in my hair, a tit-mouse light as a penny on my scalp. One corpuscular face of a grandfather of a tree whiskered in green ivy watches with his mouth set in a perpetual 'O' and shaggy eyebrows uplifted.

In my waking dream a pale, slender birch is poised on one shapely trunk of a leg, her other leg extended behind in a curvaceous arabesque. Her torso arches, arms raised into limbs, fingers that are branches now adorned in leaves. I caress her firm contours, over and around where the trunk parts, one rooted to the earth, the other back and uplifted, each toe a twig, her head thrown back so her hair too becomes a new limb climbing higher. I stroke her throat, slowly along her torso to the root, up and around the one leg of a trunk again, cupping with my hand where one parts into the other, extended limb, then press on her with slow muscle to inhale her musky pheromone.

Spent at her root, I lay reposed upon fallen leaves shaped like stars beneath a great tree, an epic poem of a tree against the blue sky. Branches near the treetops carefully cradle Bob Redman from one leafy limb to the next as they did when he built his treehouses. He reaches a hand down to me but my arms are too heavy, too light, and I must stay here on the decaying forest floor, decomposing, soon to feed the living tree.

"Bo," I whisper to a shadow moving low and swiftly, "you're forever in the park" as he vanishes, "all but the little of your ashes I tasted." And as the mushroom's magic wanes I no longer worry that the trees will disappear unless I return to them all the fallen stars.

To Make an Eden *continued*

A
t 4:30 on the morning of April 12, 1861, orders to fire on Fort Sumter in Charleston Bay, South Carolina, were issued by the flamboyant General Pierre Gustave Toutant-Beauregard, once the prized student of his artillery instructor at West Point, Major Robert Anderson who, on that early spring morning, was in command of Fort Sumter. Within days after his surrender, the shell-torn flag of the besieged fort waved atop the figure of George Washington in Union Square as 100,000 New Yorkers surrounding the statue united in outrage and sworn vengeance.

A week after the attack on Sumter, 1,050 men of New York's Seventh Regiment marched downtown for the ferry slips where they crossed the Hudson River, caught trains to Washington, D.C., and, after a few weeks of military training, were sent to war. They were nicknamed the "Silk Stocking Brigade" since so many were from New York's elite, and legend has it they paraded down Broadway carrying Colt revolvers, Enfield muskets, gleaming swift swords, and velvet- covered stools on which to sit while eating sandwiches from Delmonico's.

New York's Sixty-ninth Regiment— the Irish Brigade— soon followed, its green banner with a gold harp on it flying above the rugged volunteers. There was the Fourteenth Brooklyn, the only regiment named not for a state but a city and "who fought like devils" General Stonewall Jackson said of them, and on March 5, 1864, marching without fanfare, not even a drum but with hope that their patriotism and blood might lead to equality for all Americans, the Twentieth United States Colored Regiment.

"Give me Broadway, with the soldiers marching," wrote Walt Whitman, "give me/ the sound of the trumpets and drums!/ The soldiers in companies or regiments...flush'd and reckless...The endless and noisy chorus, the rustle and clank of muskets."

Soon Olmsted resigned his duties as superintendent to serve as the executive secretary of the Union Army's sanitation commission, a forerunner of the American Red Cross. The buildings of St. Vincent's were returned to the Sisters of Charity and transformed into St. Michael's Military Hospital. Despite the depleted work force and his missing partner, Calvert Vaux managed; the new, vast 106-acre reservoir continued to be dug, water pipes continued to be laid, and a quarter-million trees were planted by 1863 when the land from 106th Street to 110th Street was added to the park. On April 23, 1864, a marble pedestal was unveiled along the southern end of the promenade upon which eight years later would stand a statue of William Shakespeare, born three hundred years ago to the day. There was not enough money for the statue, only the pedestal, so to help finance the piece –its commission given to John Quincy Adams Ward, sculptor of my beloved and assuring Indian and his dog—a one-night-only performance of *Julius Caesar* opened at the Winter Garden Theatre on lower Broadway. Billed as a benefit for "The Shakespeare Statue Fund," the role of Marc Antony in this drama of betrayal and assignation was played by John Wilkes Booth.

Building the new park continued with renewed vigor soon after General Lee handed his sword to General Grant who returned it; the next day, in a gesture of reconciliation, President Lincoln asked the White House band to play "Dixie," the Confederate States' unofficial national anthem, but few Southerners would have sung so proudly "I wish I was in the land of cotton" had they known it was written by Daniel Emmett in New York City. First performed at the old Mechanics' Hall on lower Broadway in the spring of 1859, Emmett himself sang it in blackface.

And finally after four years of war which both North and South expected to win in ninety days, a war that killed over 625,000 Americans and maimed many more, the thinned, battered ranks of New York's Seventh Regiment marched home from places before which few of them had ever heard: Bull Run, Antietam, Chancellorsville, Gettysburg, and Appomattox Court House. Home too was the devastated Sixty-ninth –forever known as the Fighting Sixty-ninth –whose "brilliant though hopeless assault on our lines," wrote General Lee, "excited the hearty applause of our officers and soldiers" even as the Confederates slaughtered them at Fredericksburg. "Of the thousand stalwart bayonets," wrote newspaperman Charles Halpine, himself having served with the Sixty-ninth, "Two hundred march today,/ Hundreds lie in Virginia swamps/ And hundreds in Maryland clay."

Olmsted returned from military service and resumed his position of superintendent. Again the Sisters of Charity were displaced, the hospital's chapel a gallery for Thomas Crawford's sculptures; his bronze *Freedom Triumphant* stood atop the newly completed Capitol dome at Lincoln's second presidential inauguration. A charming restaurant was added, attracting some of New York's richest and most influential: financier and diplomat August Belmont, William Vanderbilt (eldest son of Cornelius Vanderbilt), along with a clientele so notorious that the Sisters asked that its name no longer be connected with the establishment. The manager of the restaurant—Patrick McCann, brother-in-law to Tammany boss Richard Croker—renamed it McGowan's Pass Tavern.

At the first snowfall of the year Fifth Avenue residents held a sleigh-ride race through the park to the tavern, the winner receiving a magnum of champagne. But similar to the fate of Central Park's Casino a generation later, McGowan's could not survive the convictions of a reform mayor. With plans to demolish the old, stalwart Arsenal along Fifth Avenue, the park's commissioner evicted McGowan's proprietor so that graceful, gabled structure could become the park's police precinct. Everything at the tavern was auctioned: paintings, furniture, even "Old Gabe," a green and yellow parrot sold for $45. But soon after his mayoral election in 1914, John Purroy Mitchel had the tavern demolished; all that is left of the Dyckman/McGowan Tavern, the Sisters of Charity residence and chapel, the museum and restaurant, are the foundations, rock upon piled rock, layers extending back nearly four hundred years. But a portion of the convent's name has survived; where fallen or rotted trees are piled is a sign at its entrance ignobly referring to the area as "the Mount Compost Road."

CHAPTER TWELVE

Blessings From Above

C arolyn Stoloff's tender poem "Afternoon by the Central Park Sailing Pond" occurs in a most popular and cheerful location, one Olmsted believed an essential purpose of the park: to commune with those we love amid the sanctity of Nature.

> We're side by side on a bench
> all afternoon "soothing"
> my mother says softly

The poet sits with her mother at the Conservatory Water, but since there is not nor ever has been a conservatory here it is more commonly known as the Model Boat Pond. There is a mood of serenity as graceful, miniature sailboats skim the water, and in the poet's imagination she becomes the small sailboat, her mother the shallow pond.

> I'd like to be that way—
> in passage, crossing my mother's
> transparent stillness
> leaving no scar.

Although just off Fifth Avenue, the Conservatory Pond is quiet, all but the highest penthouses screened by the grand, continuing row of stately American elms. The formal garden required in the park's design was to resemble an Oriental carpet, and what a stunning conservatory it would have been: two stories of glass with an entrance directly onto Fifth Avenue between 73rd and 74th streets, all reflected in the pond, the only piece not scrapped in budget cuts.

Without a conservatory the pond evolved into a fashionable spot all the more charming with the sailing of model boats. A wooden boathouse was built on the eastern shore, and men in three-piece suits and bowlers with boats eight feet tall once crowded the pond's edge where children wearing sailor suits launched smaller boats propelled by long poles and a fickle wind just as Stuart Little captained his "Wasp" in E.B. White's 1945 novel. Oddly, a bench dedicated to White is not here but directly behind Shakespeare along the Mall. Why? I don't know.

This was a world of simpler amusements, "a stirring scene, full of young, joyous life," wrote Arthur Wakeley in his article "The Playground of the Metropolis" from the September 1895 issue of *Munsey's Magazine*.

> On bright afternoons when the wind is astir the young yachtsmen of the city, in blue and white sailor uniforms, with gold anchors on their shoulders, and golden curls falling from under their sailor hats, hurry down here with their yachts under their arms. [With] sails hoisted, ships trimmed, and their owners, shouting with enthusiasm, chase after them along the plank-lined coasts.

Few men wear hats anymore, and most boys don't sail model boats even though the old wooden boathouse was replaced with one of brick where inside—home of the Central Park Model Yacht Club—dozens of model sailboats await their captains. Above the door hangs a faded print of *Lilliputian Boats in Central Park* by William Merritt Chase where small sailboats skim the rippled pond, the boys in knickers, a girl in a lace dress and matching bonnet. Except for their clothes and that no tall buildings are visible behind the treetops, the park still resembles the painting done more than a hundred and twenty years ago.

"The model yachts contend in seas sheltered/ from any wave," wrote Joel Brouwer in "Conservatory Pond, Central Park,"

> while their captains fidget
> on the concrete shore, fingers sticky
> with ice cream and Cracker Jack, less intrigued
> by the tiny jibs and rudders of their ships
> than their grandfathers would like.

On the pond's western shore sits an over-life-size Hans Christian Andersen reading "The Ugly Duckling" to an attentive duck at his feet; here on summer weekends, children are read stories and poems. Hans arrived in 1956; since then the duck has been stolen three times, twice by the same thief.

A few years after Hans appeared, Alice sitting on a gigantic mushroom joined him on the pond's northern shore. The statue is eleven feet high, her shoes tremendous, her right index finger thick as a child's wrist and shined smooth by so many who have touched it. The March Hare is trim, dapper, and, wiser than most of us, ever conscious of passing time. There's the busy, big-eared dormouse, and the grinning, mysterious Cheshire cat peers from a tree limb above Alice's right shoulder. In Alice's lap, Dinah.

The figures are modeled after John Tenniel's illustrations from the first edition of Lewis Carroll's 1865 novel, but Alice and the Mad Hatter do not resemble Tenniel's woodcuts. Alice appears older and her cheeks more plump than the curious little English girl, and this Alice is smiling, something Alice rarely does after tumbling down the rabbit hole. And the Mad Hatter doesn't appear at all mad but rather kindly, with large, happy eyes and closely resembling a stylish, older gentleman who often sat behind Alice on the wooden bench that now bears this small plaque:

> To Remember George Delacorte (1893-1991)
> Who Loved To Sit Here To Watch The Joy
> Of Generations of Children Playing With
> 'Alice' Donated By Him in 1959
> Lovingly, Valerie Delacorte

Brooklyn-born George Delacorte made a fortune creating Dell Press that published magazines, puzzle books, and comics. To memorialize the passing of his wife Margarita and as a comfort in his grief, Delacorte commissioned José de Creeft to create a statue in Central Park of *Alice in Wonderland*, which Margarita adored. The model for Alice was the sculptor's daughter Donna.

Alice was not the park's only gift from George Delacorte, the Lorenzo di Medici of New York, said former mayor Ed Koch. In the summer of 1962, along the western shore of Turtle Pond, an 1,800-seat outdoor theater opened with a production of *The Merchant of Venice* starring George C. Scott and James Earl Jones. This was now the summer home for Joe Papp's Public Theater, and the Delacorte has been giving free performances every summer ever since. Just outside the theater are two statues: the empowered Prospero summoning the tempest, his magic garment wild in the wind, and Juliet and her Romeo, entwined, slender as a ballet. Sculpted by Milton Hebald, both are gifts from Delacorte.

George Delacorte married again, and despite he and his wife being mugged—her mink coat stolen with a knife to her throat— the couple continued strolling the park. This is life in New York, he said, and to make it better is how he spent a fortune. Surely he'd enjoy how many women pose with their arms around the Mad Hatter while their boyfriends snap pictures on their cell phones.

Adjacent to the Model Boathouse is a pricey café, with good coffee and pastries, liquor and beer in the afternoons. Shaded by umbrellas on the terrace, the tables often seat the residents from the East Side, for this is their neighborhood café. On pleasant Sundays they read the *Times* or meet after a brisk walk or watch the sailboats –remote-controlled now, one lever for the sail, one for the rudder. Some might recall bringing their own children here, or at least telling the nannies to do so. Often young boys lean over the pond's smooth granite shore snatching minnows and tiny crayfish lured to the surface with breadcrumbs. Around them promenade parents with strollers, an elderly couple (she with a disapproving face, he a bit of a dandy but hobbling), Haitian care-givers and their charges, groups of awkward, mischievous, unthreatening teenagers, an Asian family posing before Alice, and on Saturday Hasidic Jews, the men in white shirts and black pants, their pale, pretty wives well-covered and with many children in tow. A young man hunched over the drop handlebars of his bike slowly weaves through the amblers. Soon an older man follows, sitting upright on *his* bike, a little dog in the basket on the back.

By the early 1990s young women on roller skates danced around the oblong pond in tight shorts and colorful tank tops wearing anklewarmers even on the hottest days because of the movie *Flashdance:* "Take your passion and make it happen." Pudgy, middle-aged men also on roller skates and wearing similar short-shorts but tube socks rather than anklewarmers listened through a Walkman to a cassette of The Village People:

> Young man, there's a place you can go,
> I said, young man, when you're short on your dough….

Gradually the Conservatory Pond lost some of its allure though never its charm. Most people sail boats for novelty now, and membership in the Model Yacht Club has greatly fallen. But then this quiet piece of

Central Park found renewal as the setting for something remarkable in which both the park and the city itself were essential. Over the next two and a half decades many thousands of New Yorkers and others around the world would be profoundly touched by this incongruous, incomparable wonder that happened here, this gift Nature gave to our city.

November 10, 1991, was the first sighting of "a very light-colored, immature red-tailed hawk" recorded in the Bird Register by sharp-eyed, reliable Tom Fiore; to this day no one registers more sightings than Tom. Though hawks have passed along this eastern fly zone heading south each autumn and back north in springtime long before even the Lenape watched their magnificent migrations, this particular hawk lingered. Its tail feathers had yet to turn that rich mahogany from which the bird gets its name, its sex unknown until another red-tail remained in the park, larger than the first and so a female. Evidently the young male had chosen Central Park as his domain, and since he was so light-colored park birders called him Pale Male.

He had won the female by dangling before her ripe offerings of freshly killed squirrels and rats and pigeons plucked from the bounty of Central Park. At times the two hawks, talons entwined, danced in a fall through the sky– a dalliance— and soon often mate throughout the days on Fifth Avenue balconies and parapets. They built a nest in a tree behind a backstop along the Great Lawn but too far out on a flimsy limb unable to hold the weight. The hawks built another nest in an elm on the east side near 70th Street, and though better anchored on stronger limbs, crows harried the birds so mercilessly that each, distracted, flew into buildings. They were rescued by helpers from the Audubon Society, cared for and released in the park, and though Pale Male remained, his mate vanished, apparently having had enough of New York.

But on New Year's Day, Pale Male's second in town, another female perched on the terraces and window guards high above Fifth Avenue. Again he courted her with tasty park delicacies and again they danced in the sky. Then something happened even more remarkable than red-tails building nests in Central Park, something that had *never* happened; Pale Male built his third nest beneath a cornice on the top floor of an apartment building twelve stories above Fifth Avenue. Stick by stick he wove the great nest over the center window ledge at 927 Fifth Avenue, between 73rd and 74th streets, facing west for the warmth of the traveling sun, his vast territory of Central Park before him.

"I told my caseworker at drug rehab that I saw a pair of hawks making a nest on a building on Fifth Avenue," a young man told Marie Winn, author of *Red-Tails in Love*. "She looked at me funny and asked, 'What have you been smoking?' "

Spring arrives in New York City with eager caution. The Easter Parade strolls Fifth Avenue that holy Sunday morning beneath outrageous bonnets in a tradition that began a century ago when flowers from St. Thomas Church at Fifth Avenue and 53rd Street were carried to St. Luke's Hospital, then only a few blocks uptown. And here in the tolerant harbor where the first Jews arrived in 1654 we celebrate our freedom from bondage.

In the Passover service, the long story to freedom is read from the *Hagaddah* ("The Telling"). After four glasses of wine, symbolic foods such as matzo and sweet charoset, after many prayers—including one of sorrow for our enslavers who suffered because Pharaoh refused to "let my people go"— there is a song of gratitude, "Dayyenu" (dī-Ā-nu): "it would have been enough" or "we would have been contented," but God gave even more. We would have been content had we been brought out of Egypt, but God split the Red Sea for us to pass. Dayyenu. It would have been enough that He spilt the Red Sea but He sustained us in the desert and led us to Israel. Dayyenu.

It would have been enough that Bryant had bullied New York with his editorials, but the City Council heeded Downing's words and chose far more acres than originally planned for the new park. Dayyenu. We were content that Olmsted was appointment superintendent but then Elizabeth Barlow headed the Conservancy. Dayyenu. Pale Male stayed in town, lured a mate, and that April 1995 when he first became a father, I did too.

Compliments of palemale.com

Part Three

I thank you God for most this amazing day, for the
leaping greenly spirits of trees, and a blue dream
of sky and for everything which is natural, which
is infinite, which is yes.

e.e. cummings

A fter baths, in their pajamas and beneath the covers, sharing a cozy room with a photograph of *Angel of the Waters* on the door, after warm milk with Nestles and while a soft nightlight glows with the face of the moon, my children asked for the same story about the Bare-foot Girl and the Prince of Belvedere.

"Go back to when her sisters warn her of the prince," Lily whispers.

"But can it kisses wash away," Skylar recites.

"Mountains, shores, the hardest stone in Greensward. Water cleanses all," I tell them, *"but can it kisses wash away?" asks one of the maiden's sisters.*

"Kisses!" cries another sister. "Why ask you of kisses? You flee the handsome soldier near the Green and run each time your gown is snagged upon a simple thorn. Why ask you of kisses?"

"Not for me I wonder but our sister might, else why is she so silent?"

"Who could sing," the Bare-foot Girl replies, "while the grackle jabbers?"

"Call me grackle, for though that name be not pleasant to the ear it is a lovely bird."

"A lovely bird I do agree though its squawks are so annoying."

"To serve as warning: give not your heart to one who will not give his in return."

This story began one summer morning in the Conservatory Garden as we watched the Untermeyer Fountain come to life. Three lovely young women in a circle, all dressed in gossamer gowns, fingertips touching, their laughter frozen until the spray in the center of their circle shot upward in the warm air and we imagined them dancing. We decided they are sisters, and one loved the Prince of Belvedere, the young Elizabethan falconer with a bird about to rise from his arm.

Soon after she arrived in the world and from a harness on my chest, I watched Lily discover Central Park. She'd close her brown eyes and inhale each soft breeze, heard the cardinal's chirp and music along the promenade. It seemed only overnight that she rode contentedly in a stroller through "Sody Park" she called it, sat in a playground's baby swing pushed by her father's untiring arms, and with a plump face full of wonder and delight nestled in Alice's rigid, comforting lap.

Lily and Alice

Within two years her fair-haired brother Skylar sat beside her in a double stroller and reason enough to leave beloved First Street for an apartment on an Upper West Side of wider streets, slower roaches, and with Central Park close by.

But almost as soon as we entered the new apartment, before a fresh coat of paint had dried on the walls and we had lined the kitchen cupboards, she walked out the door and took the children with her. I never really quite knew why; maybe because I had twenty years on her and she feared waking one morning to find herself at my age married to an old man, or maybe some people just stop loving for no real reason but the fickleness of this world despite the sworn vows and promises made. Like the first divorce the end hadn't happened suddenly, the way some of us fall in love; I saw it coming as I had many years ago only now there were marriage counselors and trial separations before she moved in with her mother thankfully just a few blocks away.

Nor was I devastated as I had been when younger. I wasn't fleeing for anywhere else, and besides, I knew with time and luck I will love again; the rough part was overnight losing two-thirds of my time with the children. Now and for years there were lawyer bills and child support, so from then on I could provide little to my children except a clean, cozy home, good food, and my love. As for sharing with them the wonders of the world, we had Central Park.

"*I'd sooner dance with a poet on the Mall,*" the second sister cries, "*a man who'd worship me and write his songs of me, than ever love a man whose head is in the clouds.*"

"*That still leaves a good amount for me.*"

The first sister laughs and the Bare-foot Girl splashes the third.

"*Why treat me with such discourtesy?*" the sister protests. "*It is your welfare that I care, to save you from the heartache sure to come with the fickle Prince of Belvedere.*"

"*Oh surely it is not he,*" the first sister cries, "*of whom our sister speaks! He'll pluck the sweetest parts of you and feed them to his birds. Have you forgotten Rosalynn, sweet Rosalynn, the Laughter of the Loch, whose heart so ached with love for him she pleaded to be spared the grief in such a life as hers?*"

"*And now,*" sighs the second sister, "*she is a willow weeping near the Pool.*"

"*And in whose safe arms starlings sleep,*" replies the Bare-foot Girl, "*where cooling shade is found on hottest days and warmth on chilly nights. Rosalynn is, though nothing like before. Her life never ended, only changed, and when I place my hand upon her trunk I still can feel the beating of her heart.*"

"*Dear sister, it is not love we warn you but rather flight with one who'll drop you from the sky.*"

"*But ah, what heights I will have known before that fall which may not come at all despite your fears. And dearest sisters, what pleasure can be found with a poet on the Mall? Does he possess a handsome, slender form with shoulders broad, or is the only effort he performs the lifting of a pen?*"

Give me a man with figure strong and light, and with him shall I dance away a night."

"It seems our sister is in love," the first declares, "and of all the castles met with argument that is the one impossible to breach. We told her of our fears," as all three sisters join hands again, "so let us worry not of matters water cleans away."

"Water to nourish us."

"To soothe and heal us," all three sing together, "sent by the Angel to us her children on this summer's day."

But before the sisters ceased their quarrel, before they touched fingertips and danced again, my children were asleep.

CHAPTER THIRTEEN

Seeing the Park with New Eyes

I stand on a great cliff of Manhattan schist, the half-billion-year-old bedrock upon which Manhattan is built. While Olmsted and Vaux worked on the Greensward Plan, a wooden bell tower for sighting fires rose on this cliff with a view of the remote and unpopulated Upper West Side. Nearby, Seneca Village and Pigtown, home to New Yorkers soon to be driven off these acres so the dreams of Olmsted and Vaux might come true.

It is a cold and cloudy morning late in March. The distant apartments to the east and to the west are visible through the mist and leafless trees. Few people are in the park, which is gray and quiet and solemn. This cliff of schist is now called Vista Rock, the watchtower replaced with a castle. No opulent French affair or the heroic fantasies of Neuschwanstein, this one is from the simpler Middle Ages, a time of dulcimers and enchanted forests.

Like the Rustic Arch in the Ramble and the North Woods' Glen Span Arch, the Castle seems to emerge from the rock. Belvedere Castle is the park's most magical artifact and its most expensive. Meant to have two towers, at $450,000, one was enough, and though less adorned as originally intended, the Castle's enchantment is not diminished. And just as the Angel and her terrace are the social heart of the park—its grand gathering place, its central plaza— and with the Ramble and North Woods our Catskills preserved in the city, a display of Nature's creation— the Castle embodies our romantic imagination and capacity to dream.

At the base of Vista Rock and the Delacorte Theater along its shore is Turtle Pond, once known as Lake Belvedere and a remainder of the original reservoir from 1842 that flowed north for nearly 2,000 feet to the stone and concrete wall we had visited once before along the 86th Street transverse road. These days I am violating park rules by standing on this cliff after hopping a rail fence meant to save me from falling to the rocks below, though before these precautionary restrictions never had I heard of someone ever falling. When I had first wound my way to the Castle through the forest, the Castle meant for magic was a ghost, abandoned and abused, boarded up, graffiti white and insane on the stone walls. But even then the Castle still retained wonder however dim, and what young Horatio doesn't wish to walk the Delacorte's stage on a summer night while gesturing towards the Castle that "beetles o'er the base into the sea"?

Today the Castle is clean and busy. Teenagers wearing Central Park Conservancy windbreakers walk the terrace with cameras pressuring visitors to have their pictures taken.

"Na, na, na," one calls loudly. "Bigger smile."

Inside, employees behind a large desk ask visitors to join the Conservancy. But I'm lucky; between the derelict dream-castle during the city's nightmare and this tourist attraction driven by commerce, my children visited the Castle at its most enchanting and beneficial. Large, black microscopes with eyepieces for both eyes and big knobs to focus better magnified the veins of leaves, the bright, round image appearing like a map of rivers and tributaries. A bird's feather under a microscope is not at all like it appears; the barbs along the shaft, called the calamus, resemble a tight forest of perfect, identical trees, and the downy feathers when magnified are white fur trees. Telescopes aimed through the Castle's windows focus on turtles sunning on the rocks below or else far across the Great Lawn toward the distant tree-line.

There was a display of a turtle skeleton still in its shell, another of a bird with bones thin as toothpicks, and a large diorama of the Ramble where the children rediscover what we just explored. There were musky-fragrant terrariums and an aquarium and a bird's nest woven of mud and straw. A narrow, winding stone stairwell led to the top of the tower and a high vista, a beautiful view, a *belvedere* across the Great Lawn.

When we left the Castle, the children in the stroller are asleep before we have left the park; "a few more steps," Amy Lowell wrote in "May Evening in Central Park," "Will bring me/ The glare and suffocation/ Of bright streets."

"Aren't you tired?" I later asked, stretched out on the rug between their beds, the quarter moon smiling dimly in its socket.

"No," Lily said sleepily.

"Gentle Prince," Skylar uttered in the candlelight.

"But *I'm* tired. How 'bout just Charlie Parker loves be-bop?"

"Gentle Prince."

"Well," I begin after a deep breath, "it is the first night of summer, and there is a festival at the Castle. On that special night and for their goodness to the park, some people transform into animals when the night's first star appears in the sky."

"Good morning, gentle Prince," says Roland to his friend, "Have you told the clouds to keep from Greensward on this festive day?"

"I asked for weather mild and clear," the Prince replies. "I hope that is enough. But why are you so early up, unless you broke the night and only now go seek your rest?"

"Like your birds, I rose this day at dawn. There are preparations still before the evening star appears, and while I shall attend each task with every good intent, I think some rare and lovely creature has distracted you. Your thoughts are somewhere else."

"A great, pale bird," the Prince assures him, "gliding on thermals high above these castle walls, its red tail glowing in the sunlight."

"Pale Male," Skylar whispered.

"I think so, too," I told him.

"I do believe some rare and noble bird encircles us," Roland nods with a smile, "and before the coming of this night upon your outstretched arm it will alight. But I have never known a bird to trouble you. Some fairer form has caught your eye and snared your heart with love."

"The Bare-foot Girl," Lily whispered with certainty.

"The hawk, dear friend," the Prince protests.

"Does this rare bird upon the Meadow dance or gather flowers off the Ramble's path?"

"Daddy," Lily said sleepily, "can we visit Alice tomorrow?"

"That's a wonderland idea."

"Wonder*ful* idea," she corrected me.

"But not the zoo," added Skylar.

After a moment Lily said quietly, "I'm never going back to that zoo."

"Is he still there, Daddy?" Skylar asked.

"Maybe."

"Even though it's summer?"

Zoos have always embarrassed and depressed me despite the dignity of the imprisoned animals, and for a dismal few moments we had watched a polar bear in a tiny tank slam off the glass with his great back paws at each lap as if trying to smash his way to freedom.

In a park meant for "spiritual renewal" not "amusements" a zoo was never part of the plan, but soon after construction began, those pets too large or troublesome for some New Yorkers were abandoned on the site. The forsaken animals were caged in the basement of the Arsenal, that squat fortress along Fifth Avenue that was never demolished after all; instead, it remained the site of park offices and a depository for incongruous 'gifts.'

Twelve swans from Hamburg, Germany, paddled on the Pond accompanied by floating nests like those on Hamburg's Alster Lake. When nine swans died, Hamburg sent another dozen. Gracious Philadelphia gave a herd of deer kept penned in a grove of oak trees: nearby, a bison from Indian territory, compliments of General William Tecumseh Sherman, and the bear tied to a tree was sent by General George Armstrong Custer shortly before taking his blundering, bloody step into the Black Hills and immortality. Soon a dozen cages were quickly assembled across from the Arsenal where the zoo is today. Referred to as the menagerie, it was the setting for some most outrageous days.

In my imagination I had yet to read that morning edition of the *New York Herald* on Monday, November 9, 1874, and visiting the park I was surprised how few people there were despite the mild autumn day. Those who *were* in the park carried hunting rifles and walked warily, eyes scanning the landscape. With my hands raised I approached one great-mustachioed fellow wearing a pith helmet and holding a double-barrel shot gun.

"What's the rumpus?" I asked.

"On the watch," he replied gruffly, his eyes alert.

"For what?"

"Animals escaped from the menagerie," he declared. "Been running wild since Sunday."

I waited for the punch line or at least a smile; neither came.

"Where'd you hear this?" I asked lowering my hands.

"In the papers," he said, eyes scanning the terrain, rifle ready. "Dozens killed already."

Incredulous, I too gazed through the grove at squirrels and birds.

"I'd keep that dog on a leash," the man uttered firmly (of course Bo was with me then too). "Don't want him mistaken for a wolf."

He touched the rim of his helmet before continuing on his cautious, stealth-like way.

"And keep your eyes on the trees," he called. "Pumas can climb."

Sixty-four years before a brilliant, brash Orson Welles terrified the Northeast on Halloween with his radio broadcast of Martians landing in Grover's Mill, New Jersey, an editor at the *Herald* tried to raise public concern about the deplorable and potentially dangerous condition of the animal cages in the Central Park Menagerie. The article was originally intended to upbraid zookeepers after staff editor Thomas Connery saw an animal nearly escape from one dilapidated cage, but wanting something more dynamic to attract attention, Connery gave the idea to staff writer Joseph Clarke.

"Excuse me, sir," called a young man who approached with a repeating rifle in his hands, one finger on the trigger, "perhaps you haven't heard that—"

"Wild animals on the loose."

He nodded once aggressively: "Mayor Havemeyer has issued an order for citizens to stay indoors until a cannon blast indicates the all clear."

"But I was in the park yesterday," I would have told him. "I didn't see any wild animals running loose or hear about—"

"Read it for yourself," he cried, his anger rising as he shoved a rumpled *Herald* in my hands. He stomped off to a clump of bushes but added threateningly, "You've been warned!"

"Awful Calamity," ran the front page story with the headline, "The Wild Animals Broken Loose from Central Park" above the words "TERRIBLE SCENES OF MUTILATION."

It seems a zookeeper had been harassing a rhinoceros that broke from its cage and gorged the man to death, then smashed open the cages of lions, tigers, panthers, bears, an anaconda, and more than a dozen monkeys "playing truant through the Park and are not to be depended on when they become hungry." Printed too, a long list of those people and animals killed although the rhino couldn't be stopped as bullets bounced off his hide as if made of iron plates.

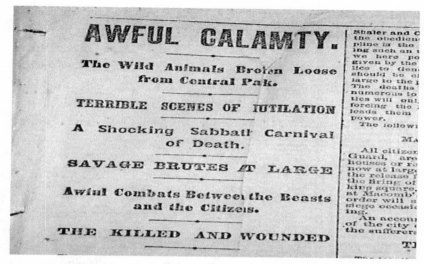

front page of *The New York Hera*ld, November 9, 1874.

A panther had mauled two policemen, then tore apart a young woman. A puma killed a little girl at the carousel. Most horrid, a lion attacked a carriage and brutally mangled four children inside. Evidently hundreds had been injured, sixty seriously, "with three most likely not surviving the night." Already forty-nine people had been killed, twenty-seven so viciously attacked that they remain unidentified.

"Wait!" I'd call to the man in the shrubs, gun barrel protruding. "You didn't read the last paragraph," so I read aloud that it's "pure fabrication. Not one word of it is true. Not a single act or incident described has taken place. It is a huge hoax." Evidently not everyone had read that far in the article before grabbing a gun, and despite the best intentions of the *Herald* reporter, cages at the menagerie remained unchanged. Rather than build secure ones, New York's notorious political machine Tammany Hall hired armed guards; this did not improve the security of the cages but did insure the guards' loyalty to Tammany, and poor Olmsted's hope to eliminate or at least restrict the zoo ended forever with the appearance of Mike Crowley.

His arrival in 1884 was big news, and we followed his health and daily activities in the *Times* and *Herald*. When sick, he received get-well cards, and we eagerly awaited his "destined bride" Miss Kitty Banana who "hails from the wild regions above the falls of the Congo River," wrote the *Times* in the summer of 1887. A year later Henry Starkey Fuller published *Mr. Crowley of Central Park: A Historie* of the first chimpanzee brought to America. Now we could gaze on our 'uncle' whose original name had been Remus after the kindly old Negro from the Joel Chandler Harris stories. The chimp's caretaker, Jacob Cook, "found the name impossible to keep in his head" and simply called him Mike.

In Mike's third Manhattan winter an attempt was made "to prevail on him to wear clothes in a civilized manner."

> The covering which nature had provided…might answer every purpose in the primeval forest of the dark continent of Africa, was hardly in good form… in the midst of the great civilization of the Nineteenth Century.

His first article of clothing was a skirt he immediately ripped to shreds as well as the "stout, canvas duck pantaloons" that followed. After several more fashion attempts, park authorities agreed reluctantly that "it was doubtful the chimpanzee's prejudices could be overcome."

At the menagerie strolled lovely Verena Tarrant in fine clothes of ribbons and lace beneath a parasol and escorted by a suitor, the lawyer Basil Ransom from Henry James's 1886 novel *The Bostonians*. When in New York they reside along stylish Fifth Avenue and West 10th Street, in stately Georgian townhouses at the north of Washington Square, once the city's most fashionable neighborhood. After a horse-drawn carriage ride—all the finest New Yorkers showed themselves in carriages through Central Park— Verena and Basil visited the "little zoological garden" which "expressed all the fragrance and freshness of the most charming moments of the year."

Unlike elsewhere in the city, here the prosperous and privileged would have encountered New Yorkers from a vastly different world. From the gruesome alleyways and crammed tenements on the Lower East Side in search of cheap entertainment and a promise of wonder, Maggie Johnson, who briefly "blossomed in a mud puddle" in Stephen Crane's novel *Maggie: A Girl of the Streets,* "discovered the Central Park Menagerie." With her, the crude Bowery boyfriend Pete who "went into a trance of admiration before the spectacle of a very small monkey threatening to thrash a cageful because one of them had pulled his tail." The names of Maggie's neighbors on those bitter streets were more likely Vito and Moishe rather than Jakey or Sean when Crane's novel appeared in 1893, but at last the varied social classes mingled if only briefly in the park.

Through a ground-floor window of the Arsenal we could gaze on Professor Albert S. Bickmore, bald and white-bearded, once a special student of Louis Agassiz, the brilliant Swiss scholar of Earth's natural history. Well-dressed and sitting at his desk with erect dignity, perhaps at work on one of his renowned lectures, Professor Bickmore is surrounded by volumes of thick books in glass cases, a large wooden bureau with many little drawers of specimens, and a slender brass microscope on the desk behind. For the Arsenal was the first home of the American Museum of Natural History until Dr. Bickmore moved his vast collection of birds, mammals, reptiles and fish, corals, shells, and many insects to the new facility across the park on Central Park West. Opening to the public in 1877, the museum eventually displayed in a glass case the stuffed corpse of Mike Crowley "hanging from the branch of a tree," the *Times* reported on January 10, 1889, "in one of his favorite Central Park attitudes." Seventeen other copies were sent across the country, and one given to Jacob Cook, Mike's keeper who tearfully had unveiled his "side partner."

Not until the mid-1930s would animals in twenty-two dilapidated cages receive a proper zoo with a monkey house, an open area for an elephant—its left ankle thick as a tree in leg irons—and a lion "serving out his life sentence in a slummy cage," wrote the poet Robert Lowell. In the zoo, "this place for lost children," Yevgeny Yevtushenko "talked quietly to America" in his poem "New York Elegy":

> Behind a wire fence, zebras munching hay
> peered, at a loss, into striped darkness.
> Seals, poking their noses from the pool,
> caught snow in mid-flight on their whiskers;
> they gazed around them, quizzical, confused,
> forsaken children of Mother Ocean
> taking pity, in their slippery style,
> on people—lost children of the Earth.

Guarding the tank where the sleek seals frolic are four large stone eagles appearing like something from ancient Rome or the Third Reich.

But they too are New Yorkers, rescued from Brooklyn Shore's First Avenue Bridge destroyed for another Robert Moses expressway. An unknown administrator sent the eagles to the newly created zoo which also now had a full-time veterinarian, Dr. Harry Nimphius, "grieved but no longer surprised by the things that visitors… toss into the animals' cages," including cigars, beanbags, razor blades, and broken glass. "Whatsamatta?" asked a woman in a 1941 *New Yorker* article "Central Park III—What a Nice Municipal Park!" by Eugene Kinkead and Russell Maloney. "He eats everything, don't he?" as she fed a hyena her patent leather handbag.

Park administrative offices are still in the Arsenal, and though we rarely visited the zoo, there under glass and hanging on a wall in the large third floor meeting room, the original Greensward Plan, ten feet long, four wide, each tree painted by Olmsted and special friends, with the original reservoir and a small art museum and with no zoo.

As my children grew—and more rapidly, so it seemed, those days and nights we spent apart—I had come to think of myself as knowing Central Park very well. My wanderings for two decades now have led from the dank depths of Indian Cave to the Castle's ramparts, from the chilly water of Lake Manhattan to hot nights of love among the leaves. I've heard Pavarotti and a bullfrog, watched the moon rise and snow fall, saw the coming winter in a junco and summer's end in a ruby-throat, and revered our city's great hawk.

By now I'd learned some names of those who made the park and some who died in it, spent hours with park people and floated in magic solitude beneath the trees, and when vaguely lost visitors asked directions I gave that and probably more than they wanted.

Like fire or a waterfall, like the city itself and like ourselves, Central Park is both constant and ever-changing: the sturdy stone arches and the turning leaves, the birds that have come and gone and return for ten thousand years, the wrinkled rock my children climb a half-billion years old. The Conservancy transformed an oval of dirt and Bo's ashes into a flourishing, tended garden, then dredged the Lake and ponds, healed the ravished, sandstone birds along the Terrace scrolls, and again curing water flows from the Angel's touch. But except briefly when the lovely dancer rinsed herself cool after swaying in the shadows in Sheep Meadow years ago, what can be found at nearly every entrance –all of them beneath tall, shading trees and easy access for strollers and schools—what for some New York children has been the only part of Central Park they knew and loved the park anyway, I had never until with my children discovered the joy and imagination of playgrounds.

Each is unique, each with something special: a concrete pyramid to climb surrounded by sand, hippos in mud (really blacktop) to their bellies, a thick rope for the boldest to swing like Tarzan between two platforms, all with fountains spraying cold water and some with basins for wading. In one east side playground, a long, curved trench of polished granite set into the earth. The children scale a log staircase to reach the top before the descent, dare devils each of them, sometimes sliding down head first, rides made all the more swift on a piece of cardboard. We called it simply The Big Slide. The entrance gates to Ancient Playground north of the Met are sculpted bronze renditions depicting fables from Aesop: the flattering fox, the slow and steady tortoise, the vain peacock, and at the bottom, the country mouse is amazed by the city's abundance but soon realizes, wrote Aesop twenty centuries before New York, how all of it "costs us dear in danger and fear." Along the edge, "Paul Manship, sculptor."

There were three 'grounds' in the Greensward Plan on which to 'play' games and sports prohibited elsewhere in the park: as Timothy "Speed" Levitch says in the outrageous documentary about his time as a New York City tour bus guide *The Cruise*, sweating was discouraged in Central Park. One playground stretched where the Met is today, another at what is now the North Meadow, and Heckscher Playground a few steps in from Central Park South. That playground was far larger than the one now and where the first playground equipment appeared in 1924, a donation from real estate magnate August Heckscher. Two slender brick pillars once served as a portal to the playground; the pillars remain though north of the playground and seem purposeless and ignored.

Another lonely remnant stands where Rumsey playground once had before lost to Summerstage: a ten-foot tall, thirteen-ton column of fine granite artfully carved into Mother Goose wearing very cool glasses and sitting astride a goose on a turtle surrounded by bas-reliefs of Humpty Dumpty, Mother Hubbard, Old King Cole, Little Jack Horner, and Mary with her little lamb. At another playground a few steps north of Alice along the Boat Pond is another playground with another carved column, also of Alice holding a flamingo for a croquet mallet. Here too is the mad Queen, the devious Cheshire Cat, and the elusive White Rabbit, both granite columns carved by the park's most exhibited sculptor.

Brooklyn-born Frederick George Richard Roth among other artists and artisans added much of the city's beauty during the Works Progress Administration (WPA) project of the mid-1930s as we struggled back to our feet during the Depression. Roth also carved the enchanting dancing bear and dancing goat in alcoves on the zoo's north and south sides, all the limestone reliefs on the walls of birds, monkeys, lions, antelopes, and wolves, but his most renowned sculpture is a life-size bronze of the legendary sled-dog that delivered diphtheria serum to Nome, Alaska, in February of 1925. By December of that year Roth's sculpture of Balto was unveiled in the park, and like Alice's index finger and the Mad Hatter's nose, the bronze upon his broad, dependable back has been worn smooth by ten million children who have straddled him (except after a summer sun baked it beyond our briefest touch). In time Balto would be preserved in books, an animated film, and, to the horror for some children if they knew, in a glass case at the natural history museum in Cleveland.

And beneath the pines and sycamores of Tots Playground a few steps north of Tavern on the Green, the most powerful New Yorker of the twentieth century underestimated the city's love for Central Park.

By 1956 Robert Moses's accomplishments such as Jones Beach and the artful system of parkways and bridges leading us there and back were known across the world, and his vision and power brought the 1939 World's Fair to what had been an ash heap in Queens. Once appointed Parks Commissioner, not even Olmsted had more unrestricted influence on Central Park. Even Fiorello LaGuardia who appointed him feared Moses could not be stopped once the mayor himself left office.

Moses saw the park's purpose differently from its creators. Rather than enriching the soul through communion with Nature, the park should provide what the populous desired: amusements and entertainment, physical recreation not spiritual re-creation, and his changes always appeared to be for the public's benefit. It was Moses who had a real zoo constructed, then he exiled the sheep which had grazed Sheep Meadow since the Civil War; legend has it that desperate men living in Hoover Valley would steal sheep for food. The Sheepfold where the animals spent the night eventually became Tavern on the Green.

To the north the park's nursery was dismantled and replaced with three stylized gardens. Roadways were widened to better serve cars, the beautiful Marble Arch leading to the promenade beneath the roadway leveled because it impeded traffic flow. Athletic fields appeared on the North Meadow, the Casino destroyed and replaced with a playground, then twenty-one more were built along the park's perimeters. He filled in the Old Reservoir and created the Great Lawn—the best change ever made to the Greensward Plan—and rather than additional, inexpressive busts of the renowned, Moses wanted sculpture meant for children: courageous Balto, gentle Hans Christian Andersen, Alice and the zany characters from Wonderland. He also had the names of the park's entrances at last carved into the perimeter wall.

The northern reaches of the Pond were drained to build Wollman Ice Rink, the meadows on the Great Hill paved for badminton, shuffleboard, and bocce courts, and a center for the elderly with horseshoes and a TV-radio room was planned for the Ramble. Only under the guidance of Elizabeth Barlow would many of the changes wrought by Robert Moses in the previous four decades be restored though she also understood the park "has to be responsive to people's current needs." In *The Park and Its People: A History of Central Park*, Roy Rosenzweig and Elizabeth Blackmur wrote that Ms. Barlow "managed to couple Olmsted and Vaux's pastoral vision with a bit of the realpolitik associated with Robert Moses...."

In the spring of 1956, at Central Park West and 67th Street, Moses had cut from the wall surrounding the park a driveway into Tavern on the Green, then planned to pave some of paradise for a parking lot: the small play area just to the north. One day Roselle Davis, who often brought her children to this playground, found blueprints reading "Detail Map of Parking Lot" inadvertently left on the lawn. She spread the word and a protest group gathered at the playground; soon the "Central Park Mothers" as the papers called the protesters chained themselves to trees while the whole city watched—but not at midnight when Moses had a fence erected around the area behind which he planned, as always, doing whatever he desired.

The papers cried "sneak attack," and the subsequent outrage and avalanche of bad publicity eventually led Moses to do what he'd never done before; he backed off. As compensation for the few trees destroyed and to restore his previously unsullied image, he had Tots Playground constructed but it was too late. Seen no longer as the master builder with only the public's benefit at heart, he was exposed as a bully and deceiver, concerned with his own interests and those of a few wealthy patrons of a restaurant. Although Moses continued wielding uncontested power for another decade, the conflict in Central Park was Moses' " 'Black Friday'," wrote Robert Caro in his epic, disparaging biography *The Power Broker: Robert Moses and the Fall of New York,* "for he had lost his most cherished asset: his reputation."

Early on a golden Saturday afternoon late in summer I entered for the first time the Swedish Marionette Theater along the West Drive. It is a dark wooden cabin set amid pine trees where I sat uncomfortably upon the small benches inside where my children saw their first live theatrical production, a precious, clumsy performance of *Rumpelstiltskin.* Within its blue box of a stage the young audience entered in their imagination, bewitched by the smaller-than-life stage sets and the marionettes moving so lightly as if on their tiptoes. We left happy and restless, then wandered behind the cottage to the Shakespeare Garden, its tiered walkways winding through flowerbeds blooming with seasonal flowers mentioned in Shakespeare's plays; small plaques and applicable quotations are set in rich, weedless beds beside them: "This bud of love, by summer's ripening breath" or "There's rosemary, that's for remembrance." A mulberry tree in the garden's southwest corner began as a cutting of a tree from Stratford-upon-Avon. Even city poet Frank O'Hara who "can't even enjoy a blade of grass unless I know there's a subway handy," wrote in "Here in New York" how the Shakespeare Garden glistens "with blood, waxen/ like Apple/ blossoms and apples simultaneously. We are happy/ here."

At the Whispering Bench I sat at one end of the curved granite and they at the other. Lily whispered, "Daddy can you hear me?" then Skylar blew a raspberry. As we continued on our way my little girl soon wandered off the path (revealing her character even then) searching for the lost or unusual, while my son trailed, his keen eyes alert to his surroundings. When I turned back to him he was motionless, focused at a point a little to my left and slightly above us.

We had seen him before gliding effortlessly beneath the clouds on broad, outstretched wings as I rowed the Boating Lake far below. In the Ramble one bright afternoon he displayed himself boldly in a tall oak tree though the children's struggle with binoculars soon bored them; they smiled weakly and moaned, "We see him fine, Daddy" before scurrying

compliments of PaleMale.com

off. But now we stood right beneath him calmly perched on a low limb as if to finally show himself ten feet away.

Skylar hadn't moved, transfixed and faintly smiling. Lily quietly returned and whispered, "Is that Pale Male?"

His noble head was a soft brown like sand, his chest of white feathers streaked with darker brown, shoulders broad with his wings folded behind him. He remained immobile, staring straight ahead, but then he peered down, tilting his head at different angles as if for a new perspective of us reverentially below.

We were only three of many New Yorkers captivated by this bird, but if Pale Male recognizes anyone, it is tall, slender, misanthropic Lincoln Karim. He too is a hunter waiting hours for his shot, in heat or cold, dark winter afternoons, through rain, even Sundays, then he posts what he captured on his website the next morning. When Pale Male and I first became fathers that April in '95, Lincoln appeared on the Model Boat Pond's shore with a tremendous camera on a sturdy tripod, a shiny blue barrel of a telescope birders called the Hubble.

Sometimes he posts close-ups of other birds or a squirrel or insects greatly enlarged, impossibly colored and armored like machines, even photos of a rat: to Lincoln not the vermin of lore but one of Nature's creations and, if not poisoned, a fine meal for a red-tail. Also, photographs of kites and balloons snagged on trees, and one of a pigeon dangling in air, its wing ensnared by one of those strings. Lincoln also posts letters to the mayor demanding removal of all rodenticides, an end to automobile traffic in the park, for maintenance crews to use only electric-powered carts and a return to brooms rather than loud, gas-engine leaf blowers, and letters to the Conservancy, its president Doug Blonsky paid $432,000 a year to head a nonprofit organization. After park worker Manuel Sobral was killed in February 2016 during a landscape project in the Ramble, Lincoln petition for a memorial.

Lincoln remains unwavering in his devotion to park vigilance and Pale Male. This spring, twenty-two since those first baby hawks were born along the side of a New York apartment, three more young have added to the legacy. Far fewer people anxiously await the sight of white, furry little heads peering from the nest, of meals brought to them several times each day by their father, the eyasses' growth and fledging, their summer discovering Central Park, their father's care until they can hunt for themselves and he drives them from his territory, but each morning with coffee I check to find what Lincoln has saved for all of us.

CHAPTER FOURTEEN

Garden of Song and Saffron

A t eight o'clock each morning, whatever the weather and even on holidays, atop an arched passageway between the zoo and the children's petting zoo a few steps north, two monkeys each with a mallet tap eight times on a bell larger than themselves. In an hour they'll tap the bell nine times, and they'll continue doing this on the hour until six tonight. Only after the monkeys have tapped each hour does the band play. It has been waiting eagerly and motionless on a platform beneath the monkeys, and while playing the band members circle the bell on an oval track. Elephant plays accordion, Bear's on tambourine. Kangaroo and her Joey blow horns with Goat on panpipes. The esteemed Penguin beats the drum while Hippo, most delighted, plays the fiddle. Created by Andrew Spadin, the band gives free concerts every hour performing only children's music except in December when Christmas carols are added to their repertoire. The clock too was a gift from George Delacorte, the archway designed by Edward Coe Embury whose father had helped design the park's first real zoo thirty years before.

The carousel's calliope waits until ten o'clock before beginning its happy jumble of snares and pipes: "Let Me Call You Sweetheart" or "Lara's Theme" or else "The Good Old Summertime" in the summertime. Schaefer rock concerts once blasted from Wollman Rink, a string quartet at the Conservatory Garden performs concertos on Tuesday afternoons in June, and an old man named Chester rides along the Harlem Meer on a shined and sturdy Schwinn with reggae turned up loud on his radio bungie-corded to the rack over his rear tire.

On Sunday afternoons along Lake Belvedere we dance to medieval music under the protection of Prince Valiant with two great crossed swords. Actually it's a very large King Jagiello on a great, armor-clad horse that once guarded the Polish pavilion at the 1939 World's Fair in

Queens. For ridding their beleaguered nation of the Nazi evil, Poland gave us the king in gratitude though I wish his magnificent might were displayed elsewhere other than the park.

One Christmas Eve, with only a few of us creatures stirring through the park on way to other festivities, a tall young man in formal wear sang Christmas carols in his Irish tenor inside the reverberant Angel Tunnel. His top hat remained on his head—not in front of him for donations— and after a hearty rendition of "Good King Wenceslas" he took off his hat, bowed with formality, then wished us all "A Very Merry Christmas" before we wound deeper into the holy night.

Shortly after Bush fouled any sympathy the world briefly had for America following 9/11, Warren Dastrup strums his guitar while sitting on Umpire Rock near the carousel angrily singing his "Mass Deception" in a voice that is otherwise melodious and gentle when singing his children's songs. With dark, intense eyes and hands strong as a construction worker's, this ragged balladeer sings of our "righteous wrath" when "we got shot in the back/ with weapons of mass deception, /And now we're mired in Iraq." His music conjured up a spirit that drifted through the park during a month of summer nights of harmony and understanding in 2008 when *Hair* packed the free seats of the Delacorte Theater. A dozen strangers until those moments met on the terrace of Belvedere Castle at curtain time and together we sang along and cried for lost loves and friends long ago.

Someone's always singing John's music in Strawberry Fields (except when the Conservancy tried enforcing there a "Quiet Zone" rule in a garden dedicated to a musician). Occasionally "up come a man with the guitar in his hand" just as John had written about him in the song "New York City." He is David Peel; years before, John and Yoko performed in his raucous, irreverent "New York City Hippie," but today he plays quiet renditions on a steel guitar across his lap; here the mood is often reserved, like the songs "And I Love Her" and "Across the Universe" and "Norwegian Wood."

"How 'bout 'Yesterday'?" asks a sweet-faced kid with a thin hoop through one nostril.

From the corner of her black lip-sticked mouth his girlfriend whispers, "Paul wrote that, stupid."

For over twenty years now along the Boating Lake's western shore,

David Ippolito plays acoustic guitar directly across from a bench in memory of John Denver. Charming and friendly, David sings James Taylor, the Beatles, "American Pie" and a decent rendition of "Thunder Road." In his own "Singin' in Central Park," he'll "play what's requested/ All afternoon if I don't get arrested," so—

> Sit down in the shade or hang out where it's sunny,
> You got it made 'cause you don't need any money
> When the people on the hill are singin' in Central Park.

Central Park has inspired nearly as much music as poems and paintings; in 1867, band leader Harvey Dodsworth composed the Sousa-like "Central Park March." There's the easy jazz piano in Cyrus Chestnut's "Strolling in Central Park," Nina Simone's "Central Park Blues" like Bach playing jazz, and in his moody, atonal "Central Park in the Dark," Charles Ives composed what we'd hear if sitting on a park bench one summer night in 1906. *Up in Central Park* opened on Broadway in 1945 (later made into a film) set in the "Boss" Tweed era with songs "A Walk on the Promenade" and "The Big Back Yard," and "Carousel in the Park" where "children and nurses empty their purses to ride to the music."

One night each summer the New York Philharmonic and on another night the Metropolitan Opera give free concerts on the Great Lawn. We spread blankets beneath the warm Manhattan sky and bring baskets with wine and food from Zabar's or Citarella's or just a sandwich from Subway, and the varied city listens. In Claudia Menza's poem "At the Opera in Central Park" there are "proper ladies/ in the folding chairs" and "five Chinese girls/ in a circle" and a young man sitting on the hard edge of a trash can instead of "down on the blankets" where people are "packed foot to butt/ not me/ I'm free." And for one summer day a year the park sways to salsa when the largest Puerto Rican population of any city in the world takes over Central Park; even the mayor is Puerto Rican that day when I become Esteban Lobo.

John Boyd and his family arrive early at the Angel Tunnel to sing gospel until the middle of the afternoon. Along the Model Boat Pond a man squeezes and stretches out music from an accordion, while SummerStage rollicks days and nights with Charlie Parker or Flávio Renegade, Funkmaster Flash, Tito Rojas, or a very cool klezmer band; on the day after his dad would have turned one hundred years old, Arlo Guthrie sang in the middle of "the New York island" while I sat on a bench along the promenade singing in "this land made for you and me."

Beneath an archway—each shaded, unique, and named whimsically Willowdell or Driprock, Trefoil or Denesemouth or Winterdale—two young Juilliard students (one on violin, the other flute) play Telemann, cases lined with royal blue velvet open to our generosity. At another tunnel, a silver trumpeter in a pork-pie hat blows the love theme from *The Godfather*; had I grapes I would put one in each cheek and talk like the Don, then laugh sympathetically for my poor myself back then who could have never imagined it would all turn out like this.

Along the promenade, three young men with fiddle, guitar, and mandolin (and a tambourine around a boot) play lively bluegrass but also sweet, sad "Lorena" loved equally by Billy Yankee and Johnny Reb.

> A hundred months have passed, Lorena,
> Since last I held that hand in mine,
> And felt the pulse beat fast, Lorena,
> Though mine beat faster far than thine.

Nearby, a Chinese man named Joe (at least that's what his CD says is his name) plays the delicate, high-pitched Erhu, a two-string fiddle sounding Asian even when he plays "Danny Boy." On the northern end of the promenade, Mr. Ralph Williams plays a very soulful saxophone.

Initially Olmsted had wanted only light classical music played in the lovely music stand upon the promenade. He believed the popular music of the day not sufficiently uplifting and that park visitors needed to be educated about how to use a park not meant for hardy pleasures.

By 1905 the concerts were financed by merchant and banker Elkan Naumberg who believed that this gave him the right to destroy the music stand in 1922 (though colorfully preserved for us in a painting by Edward Middleton Manigault) and pay for a new, far larger one of concrete in the shape of a large, upright half-shell: "presented to the people of New York" reads the inscription along its base "and its music lovers." Its premier concert on September 29, 1923, featured a sixty-piece orchestra playing "The William Tell Overture," selections from *Carmen*, Beethoven's Fifth Symphony, and a new march titled "On the Mall" composed by Edwin

Franko Goldman: "there's a place to go/ where there's rest brought by sweet music's flow." The eighty-four year old Naumberg, with a white goatee and smiling through pince nez, sat delighted in the front row. Just beyond the band shell, past the redolent, entwined wisteria vines, the Casino catered to the wealthy, the glamorous, and the powerful.

In the coming years, Duke Ellington played the band shell, Benny Goodman and Irving Berlin too. The edifice shows its age now and often merely shelters teenagers smoking weed and strumming guitars, but on special Saturday summer nights Carlos Konig and his friends play Salsa in the band shell where before them dance beautiful, sexy Latin people and Anglos trying to be beneath the somber countenance of Beethoven across the promenade, his chin lowered, resolute, "in a place of whispering leaves and gloom" as English poet Alfred Noyes wrote in "Beethoven in Central Park." Despite the sensual music and swaying steps, the great maestro is "alone/ With his own grief, and his own majesty."

On summer Sundays nights along the promenade we hear throbbing, trancelike rhythms from Africa and the Caribbean Islands beaten on congos and bongos, djembes and the batá by Chaka Chocolate and other men and women with bandaged fingers and furious hands. Others shake maracas and a tambourine, tap a cow bell and a triangle as the world's most international city unites in this primal summer dance. No one asks for money though a DVD is on sale for $5: people simply gather in the park on weekend nights with their drums, in dreadlocks and straw hats and Bob Marley t-shirts to make music. Women sway gracefully in brightly colored garments and a shirtless old man to the side jumps and gyrates.

Each warm weekend on the concrete between Beethoven and Sheep Meadow to the west is a twirling, counter-clockwise circle of motion and music. This is Central Park's makeshift roller disco where tall, synchronized black men skate together while a blonde woman glides and spins and leaps as if on ice, even wearing the provocative outfit to the music of Donna Summer.

> They said it really loud
> They said it on the air
> On the radio....

Once blasting only from a boom box someone skated to the park, music is now cranked up by a genuine DJ with three turntables and large speakers arriving in a step van with Lady Liberty painted on the outside lifting not a golden torch but old-school roller skates.

Often at the Terrace along the Boating Lake's shore far from the disco beat, Arlen taps lightly with thin wooden hammers the strings of a dulcimer playing distant, enchanting tunes: "Shetland Reeds" and "Epping Forest" and "The Battle of Augrim." The sounds carry us back a thousand years, as does the sight of gentle Arlen wearing the soft, velvet hat and embroidered shirt of a troubadour (though jeans and work boots too). While playing, Arlen sighs, takes small breaths, seems quietly awed by the gentle sounds emanating from the dulcimer.

At times performing with him, Meta plays a harp. She has played in other city parks and in subway stations during winter and for passengers on pleasure cruises around the world but much prefers Central Park. Getting here from deep in Brooklyn is a long journey made all the more arduous by pushing the bulky instrument, far larger than she, in a cart with wheels much too small along cracked sidewalks.

Meta is plump, with dark, unruly hair and jolly eyes, and even before one string is plucked we are bewitched by the harp's magic, its curves and carvings, like a great gold swan set upon the Terrace. And when she plays —Pachelbel or Bach or "The Sound of Music" when requested by tourists, and always "Für Elise" for me— the ducks on the Boating Lake cease their squabbles and the squirrels sit up to listen. She smiles softly and utters a quiet "Thank you" to each person who drops coins or a dollar bill into the cloth bag set beside her CDs for sale though many people merely listen, take her photograph, and move on as if she's but one more park curiosity. When she rests her nimble fingers and if the wind is blowing and if we sit very close, we can hear the strings still singing.

Now imagine the park in winter soon after the ball atop the *Times* tower officially brought in 2005. Workers busily prepare the enormous conceptual art project by the artists Christo and Jeanne-Claude who for fifteen years have been trying to create "The Gates" in Central Park, the project's name an allusion to the park's original formal entrances carved into the perimeter wall. Thousands of "portals" were planned along the walkways, each waving with saffron fabric. At last New York City had permitted the installation on the strict conditions that it would not be permanent nor harm Central Park in any way. Immediately the project was attacked by some park lovers as antithetical to the Greensward Plan since the park was meant for neither entertainment nor amusement. Bike riders condemned it as a safety hazard for limiting our space on the walkways, and a few birders' ruffled owing to the disruption the gates might cause Pale Male's hunting grounds. The park would not profit financially except from the sale of sweatshirts and hats, but hotels and restaurants capitalized creatively on the expected boom when tourism was only recently recovering from 9/11. One hotel with a park view provided binoculars to each guest, while a restaurant served mussels in a saffron cream sauce.

Financed entirely by the artists, the installation would cost an estimated $21 million, which outraged some people: how many hospital wings or crumbling classrooms or struggling families could be aided by such a sum spent for something so impractical, temporary, and indulgent. Though restrictions on entertainment in the park had been tossed out long ago and the world's most adaptable red-tail hawk could pluck his next squirrel or pigeon from the tree-tops and we weren't really supposed to cycle on the walkways anyway, I dreaded the huge crowds the event would bring into the park. Besides, I begrudged Christo's art since the late summer of 1985; with sand-colored canvas, he wrapped Pont Neuf, the oldest bridge crossing the Seine, just when I saw Paris for the first time except in my dreams. Of all the bridges over the river, Pont Neuf was the one I least wanted to see under wraps.

But my girlfriend with whom I was traveling on her way to see family in Munich had often visited Paris and enjoyed the spectacle.

"Ach, deez alt bridge," she said disapprovingly. "Unt now," and her eyebrows lifted, "zee bridge is made new, ja?"

For weeks the park teemed with volunteers receiving instructions from people scooting from group to group in golf carts, cluttering walkways and eating in crowded, boisterous shifts at the Boathouse. Press photographers and film crews were everywhere. Christo and Jeanne-Claude surveyed the process on a slab of rock overlooking Wollman Rink; they appeared thrilled, thin, interesting, wrinkled, Jeanne-Claude's hair bright orange and Christo's eyes so lively.

And finally on a chilly February 12 beneath a bright sky during a photo-op with Mayor Bloomberg, Christo and Jeanne-Claude unfurled the first gate: across two saffron-colored poles each sixteen feet high and straddling the walkway was another pole from which unfurled saffron-colored nylon fabric that hung or, ideally, fluttered above us. Throughout the park for the next few hours, spaced twelve feet apart, 7,502 more "gates" were unfurled, varying in width from five feet six inches to eighteen feet and covering twenty-three miles of park walkways with 1,076,391 square feet of saffron fabric.

There were gates at all the park's entrances, around Sheep Meadow, down the promenade, encircling Bethesda Terrace, the Great Lawn, the Harlem Meer and Lake Manhattan, gate after saffron gate winding along every walkway except through the Ramble and the North Woods. Gates led to every tunnel and waited at the other end, crossed Gapstow Bridge and lined the Pond, marched through the zoo, behind the museum, even reflecting in the museum's back windows while young volunteers handed out two-inch squares of salmon-colored fabric as souvenirs. But soon it all seemed repetitive after the first three thousand and crowds overwhelmed "The Gates." Thousands of visitors posing for photographs caused bottlenecks along the walkways, international film crews narrowed the paths even more, and one young man videoed the event while weaving through the gates on roller blades. I headed home and didn't think much more about it.

For the next week I avoided the park, but one Sunday morning a light snow began to fall, turning heavier in the next hour until two inches coated the fire escape railings outside the window. The sooner we arrived, the more the park would be only ours, so we bundled in boots and jackets, mittens, scarves and woolly caps until my children resembled little gnomes. With birdseed and peanuts for squirrels, we headed into the snowfall on our old sled with steel, red runners and "Paris Champion Fastback" in faded letters along the wooden slats: for back-up, a large, blue plastic saucer.

Even a Midtown workday turns quiet during a snowfall, muffled and slow, but no place is more hushed than Central Park where the snow doesn't quickly turn to dirty slush. Having forgotten about "The Gates" I understood everything when we arrived; in the white park a ribbon colored like the sun wound along the walkways. It dipped and gently curved, rose and then descended again, motionless and glowing in the unblemished snow. My children were dazzled.

"Who *did* this?" Lily asked, hushed and enthralled.

Along the West Drive as we trudged the saffron-ribbon shore of the white lake, a black limousine ground the snow beneath its slow-turning tires. The back window was down, and two pale, wrinkled faces smiled out into the cold air: an old man, his bright eyes beaming, and a woman with hair only a shade darker than the gates.

The physical labor of creating Central Park began at 6 a.m. six days a week, lunch for an hour and the hard day finished at 5. If a laborer lived far downtown where most did, he had nearly a four-mile walk just to Fifth Avenue and 60th Street. He'd leave for work at 4:30 if the weather's good though hitching a ride on a mule-drawn cart costs a dime, a full hour's pay for some. Same price for heading back, but after laboring for ten tough hours and, like every day, getting injured somewhere on his body, most paid for a bumpy ride home.

Edward Kemeys arrived in New York because eight hundred miles west he had heard of work for able-bodied men clearing land for a vast public park. He was twenty-four years old, a slender six feet tall, with clear, gray eyes, dark hair, and an enormous mustache drooping across his youthful face. His own farm had failed despite the rich Illinois earth and good rains, but he could handle an ax, and so for $2 a day he and three thousand others drained quicksand, pulled tons of poison ivy before burning it, and moved enough one-horse cartloads of soil to stretch one and a quarter times around the world. Some men got the rash from the oil left in the smoke of poison ivy, and though a worker could miss a day or two of work, any more than that without a strong Tammany connection meant he would most likely not have a job when he returned.

For many laborers the most unnerving work was blasting through bedrock; more gunpowder was used creating Central Park than the 620 cannons firing hot for three days at Gettysburg. Men took shelter and plugged their ears once the red flags were raised indicating an impending explosion, but if close to the impact it pounded into their chests and knocked the breath away. Luke Flynn, the first man killed working the land, died from a blast in the autumn of 1858, and a boulder that traveled five hundred yards after a detonation killed Timothy McNamara.

But Kemeys remained untroubled by the explosions, having been a captain in the Union artillery corps during the Civil War and, like many working on the city's new park, unendingly grateful to be still on Earth.

Often the construction site was shrouded in morning fog where from within Kemeys heard the clatter of wagons pulling cumbersome loads, a blacksmith's hammer, calls that carried far in the chilly air. Through the mist he watched the brief glow of an explosion moments before hearing it, and this reminded him of the battlefield smoking from cannons and muskets where he killed a dozen charging men with each of his deadly orders to fire. The smoke from gunfire had gratefully appeared like a shroud above the carnage within, hiding the ghastly sight. The recollection troubled him, but by noon the sun had burnt off the fog and it seemed a curtain had lifted on a newly formed meadow or another graceful bridge spanning a bridle path, the area so artfully transformed Kemeys could not recall how it had looked before.

On mild days an unusual sight drifted above the workers; from his "Balloon Amphitheater" near ARTISTS' GATE at Sixth Avenue and 59th Street, Professor Thaddeus Lowe gave aerial tours in his hydrogen-filled balloon *City of New York*. The professor had done reconnaissance for General McClellan with views high above Civil War battlefields in his *Eagle* which undoubtedly moved far faster than did the Grand Army under its tentative commander. Now in peacetime Lowe provided lofty park tours, the balloon's boat-shaped basket hoisting terrified, then delighted passengers dazzled by the new water bodies, winding drives, bridges and meadows two hundred feet below.

One afternoon Kemeys watched a man sculpt in wax the head of a wolf. Soon he tried what the sculptor had done, his model an Alaskan husky owned by a fellow laborer. Before long he made a sketch of a mountain lion coiled on a rock, ready to attack; years would pass before his piece was fully realized, and by then the acres he cleared had transformed in ways unimaginable in his hard, thankful days after the Civil War.

CHAPTER FIFTEEN

The Magic of Osseo's Log

Each visit to Central Park gave something special: the children splashing in the Angel's basin, a young woman playing guitar in Glade Arch, Pale Male perched above us.

"And seeing the little wolf," Skylar told us one night.

"You saw a little wolf?" Lily asked eagerly.

"Maybe just a big dog running free," I told him

He smiled quietly and nodded, "It was a little wolf."

Only later did I understand the little wolf was not conjured up in my son's imagination; he had seen a spirit, elusive and austere, winding its way through Central Park.

Early in the spring of '99, word had excitedly spread that a coyote roamed the park. Another appeared in the winter of 2006—the one my son had seen—and another four winters later. Most likely they journeyed from Westchester County, through vast Van Cortlandt Park in the Bronx and onto the island along the Amtrak line at Spuyten Duyvil. Perhaps they wound south through Inwood Hill Park, then down Riverside Park, and certainly across the quadrangle at Columbia University where one was spotted. Once arriving, miraculously, in Central Park, each made its lair in the same place: not the remote North Woods or the Ramble but in Hallet Nature Sanctuary which Bo had also discovered and, with Bob Redman in the branches above, where I had passed a summer's night years before.

Each coyote was eventually shot with a tranquillizer gun. The first ended caged in the Queens Zoo, but the second died before release: from heartworm, we heard, or a poison rat or perhaps the trauma and abuse of its capture. The third was trapped in TriBeCa far downtown after surviving nearly five miles of Manhattan traffic and released "at an undisclosed location."

I spent cold, dark hours lingering at the southwest corner of the

Pond where they were seen leaving and returning to the Sanctuary but saw a coyote only in photographs and videos that hardy, resilient photographer Bruce Yolton posted on his website *Urban Hawks*. Bruce too was excited at the coyotes' appearance and "with educational effort, I think man and coyote have a good chance to leave [sic] together with minimal conflict in the Big Apple."

Coyotes in the park brought me nearer to my Indian fantasy of these tamed acres but I worried for the animals; before the first corgi was fully digested the city would never allow it despite Bruce's hope. Coyotes, red-tail hawks, and the common loon paddling Lake Manhattan all indicate the good health of the park, but this also tells how little of the natural world remains outside the city. As more animals try adapting to urban spread, the wonder given us by close proximity to these creatures might be the only benefit to their impending peril.

One Sunday morning my children made their first visit to the North Woods. We entered at STRANGERS' GATE (106th Street/Central Park West), the park's most dramatic entrance known originally as IMMIGRANTS' GATE but that sounded less friendly and far less romantic. A roadway rises up a hill to the left, the staircase to the right is wide and steep and cut from the jagged rock face rising above us. That day the summer season began at Lasker Pool, and from high on a ridge we could smell the chlorine and watched sunlight sparkle on the pool's clear water. Along the wooded pathways of the Ravine Skylar found a fallen oak tree, huge and hollow, uprooted long ago by a storm buried half in mosses and the dry, dead leaves it once held so loftily. Pointing at the log's gnarled opening, Skylar said, "I go in."

"Well," I warned him, "this is Osseo's log," and he hesitated. Lily ceased her explorations and listened, then I told the Ojibwa legend of old Osseo who married the young and beautiful Oweenee.

"Like you and Mommy," Lily said.

"A little," I replied, "but Osseo was *very* old, wrinkled and bent over. Well, one day as he and Oweenee walked slowly together through the forest, Osseo saw a fallen oak just like this one. He crawled inside and Oweenee followed, but when he came out the other end," and I pointed where he would have emerged, "Osseo was young, standing straight and strong, his face unwrinkled."

Their eyes widened.

"But when Oweenee crawled out," I whispered, "*she* had grown old, bent over and wrinkled."

"How old?" Lily asked.

"Grandma Ellie old," I said.

As old as my mother gave even my adventurous boy apprehension. He looked at the log, glanced back at me with a taunting smile, then put his hand very near the log's entrance ("Hey!" I cried) and withdrew it. He did so again, quickly now, but then he placed his outstretched arm inside and kept it there, waiting to see if Osseo might pull him in or if his hand would wrinkle.

But perhaps being so near the opening Skylar inadvertently breathed in a portion of the log's magic and from there spread to his sister. This change did not occur in the brief time it would take to crawl through a fallen, hollowed tree, but, like the song "Sunrise, Sunset," it does seem almost like seedlings to flowers overnight.

Though my children loved all the park, as with Bo, me, and Olmsted, the Ramble was most special, most sacred. Here they whisper and tread carefully when we leave the walkway, never harming the forest or touching anything Nature didn't create. Into their pockets I placed fallen chips of cedar bark wherein the Cherokees believed lay the souls of their ancestors, and when they sit very still the animals come to them. I scattered seed for opportunistic birds, and soon a titmouse and chickadees pick from their outstretched palms with tickling talons, my children almost giddy with joy. Squirrels quickly arrived, sitting up close by, their little front paws together as if begging before they snatched peanuts from our fingers.

"Daddy, why are some trees still green?" Lily asked the pines one winter day.

It had something to do with chlorophyll and photosynthesis, but I knew an older reason.

"Long ago, as the days grew shorter and the nights were chilly, a sparrow was too injured to fly south."

Skylar clicked his tongue a few times, lured a squirrel and tossed a peanut.

"The little bird asked each tree for shelter," I went on, "but only the pine said yes, and so the Great Spirit had all the other trees lose their leaves for the winter."

Here in the Ramble, with its groves and rock outcroppings and thick brush, the children first wandered from my sight. They were eager to be on their own, initially together, then separately as they explored over a rise or climbed a slab of rock where we'd meet at the top on the other side. Lily would lead her little brother to what she knew better though he soon wandered on his own, but when my seven year old daughter disappeared behind that boulder she emerged near the Gill wearing a lavender t-shirt with butterflies, not the pink hoodie that would have been too small for her at ten years old now. The beige cargo pants and sky-blue t-shirt Skylar wore when climbing those rocks were now black sweatpants on the other side of the ridge where he stood with a long branch of a spear, my little boy emerging now as a young hunter.

One drowsy afternoon I munched peanut butter and jelly sandwiches with toddlers in the shade of a Strawberry Fields meadow, and though the elms along the promenade seemed no taller than two decades before when I first saw them and Alice appears as she did when my little daughter had first sat in her bronze lap, suddenly, or so it seemed, I stood with Lily near the IMAGINE mosaic as hundreds of people celebrated John's life and my teenage daughter sang all the Beatles' songs. And as my son and his teammates of the West Side Hawks—confident, relaxed, gifted boys in red, white, and blue uniforms—took the field of the North Meadow for warm-ups before a baseball game, it seemed only last summer, with his glove in one hand held close to his heart and his other hand in mine, when that little boy beside me at the stop-light looked at the park and declared, "I'm dying of baseball happiness."

On *Sesame Street* the Count walked the terrace of Belvedere Castle, Big Bird crosses Bow Bridge, and along the promenade we rested on the bench dedicated to Jim Henson "Who Loved This Walk in the Park." In summer Wollman Rink converted into an amusement park called Victorian Garden where the children flew bi-wing airplanes circling twenty-feet in the air, plunged down an inflated rubber slide, and rode a little red roller coaster three-cars long. The carnival lights grew brighter as the sky darkened, and after closing time the teenagers who operated the rides let all the children ride for free again and again.

Late on a warm afternoon when shadows stretch east in dark, shimmering waves across the Boating Lake, we crossed Bow Bridge into the green, leaf-thick Ramble on our way home. The children meandered to a rocky gorge where, hidden by rocks, the source of water flows into the Lake. Here they squat beside the clear stream, dip their hands on summer days or turn fallen leaves into miniature boats. In the sky deep blue near sunset we saw the quick, jagged flight of bats low enough for us to hear squeaks from their radar, and above us in a knot hole, first one then twothreefourfive raccoons emerge, slow and sleepy but already masked for their night's marauding of trash cans.

In the gnarled stumps, knotholes and curves of bark, the children detect the faces of the trees. When they lift a log from the forest floor, tiny, fascinating creatures hurry away or burrow deeper into the life-filled earth. Sometimes Lee Rogers tends the bird feeders. Solitary, dressed like an explorer with her pigtails and walking stick, she either strolls the Ramble with long, noble strides or sits in the Boathouse café with pencils and watercolors drawing on a tablet what she has seen in the forest. She supports herself by selling her very detailed pictures to other park people, mostly birders who chip in $100 for an original; a color photocopy is only $10.

And one winter afternoon —the trees bare except for the evergreens and the holly—my children and I were tramping off the Ramble's walkway when a briefly terrifying moment transformed to wonder. What appeared to be every squirrel in Central Park ran slowly past us. Hundreds of them all trotting the same direction through the dry leaves, hopping fallen branches and scooting over stumps, squirrel after squirrel not begging peanuts or fleeing a forest fire but casually, as if on their way to an arranged squirrel gathering at the Boathouse. Initially I feared we were being swarmed, eaten alive by vengeful Nature at last getting back at humanity, but my children were delighted and unafraid from the first instant the little creatures appeared, smiling with astonished delight. When all the squirrels had gone we resumed our wandering which sometimes led to one of the park's most enchanting artifacts.

From just below Sheep Meadow we hear its clattering calliope. There is a balloon man (neither lame nor goat-footed) at one booth, another sells fresh popcorn, and as a sort of greeting, two black posts with tiny horses encircling them lead us to the ticket booth.

The park's first carousel in 1871 was powered by the strong arm of its conductor who turned a hand crank to get the horses moving. Later, in a circular pit beneath the structure, a mule or horse, perhaps even blind, took over the task, the poor creature finally replaced in 1912 by electricity. The original carousel was a lovely, delicate structure enclosed in an airy shelter, and though destroyed by a fire in 1924, that first Central Park carousel remains with us to this day on each can and bottle of Dr. Brown's Black Cherry Soda.

"Daddy, you ride with us," Lily said while pulling me through the gate.

The carousel that replaced the first one was lost to flames in 1950 but immediately another was built. Like the house of the third little pig, this one is sheltered in brick, tenement-red, permanent and restricting as if we're riding indoors. But the fifty-seven nearly life-size horses are wondrous, grouped four abreast with the smallest on the inside to the largest on the outside. Hand-carved by Solomon Stein and Harry Goldstein, immigrant Jews who began by carving flowers on ladies' combs, the horses and two elaborate chariots were completed in 1908, ridden a few years at Coney Island before placed in storage but rescued in 1951 from an abandoned trolley terminal. Their paint is bright and thick, the reins of real leather, and these horses aren't peacefully prancing nor rise and descend in a tranquil trot; these are raging nags in full gallop, stomping steeds with fetlocks gobbling ground, heads thrown back, furious manes waving motionlessly, eyes wide, teeth bared, tongues hanging out from these wild, whirling rides.

My children always carefully chose their horses, hurrying from one to the next before losing it to another child, Skylar astride a fiery-eyed black charger with silver-scaled armor plating and Lily on a white stallion, its mane the color of honey. The ride begins slowly but soon picks up speed, and Lily was always a little frightened though she'd never admit it, sitting straight in the saddle, unsmiling, her brown eyes wide as she held the pole with both hands. Holding neither the pole nor the reins, Skylar rode with palms up near his sides in apparent surrender like William Wallace in *Braveheart*. It was at the carousel that Holden sat on a bench, in the rain I remember, watching his little sister Phoebe "going round and round." He started crying because he "felt so damn happy," and I understood why. Holden loved the glass cases at the Natural History Museum because each time he visits, everything has remained the same; he wishes to put what he loves in glass cases to keep them from changing. The carousel ride made it appear as if time had stopped, that the children remained in one place, even going backward as they ride away in a circle. Osseo's magic had no power here; here, briefly, the children did not age, or at least as near as Holden and I would get to holding back time.

But the ride ends, the earth turns, dusk encloses the park with fading, mysterious light. Back home, after baths and supper, between the sheets, my children listened to the story of the park's magical summer night when *candlelight glowed from the Castle windows. Soft, plucked notes from Meta's harp and those tapped from Arlen's dulcimer wound through the festivities when park lovers transform into animals. Squirrels nibble cashews and pecans from the banquet table because everyone knew they weren't really squirrels. A pair of mourning doves —coy and delicate and in love—sat on the parapet, a Great Horned Owl in a window, and someone had chosen to become the huge snapping turtle from the Boating Lake.*

"What animal would *you* be, Daddy?"

"I would stay a man so that I might dance with Betsy Barlow."

"I would be Pale Male," Skylar decided, but Lily said, "You can't be Pale Male, Skylar. Only Pale Male can be Pale Male."

"Then I'll be his son."

Lily always chose a different animal but each time I told this part of the story Skylar was Pale Male's son except once when he became the mountain lion coiled on a rock ledge over the East Drive.

"And I'd wait for you," he whispered low and sinister, "until you ride by on your bike."

"Daddy, can people become statues?"

"If we want them to."

"Then I want to be Alice."

"That's a wonderland idea."

"Da*ddy*!"

And the Prince danced with the Bare-foot Girl until the first star vanished from the sky. Butterflies and hummingbirds disappeared through windows into the brightening darkness and the coming dawn; knowing how far it was to the Boating Lake, the turtle had left some time earlier. Anyone seeing the Castle the next day knew magic had happened here as music from the harp and dulcimer still glittered above the turret.

Sometimes I too fell asleep, waking momentarily confused before dragging myself from the floor to find the children, like those in *Extremely Loud and Incredibly Close,* peacefully dreaming of Central Park.

In Jonathan Safran Foer's novel, the young narrator's father tells the story of New York's Sixth Borough, an island like all the other boroughs except for the Bronx fastened to America's mainland. Central Park used to be on the Sixth Borough—"It was the joy of the borough: its heart"— but gradually the Sixth Borough began drifting away, and though nothing could be done to save the borough, an attempt was made to salvage the park.

> Enormous hooks were driven through the easternmost grounds, and the park was pulled by the people of New York, like a rug across a floor, from the Sixth Borough to Manhattan.

Children in the novel lay on their backs as the park is pulled to "its current resting place" until every child "had fallen asleep, and the park is a mosaic of their dreams."

One humid, over-cast morning early in September, we were heading to the Oven, that sloping gorge on the Ramble's eastern side where a stream trickles into the Boating Lake. Here birds often bathe and, hopefully that day, we might spot hummingbirds. Soon the sky darkened and that fresh, green fragrance permeated the Ramble.

"*Petrichor,*" Lily said, then carefully explained how the leaves— anticipating the cleansing, life-giving rain— release oils containing that marvelous aroma. When the soft drizzle turned harder we scampered for shelter in the Angel Tunnel where a few other visitors had the same notion, all of them silent and dazzled and staring at the ceiling.

A gleaming carpet of polished tiles spread above us, white and gold, blue and ornately patterned in repeated panels. They covered the entire Angel Tunnel, from the steps leading to the promenade and across to the seven arches open to Bethesda Terrace. Vaguely I remembered this dark, smudged ceiling more than twenty years before, with empty spaces where tiles had already fallen. One day they all had vanished; well, I thought, that's New York: a building is demolished, a tree cut down, and I never thought about it again until that rainy summer morning.

For the tiles had been removed by the burgeoning Central Park

Conservancy in a valiant effort to restore a treasure most of us, even park people, could never have imagined. An estimated $1,000,000 would be needed to repair all 15,876 tiles, but "For us not to restore the tiles," Mayor Ed Koch said at the time, "you'd have to be a Philistine." Forged in the renowned Minton Tile Company in England, these clay tiles had always been cast in their intricate process for cathedral floors; never until Central Park did they adorn a ceiling. The tiles were installed in 1869 when the roadway above carried artful carriages, equestrians on handsome horses, bicyclists riding "penny-farthings" (those with the enormous front wheels), and the leathered footsteps of vanished New Yorkers. A century later, with pounding automobile traffic and both the park and city's general neglect and deterioration, tiles cracked, water damage loosened the holdings and many fell to the floor, shattered into fragments dusty and forgotten.

And in September of 2007, costing seven times the estimate but financed by the estate of Evelyn M. West, with over a thousand carefully reproduced, the gleaming tiles returned; once more we marvel at one of the park's most stunning gifts to the people of New York.

We never saw a hummingbird though said we would try another day but never have. No matter; for parents and children the park always evolves into memory.

In "Central Park, May 1980," Hilda Morley wanders "through the park of/ my childhood" finding her past in "those hiding-places,/ those rocks" that link her to "that father/ carrying a little girl on/ his shoulders/ and to the little girl herself,/ myself." Ursula Le Guin too hears a reminiscent echo of her father in Central Park; in "Central Park South, 9 March 1979" she wonders "did he walk here as I walk/ between the weary horses and the trees" and then imagines when "he was ten.../ in 1886, cap and bare knees" as "he/ ran, on the paths there, by the lake."

In "A Sunday in Central Park, 1900," with a growing son's impatience, poet Alfred Kreymborg grudgingly walks with his father "when Central Park begins to bloom." A German immigrant, his father asks *Hast du schon einiges gesehen/ so hold and schön und rein?"* (have you ever seen something as/ fair and pretty and pure?). Not to disillusion him, "and so I answer, *Nein*". And riding with his father through Central Park, the young narrator in Thomas Wolfe's short story "In the Park" sees "all the leaves and buds are coming out" and "there was just a delicate shaving of moon in the sky" and "it seemed to me the loveliest thing I had ever seen, and when I looked at my father, his eyes were full of tears and he cried out, 'Glory! Oh glory! Glory!' "

More than anywhere in the city, the park conjures up recollections from our past because so much here has remained as we remember it. Photography books of the city "then and now" show drastic changes in Times Square, the Upper West Side, SoHo, and the waterfront, but most of the park remains as it was in our imagination. These familiar visual remembrances bring us closer to those with whom we shared these cherished places; if not standing still, here time slows down, but why, contrarily, do the hours in the park pass so quickly? Because one day while strolling the park's east side Lily and I revisited the playground with the granite trench of a slide. At the sight of it Lily stopped, stared, then whispered, both amazed and disappointed, "But Daddy, it's so small. Why did we ever call it the Big Slide?"

Lily and Alice too

CHAPTER SIXTEEN

Garden of Remembrance

No other city has changed so rapidly, so continuously, or as unalterably as New York; this is both our strength and loss. Constantly evolving, progressive and inventive, the city also too quickly rids itself of the old, leveling our past with a wrecking ball and building over it. "Change has often been more characteristic than improvement," wrote Nathan Silver in his gorgeous, ghostly *Lost New York*. Even New Yorkers who never saw glorious old Pennsylvania Station bemoan losing it and take a grateful breath that its fate wasn't repeated on Grand Central.

In Central Park the oldest artifact is an obelisk stolen from Egypt while New York flexed its self-importance at the end of the nineteenth century. The seventy-foot-tall, 224-ton piece of granite celebrated the reign of Thutmose III and stood for three thousand years before the Temple of the Sun in Heliopolis, near what is Cairo today. New Yorkers know the obelisk as Cleopatra's Needle because the resourceful queen moved it to Alexandria to adorn a temple she built there for Marc Antony. But since Paris, London, and Rome had stolen an Egyptian obelisk, then New York should too. Master showman Cecil B. DeMille promoted his 1934 film *Cleopatra* by financing a translation of the hieroglyphics set in plaques at the monument's base: "User-maat-ran, Son of Ra," it reads in fading stone, "protector of Egypt" who "with strength smites the rulers of foreign lands." DeMille's cinematic extravaganza starred irresistible Claudette Colbert "who spent many happy hours in Central Park" reads a small silver plaque fastened to a bench dedicated to her on the terrace just north of the Model Boat Pond.

Central Park's obelisk appeared in advertisements for Vaseline, cold cream, Pan Handle Tobacco, and on the logo for the old St. Nicholas Hotel once on Broadway and Spring Street. The lower third of the hieroglyphics—perfect upon arrival in 1881—has faded badly from our extreme weather and years of toxic car exhaust rising from the East Drive where the obelisk stands; ancient relics far less monumental are protectively displayed in the Metropolitan Museum's glass cases a few steps away.

There is stone and iron in Central Park placed long before William Cullen Bryant began pressuring city officials in 1844 for a great public park, older than the old reservoir's wall along the 86th Street transverse road, older than the spike pounded into the schist by the Grid surveyors, older than the United States. When embittered and outraged colonials sent a letter to their distant king in England declaring their independence, George the Third refused to give it and a revolution began. The British were determined not to lose the Port of New York, essential for his supply lines and the military capital of its province. A series of three fortifications were constructed along a high ridge in what is now the park, each with a commanding, unobstructed view over the northern part of the island.

As I stroll the quiet shore of the Harlem Meer where Canada geese paddle through algae-covered water, just above me well-disciplined British troops with their thick scarlet coats and cocked hats once pointed their cannons and long rifles at what are now high-rises along Fifth Avenue and Central Park North. Joining the English, a thousand blue-coated Hessian mercenaries with gold, coned helmets. For several harried hours on September 15, 1776, after their bloody defeat at the Battle of Long Island, a retreating General Washington and his embattled troops fled New York for the remainder of the Revolutionary War through this gentle ravine. Washington knew how important it was for The Cause to capture New York though he never would, but after seven years of blood and hardship, the Continental Army under the command of General Henry Knox triumphantly returned through this same passage in what is now Central Park.

Those defenses were never used against the colonials, for the war ended before a shot was fired in New York. But soon the newly formed United States were again at war with England (the United States would not be referred to in the singular—'was' in this case—until after the Civil War). This time the conflict was over the kidnapping and forced conscription of American sailors in England's navy. Those three fortifications meant for use against the colonials were seized by American citizens for use against their former oppressors and named Fort Clinton, Nutter's

Battery, and Fort Fish. A fourth installation, a new blockhouse, was built a few hundred yards to the northwest as defense from a possible British invasion in the War of 1812.

With the northern part of the island now fortified, cannon emplacements to protect the harbor were constructed on a small island made of landfill off Manhattan's southern tip. Those twenty-eight guns too were never fired in war, and soon the island fortress called Fort Clinton was entirely enclosed by landfill and became Castle Garden. In the years to come the fort processed eight million immigrants until the completion of the massive facility on Ellis Island. Castle Garden was an aquarium for a while until one opened at Coney Island; it is a visitors' center today where dock ferry boat for rides to Ellis Island and the Statue of Liberty.

But the outposts to the north did not fare as well. Where Fort Clinton once stood, at lamppost E0503, wooden benches encircle two cannons, one facing north, the other east; salvaged from the wreckage of the H.M.S. Hussar that sank in 1780 in that turbulent, treacherous strait of Hell Gate between Queens and Wards Island, neither were ever in place to defend Fort Clinton. Nutter's Battery, now a low stone wall broken intermittently near lamppost 0736, was named for the man on whose land it once stood, and Fort Fish is now only a white marble bench "In Honor of Andrew Haswell Green" who was not the "Directing Genius of Central Park In Its Formative Period" despite the chiseled inscription. He *is* considered "Father of Greater New York" for his efforts to consolidate the five boroughs into one great city, and the five young trees planted behind the bench represent each borough. What was left nearly intact, solid and silent today, is Blockhouse #1.

It has the high ground overlooking, appropriately named, WARRIORS' GATE at Central Park North and Adam Clayton Powell, Jr. Boulevard (Seventh Avenue). With the forest along its perimeter the blockhouse is hard to see from the walkway and undetectable from the Drive. But find traffic light #20 near lamppost W0606, take this walkway into the woods to lamppost 0715 and, a hundred feet to your left, rock on rock thirty feet high, what had been formidable two centuries ago.

In the *New Yorker*'s first issue on February 21, 1925, a poem appeared about the Blockhouse written by Arthur Guiterman, a founding member of the Poetry Society of America. Like this old military outpost, Guiterman too has been largely forgotten despite "the most American of all poets" a century ago, but as Olmsted allowed these old relics to remain, the poet preserves our past while giving tender tribute to Central Park in the "Block-House in the Park" that "never knew the crashing brunt/ Of musketry or cannon-ball/ Awaiting war that never came.

> A virgin fortress still I stand;
> But now, unscathed by hostile flame,
> I guard a gate of Fairyland.
>
> For, while my gloomy watch I stood,
> Unmarked the leafy marvel grew;
> Behind me spread the mystic wood—
> A place of dreams where dreams are true;
>
> Where boyish cohorts, undismayed,
> Deploy beneath the friendly trees
> To take my cliffs by escalade.
> May all their wars be such as these!

Whenever walking this rugged, remote area of the park where once forts stood their high ground, I am grateful they were never under attack or fired cannonballs at other young men no matter the allegiances. Park Commissioners decreed in 1867 that Central Park "was not an appropriate place for sepulchral memorials" that might "sadden or oppress" park visitors. But in the years following the Civil War, memorials commemorating the bravery and sacrifice on both sides of the newly unified states were dedicated in town squares and along main streets, in front of courthouses and in city parks from Cumberland, Maine, to Fort Myers in Florida, at Snow Hill, North Carolina, and Summer Hill, Illinois, at Hot Springs, Arkansas, and Cold Harbor, Virginia, on the battlefields at Gettysburg, Chancellorsville, Lookout Mountain, and the first memorial dedicated at Berlin, Connecticut, in 1863, to its local young men lost in the war: "How Sleep The Brave Who Sink to Rest, By All Their Country's Wishes Blest." Despite the commissioners' degree, *Civil War Memorial of the Seventh Regiment* was unveiled one mild June day in 1874 in Central Park.

John Quincy Adams Ward was asked to create a tribute to the

common Union soldier, a volunteer or reluctant but patriotic conscript that better represented Olmsted's ideal of a park for the average person. Originally intended for WARRIORS' GATE, a young soldier on a pedestal stands at ease along the West Drive at lamppost W6803 between Tavern on the Green and Strawberry Fields. Gazing into the distance and leaning on his long musket, bayonet sheathed, he is not ready for battle but seems reflective, peaceful, perhaps thinking of home or a young woman he may never see again. "Pro Patria et Gloria" is inscribed on a shield along all four sides of the pedestal, "For Country and Glory."

Ward's model for the piece was Steele MacKaye who rose to the rank of Major during the war. The memorial honors the fifty-eight members of the Seventh who never returned after that distant, buoyant spring day in 1861 when they marched to war with sandwiches from Delmonico's and belief in their invincibility.

Though unintended, the soldier looks off to Sheep Meadow, originally meant for military parades. But after four years of war, when "every drop of blood drawn with the lash," said Lincoln at his second inauguration, "shall be paid by another drawn with the sword," no one wanted any more martial displays. Ward's gentle, eternally young soldier today watches not armies in formation but young men throwing pickup lines and footballs, and a lovely woman dancing in the shadows.

The largest memorial in Central Park is a quiet, neglected grove of tall oaks marked only with a boulder carved with the words "To the Dead of the 307th Infantry A.E.F." On the reverse side, the names of each member of the 77th Division. Once shaded by trees older than Central Park, Hurricane Sandy hit this grove very hard that Monday night in October 2012. Beneath the thinned canopy, bronze, dim tablets lay at the base of the remaining trees, one plaque for each company of the 77th. It is a lonely grove with rarely a visitor despite only steps from the promenade and SummerStage. There is a solemnity here; those small plaques at the base of each tree represent headstones of the 590 American officers and men who fought with the French and English between 1917 and 1919 during the Great War. "What they saw and what befell them," writes Cal Snyder in *Out of Fire and Valor: The War Memorials of New York City,* "has passed from the living memory of the city more than a generation ago. Only the neglected grove [in Central Park] attests to the fire that consumed their young lives...." Today as we kick fallen acorns at our feet this grove seems remote from the city, the park, and the war in which these valiant men fought.

On Fifth Avenue at 67th Street just outside the park's perimeter wall is another memorial to the Seventh Regiment and its 107th Infantry who fought in World War I. On a long pedestal, then rising on thin steps, are seven larger than life bronze soldiers in a rugged line. The bronze surrounding their legs appears on fire. The middle three are attacking, bayonets fixed, the one in the center raised slightly higher than his compatriots beside him. One soldier to the left and another to the right of the charging three each supports a wounded soldier, one nearly dead, the other badly wounded though with a grenade in his left hand, a hand, like all the soldiers' hands, modeled after the artist's own. Created by Karl Illava, a sergeant in the 107th during The Great War, the memorial sculpture is powerful and haunting, capturing the aggression, the suffering, the bravery and compassion of those young soldiers of a century ago.

A gilded bronze bust at ENGINEERS' GATE (Fifth Avenue/90th) memorializes our youngest mayor John Purroy Mitchell; after losing re-election in 1917, his "one wish," he said, "is to get over to the western front, where I can do some work that will count." Soon after enlisting, he died in a training accident on Long Island; Mitchell Field is named for him.

In Wagner's Cove tucked in the southwest corner of the Boating Lake, an oak tree is dedicated to silent film actor and director S. Rankin Drew; he had volunteered for the American Ambulance Corps but "Killed in Action May 19, 1918." Near the bust of Friedrich Schiller at the northern end of the promenade is another tree to him dedicated two years to the day after he died in France. Nearby, a few steps behind the uninspiring bust of Johann Schiller along the promenade is a flagpole "In commemoration of the heroism and sacrifice of the city employees who fought in the various wars of the United States." Beneath the American flag, the black POW/MIA flag.

And there's the tree in the grove along the promenade remembering Joyce Kilmer.

At the Model Boat Pond a few steps north of the café is a stone on the ground with a bronze plaque:

> These Trees
> Honor the Memory of
> Richard Saunders Scott
> Born Massachusetts 1904
> Died North Africa 1942

Though this captain of a heavy bomber group lays in a Tunisian cemetery, his spirit quietly remains in Central Park. And Bethesda Terrace has another name: inlaid on the Terrace floor half way between the Angel and the Angel Tunnel, a bronze plaque:

> Navy Terrace
> Named in honor of
> The Men and Women
> Of New York City
> Who Served Their Country
> During the World Wars
> In
> United States Navy
> United States Marine Corps
> United States Coast Guard
>
> Dedicated May 24, 1947

To the west of the Terrace's regal staircase is a gentle hill with oak trees along the walkway. This is "Navy Walk." A bronzed, greened plaque inlaid into the earth reads:

> Trees Planted Along This Walk
> Commemorate the Many
> Naval Battles of World War II
>
> Dedicated May 27, 1947

There is a similar, tree-lined walkway just east of the eastern staircase though its plaque is missing.

There is no memorial to the 110,000 American soldiers killed in Korea, Vietnam, and the Middle East wars.

Although prohibiting memorials was well-intended—to keep out anything that might distract us from Nature's restorative powers—the 1867 degree passed before Central Park became so special to so many.

Here we have exchanged sacred vows of love for each other, shared our dearest intimacies and most cherished recollections, for in Central Park we often find the best of our fragile, enduring selves.

At SCHOLARS' GATE (60th Street/Fifth Avenue), along Wien Walk on the path to the zoo, the third bench on the western side has four small, inlaid plaques: "We Honor All Those Who Perished on September 11, 2001," reads the first. The second, third and fourth are "For the Heroes of" the fire department, the police department, and Port Authority. Near the softball fields close to the Ballfield Café is a bench "In Tribute To the Firemen of O'Hurley's 2001 NYSBL Team Who Gave Their Lives on Sept.11: Steve Mercado, Jimmy Giberson, David Arce, Mikey Boyle, Kevin Brachen."

Inlaid in the stones in front of *Hans Christian Andersen,* a plaque "In Honor of The Children Who Lost Their Parents on 9/11/01." In Strawberry Fields, a bench from the people of Liverpool "To All Who Lost Their Lives on 9/11/01". The rescue dogs of 9/11 are honored on a bench just north of the zoo.

A bench for Amy Hope Lamonsoff is in Strawberry Fields, a memorial within one. Along the north side of the Pool above 100th Street, a bench for Ann Walsh McGovern. On the east side of the Great Lawn, a bench for Peter R. Kellerman, and one for Bill Godshalk at the northwest corner. Beside his, a bench to Derek O. Sword with the words, "To the world you were one person, To me you were the world." Though we do not know who wrote this, Derek will. One bench near lamppost W9213 is for Gregory Rodriquez. West of Sheep Meadow, one in memory of Scott Mitchel Schertzer, one for Douglas B. Gardner, and one for Margaret W. Seeliger. Along the promenade is a bench for Brent James Woodall, and Nauka Kushitani, and Gregory Richards. At the end of the promenade, just east of the single staircase leading under Olmsted and Vaux Way (72nd Overpass), two benches "Remembering Josh With Love" and beside it, "Remembering Uncle Josh." All died at the World Trade Center.

Inside the park entrance at West 67th Street is a bench for Nigel Thompson. There's one to "Beloved JMR" nearby, and for Vincent Kane, and near his, a bench to Taimour Khan. On a bench facing the East Drive just north of lamppost E9101, a remembrance for Neil D. Levin. North of King Jagiello's statue, a bench for Michael J. Armstrong.

Between the art museum and Greywacke Arch is a bench to Vincent M. Boland, and one on the walkway for Jason M. Cefalu behind the Alexander Hamilton statue. Near lamppost E7204 just west of Fifth Avenue, Timothy J. Coughlin is remembered, and so is Brooke Alexanda Jackman along the shore of the Pond looking toward the Sanctuary. One in the Ramble is for Linda C. Lee, for Laurence M. Polatsch near the Boat Pond, and a bench north of Alice for Scott M. Johnson. A little to the north of the James Levine Playground, a small boulder is dedicated to Scott H. Saber. Across from the Boathouse along the East Drive, a bench for Nancy Morgenstern, and just passed the pergola near Strawberry Fields along the Boating Lake, one for Aaron Jacobs. They too died at the World Trade Center.

A plaque at the promenade just south of the SummerStage reads,

> May These Trees
> Stand Tall Forever
> In Memory of My Wife
> Dorothy Inez Andreas.
> December 1996

The restoration of the walkway from the southern tip of Bow Bridge to the Terrace as well as ten benches along the walkway were financed by Charles Bronfman in memory of his wife, Andrea. A fighter for social causes and especially women's issues, she was killed by a car in 2006 while walking her dog along Fifth Avenue. Across from these benches is a boulder: "Andy" reads the plaque, "I Love You" from "Charles" written in bronze script.

Inside the park at 90th Street and Fifth Avenue, between the roadway and the track around Lake Manhattan, a life-size bronze statue of a slender, bearded man wearing a running suit and shoes checks his stopwatch. He is Fred Lebow, organizer of New York's first marathon in 1970; after four laps around Central Park, 55 of the starting 127 runners completed this grueling race that had killed Pheidippides twenty-five centuries earlier. Fred raised millions of dollars for cancer research before dying of cancer in 1994, but each year before the New York City Marathon his statue is moved across the park to the finish line so Fred can permanently check the times of the 45,000 running through all five boroughs now.

Three young trees east of the Center Drive behind the Shakespeare statue are dedicated to Penelope London. The Whispering Bench in the Shakespeare Garden is for the "Founder of Outdoor Playgrounds" Charles Stover. Three small plaques near the Model Boat Pond remember Kate Kaurate, only eighteen. In the Ramble before the Gill trickles to the Boating Lake is a small bridge made of limbs from the park's fallen trees. A modest plaque on a boulder off the walkway tells us that this bridge is in memory of Timothy Laupot, who died when he was twelve. And fastened to one of those small posts with the carved horses in miniature leading us to the ticket booth at the carousel are words similar to the lullaby "All the Pretty Little Horses."

> Hushaby
> Don't you cry
> Go to sleepy, little baby

Across from it, on a similar post, a memorial to Michelle Bernstein, three when she died.

> When you wake
> You shall have
> All the pretty little horses

While my first child grew that spring of 1995 and Pale Male nurtured three of his own, their growth, maiden flights, and first summer exploring Central Park were filmed by a young Belgian named Frederic Lilien and released in 2002 as a fifty-two-minute documentary for PBS. Seven years later an extended version premiered as a feature film at the Angelika movie theater downtown. *The Legend of Pale Male* included the heartbreaking and then triumphant part of the story when the building on which Pale Male lived had him evicted. But as Robert Moses had discovered trying to replace with a parking lot a single Central Park playground, outraged New Yorkers aggressively object to any interference to the park's beloved celebrity. Rowdy demonstrations outside the building's luxurious doors at last led to the construction of a platform where the nest had been, and soon Pale Male began weaving another one on it. Missing in the film was the co-star of Frederic's first film, a tall, gentle man with his long hair in a ponytail. Knowledgeable and reverent of Nature's creations, especially those in the park, Charles Kennedy "worked as a jeweler for a number of years," he wrote, "with gorgeous stones, minerals, fossils, natural crystals."

> And that's what birds are—only they move. They are
> these exquisite gemstones, many the weight of a nickel,
> that can migrate for many thousands of miles and arrive
> here on this tight little island.

His book of essays and photographs *Pale Male and his Family* is less renowned than his dear friend Marie Winn's *Red-Tails in Love*, but the memoir is tender and generous toward all those following the story of our remarkable hawk. Charles died of cancer in October of 2004; he was sixty-four. But sit on a bench during a winter morning and watch the birds at the dangling feeders Lee Rogers tends in the Ramble's Evodia Field. There are starlings and sparrows, doves and grackles, a striking Sapsucker, a tit-mouse, male *and* female cardinals, finches, and more sparrows all probing on perches for seed into a plastic gallon milk jug, sucking the nectar from half an orange impaled on a branch or else pecking the nourishing suet in a green net. On the plaque of your bench, one of Charles's poems.

> *Empty milkweed pods*
> *Week since a butterfly*
> *Maybe there'll be owls*

Poor health the last two years of his life kept Samuel Menashe from visiting the park. He died of heart disease in 2011. The plaque on the bench he loved along Lake Manhattan is dedicated to the painter Helen Frankenthaler who as a girl often came to Central Park with her chalks and paper, eventually painting a colorful abstract of the park. A bench to Samuel can be found on the Ramble's eastern edge not far from the mountain lion. Beneath Samuel's name, a passage from one of his poems: "Stay…Here you can wait forever…."

Alberto Arroyo, the kindly old man who greeted visitors at the reservoir's running track, had died the year before.

Between the western shore of the Model Boat Pond and the benches beneath the sycamores Rik Davis set one powerful spotting scope focused on the nest above the Fifth Avenue-top-floor-center-parapet window and another aimed at a different ledge or an antennae where Pale Male or his mate might perch. Between the telescopes a table displayed Rik's various-size photographs of Pale Male. On moon-less summer nights he'd set up telescopes along the Great Lawn where we gazed at Saturn (my favorite planet after Earth) close enough to detect each separate ring, but best was sitting peacefully beside him on a bench at the Model Boat Pond, enjoying the day whatever the weather. If there were no hawks, Rik watched pretty women walk by in their summer clothes; despite resembling a bearded, burley mountain man, he had been a fashion photographer before drawn to even more compelling subjects. He'd speak with anyone who gazed with interest through his spotting scopes, even wisecrackers wondering if we were spying on celebrities, which, in a way, we were. If neither hawks nor pretty women, we watched dragonflies skim inches above the Boat Pond.

On an afternoon late in May of 2012, I stopped along the Boat Pond but Rik was not there, which was unusual since he sat on a particular bench nearly as often as Hans Christian Andersen sits on *his* bench nearby. At my next visit I knew something was wrong. A bouquet of white carnations lay where Rik used to sit. Nearby, his old friend Conrad told me a heart attack had killed him at home three nights ago. For a while taped to his bench was a laminated note card with Rik's name though it was soon removed.

In February of 2013, Starr Saphir—that slender, sprightly birder with the light-blue-bandana leading tours even to the North Woods in its most troubled days— died after a long, valiant battle with breast cancer; her illness "heightened my joys in life," she declared, "because I know that not only is it not to last forever, it's not going to last that much longer." And in the summer of 1986, bearded, elfish Lambert Pohner died. Along with Sarah Elliott he had given me my first birding lessons despite his preference for Bo. Now I too put a feather in my hat band as he did.

Nick Wagerik often went birding with Sarah or Marie Winn. He was tall, slender, sweet-faced, and always with a backpack crammed with field guides for birds but butterflies too; in Frederick Wiseman's documentary *Central Park*, Nick speaks knowingly of Monarch migrations while standing beside Sarah in the Conservatory Garden. He was one of the few park people I'd see at unusual times and places throughout the park. Most park people keep to their comfortable areas the way many New Yorkers know only their own neighborhoods; I knew a woman from First Street who never went above 14th. But Nick, focused and solitary, probed through the reeds along the northern shore of Turtle Pond, followed the erratic flights of butterflies near the Pool, searched in the park with a flashlight after dark for moths. We picked up children at the same school at West 84th Street; those children were always happy to see him and he appeared very content with an explorer's hat on his head as if he'd been in the park all day, but he died unexpectedly in September 2013. And in 2015, that bearded man dressed in purple who brought beauty and nourishment in the form of a flourishing garden on the Lower East Side, a garden growing healthy for twenty years with the horse shit of Central Park, the man who believed amid the worst days that there could be better ones ahead, who—along with hundreds of his neighbors— helplessly watched as the city bull-dozed his garden for a gentrified residence, died while bicycling across the Williamsburg Bridge. He was 84, his name Adam Purple.

Death is a frequent visitor to Central Park. Someone dies and we feel a hole in our hearts at seeing that empty bench or at a melody not rising above the Terrace or at sighting a Cerulean Warbler briefly in the park on its long flights to and from the Andes. Like in Thomas Grey's country churchyard, those we love were not "on the custom'd hill" nor "near his fav'rite tree…Nor at the woods was he." But here we feel a little closer to them, especially at solemn twilight when the light changes, birds roost and chatter and grow quiet, when many visitors return to the city and leave the park to us. That once ragged oval from where I always pinch the soil is now the blossoming 'Olmsted Flower Bed' despite his wish to have no formal garden in the park, while in the northern reaches of the park a remote, fragrant, melancholy area has evolved into its own sacred garden.

The Conservatory Garden is actually three gardens with no conservatory. At one time an enormous greenhouse nourished the bulbs and plants soon to be transplanted through the park, but Robert Moses had it razed in the 1930s and replaced with these gardens. I usually enter by the back door. Just before the roadway descends with a mighty left curve, a walkway on the right (lamppost E0503) leads down a steep slope to a piece of the park enclosed by a black iron, Paris-garden of a fence.

Behind the gardens, a rocky foundation stone on stone supports a hill of earth. It too is a memorial of sorts, for these are the remains of the Convent of St. Vincent, Mrs. McGowan's tavern, the Dyckman's before that, even the old English halfway house—still here, like so much of the city's story and, like life in New York, stacked on top of another.

Just inside the garden's gate, redolent of lilacs in the spring, is a small plaque fastened to a bench that tenderly casts the mood of this tranquil place.

> "My Father Charles Vorisek
> Loved and Inspired Me to Love
> Central Park"
> Helen Vorisek Chaplin

But for our first visit to the Conservatory Garden we must enter by way of the grand, formal gates at Fifth Avenue and 105th Street, a piece of Cornelius Vanderbilt's grandeur from his colossal, 150-room mansion at Fifth and 58th where Bergdorf's is today. We, the small and meek, pass through what once welcomed a procession of old New York's most powerful, influential, greedy, and corrupt.

As soon as we enter the Vanderbilt Gate we feel an aura of quiet splendor. Before us stretches an immaculate green lawn, lined on both sides with crabapple trees that form a sort of floral boundary separating the adjacent gardens. At the far end of the lawn is a basin where a stream of water shoots high into the air, its soft mist sprinkling us on breezy days. Behind the basin, on tiered hedges, staircases take us up to the park's largest wisteria pergola. The vines grow through the supporting trellises in wondrously torturous ways; at our feet, thirteen large medallions commemorating the original thirteen unified states.

The garden is of Italian style. The one to the north is French, to the south, English. The six acres spread horizontally along Fifth Avenue were designed by Gilmore D. Clarke with assistance from his aptly-named wife Betty Sprout. Clark's success with these gardens led Robert Moses to appoint him the task of creating at last a genuine zoo in Central Park, but his greatest collaboration with Moses was designing the 1939 World's Fair held in Flushing Meadows, Queens. Before its transformation into "The World of Tomorrow" with its distinct symbols— the tall, slender

Trylon and the circular Perisphere— this area had for over a decade been "a solemn dumping ground," wrote Scott Fitzgerald in *The Great Gatsby*, "a desolate area of land, a valley of ashes." When the Fair closed in October 1940—its bright promise of the future darkened by another, even more terrible world war—everything was dismantled, the towering, white obelisk and colossal sphere melted for weapons. But the benches that once lined the broad, busy promenades in 1939 are now beneath the Garden's crabapple trees.

In the French-style garden to the north, flowerbeds thematic to the season encircle a wide pedestal in a pool of water, its spray dampening three dancing maidens. They are joyous, beautiful, perhaps Zeus's daughters The Graces, their thin, clinging coverings even more alluring when damp from the spray around which they dance, fingertips barely touching. A gift from the Yonkers estate of Samuel Untermeyer, these are the three sisters of our bedtime story, one the Bare-foot Girl who loved the Prince of Belvedere.

To the south, the English garden of winding beds of wildflowers is less orderly and groomed than the French-style garden though carefully tended. Along the edge of a shaded pool are bronze renditions of Mary and Dickon from Frances Hodgson Burnett's novel *The Secret Garden* sculpted by Bessie Potter Vonnoh. Dickon reclines, playing his flute, while Mary stands beside him holding a birdbath where real birds often join the one of bronze perpetually sipping from the bowl.

Like these gardens, Burnett's story of Nature's healing power has a spirit of melancholy where many of us along the quiet walkways seek that remedy. For often in good weather the gardens are visited by patients from Mount Sinai Hospital directly across Fifth Avenue. The ailing, often elderly accompanied by hospital staff or friends or family sit in wheelchairs in the warm sunlight, gaze on flowers and listen to chattering birds. The names on plaques of the garden's benches are those of people who spent pleasant hours here, perhaps some of their last, the roses "maintained in memory," reads a plaque on the slate walkway, "of Rose F. Tishman." The gardens are quiet places to grieve: "Hearing the news, we headed for this garden,/ a children's picture book."

We'd planned to bring him here. In an arbor,
crabapple trees enclose us like a vault

In her "Elegy Written in the Conservatory Garden," Grace Schulman finds not only solace here but also the spirit of the one for whom she grieves.

> He is the blurred form moving through warped trees
> like fingers on a harp.

The poem mourns the death of Irving Howe who appears "behind a screen of roses,/ fragrant, pink-to-gold in the sun...." Many immigrants Howe wrote about in his monumental, compassionate volume about the Jewish experience in *World of Our Fathers* found reprieve from sweatshops and tenements beneath the peaceful, restorative trees of Central Park. Walking this garden after her dear friend's death, Ms. Schulman is reminded of her own mortality, finding what Olmsted hoped to preserve in the city, Nature's enduring spirit of death and rebirth.

> We stand, as though to visit him again
> and touch a magnolia tree that may live forever,
> with our thumbprints gleaming on its trunk.

"When good New Yorkers die," wrote architecture critic Herbert Muschamp in *The New York Times*, "they go to Central Park. We, the living, go there ... to become more worthy of life in paradise."

To Make an Eden *continued*

When the city bought the land that after twenty years and millions of man-hours evolved into Central Park, the only water on the site (excluding the receiving reservoir and a putrid swamp) were the small streams Montayne's Rivulet to the northwest and DeVoor's Mill Stream trickling into the park's southeast corner. But soon underground pipes transformed many acres into the picturesque Boating Lake, the Pond, the Pool, Harlem Meer, the Loch and the Gill, all engineered by George Waring. He was born in Pound Ridge about fifty miles north of the city, and as Olmsted did, he too resigned from his park duties once the Civil War began and accepted the commission of major in the Union Army. As commander of the 4th Missouri Cavalry, Waring added support to Major-General U.S. Grant during the siege of Vicksburg. After the war he resumed his efforts on the park and was later appointed commissioner of New York's Department of Street Cleaning, a position first offered to Theodore Roosevelt who had other plans for himself. Under Waring's capable leadership and extensive knowledge of waste removal, the city's death rate from disease decreased by one-third. His street cleaners, dressed in white and paid a dollar a day, were known appreciatively as "White Wings." Waring died in New York City in 1898 after contracting yellow fever in Cuba where he had gone to establish the island's sanitation system.

It was Ignatz Pilát, wrote Clarence Cook, who had transformed these acres into "the delicate flavor of wildness." An Austrian, the park's first chief horticulturalist had formerly maintained the gardens of the Earldom of Karrach on the Danube, then the Imperial Gardens at Schonbrunn Palace in Vienna before fleeing to New York after Russia's brutal suppression of his country in the middle of the nineteenth century. This bloody turmoil brought thousands of Germans to settle in Kleindeutschland on New York's East Side.

Having seen Pilát's artful plan for the park during the design contest that spring in 1858, Olmsted offered him the task of chief horticulturalist. Pilát later redesigned Washington Square, curving the walkways, like those in Central Park, for a gentler stroll from what had been a military parade ground and a potter's field before that. He was appointed Central Park's chief gardener for life but died of consumption in 1870; he was fifty years old. *The New York Times* wrote that "The Central Park owes everything to his taste, skill and judgment."

Set upon three great mounds of schist throughout the park are three large shelters made of unhewn cedar and gnarled roots and branches entwined into a patchwork. All is open to the surroundings and the sky, but we are shaded from the hot sun by vines often faintly fragrant with wisteria. Once there were fifteen rustic shelters throughout the park, but in time they fell into disrepair. Of the remaining three, one is on a rise of rock in the Dene on the East Side just north of the zoo, one in the Ramble often sheltering the homeless, and the Cop Cot inside the park at ARTISTS' GATE (Sixth Avenue/59th Street) where lovers meet on reckless summer nights. Four smaller shelters line the Boating Lake, all of them based on originals by Anton Gerster.

Born in Hungary, an army lieutenant until his country's 1848 revolution, Gerster too had fled the impossible defense against the huge, invading armies of Russia for the United States. In gratitude for refuge he enlisted in the Union Army during the Civil War as an engineer, then later settled in Brooklyn, his woodworking shop glowing with light from a red-hot stove where he created the rustic shelters and hundreds of birdhouses and beehives and dove cots. But despite these contributions in the park he was best known in his day as Uncle Anton, his niece Etelka Gerster, the celebrated cantatrice of the New York Opera.

And there was the odd, eccentric Englishman Jacob Wrey Mould.

He had bulging, mournful eyes, a large nose, was apparently ill-mannered and with a 'questionable moral sense' for living unmarried with a woman. More importantly, Olmsted believed him "a strange genius" with, thought Vaux, "a graceful and unwearied hand"; it was Mould who created most of the park's enchanting artifacts and many that have vanished.

At twenty-six years old he left the London suburb of Chislehurst for New York in 1852 at the request of Moses Hicks Grinnell. The shipping magnate and congressman wanted Mould to design the new Unitarian Church of All Souls at Fourth Avenue (Park Avenue South) and East 20th Street, the congregation one of New York's wealthiest and the new edifice referred to as "the Beef Steak" church, its pastor Henry Bellows. Like all of Mould's designs the church was unusual, its peculiar stripe pattern leading some people to call it the Church of the Holy Zebra. Vaux and his family lived nearby, and after seeing the church (lost to fire in 1931) he asked Mould to join the project creating Central Park.

He designed the handsome stables along the 86th Street transverse road (the old section of what is now the park's police precinct), the fairy-tale-like structure known as the Dairy, and Tavern on the Green, originally the Sheepfold where slept the two hundred sheep that munched the meadow across the roadway to the east. He designed the delicate, cast-iron Ladies Pavilion near the massive chunk of schist known as Hernshead along the western shore of the Boating Lake; before the intrusion of the *Maine Monument* it had sheltered waiting commuters at Columbus Circle. The airy, enchanting carousel (lost to fire) was his creation, and the original Mineral Springs where in my dreams I had danced with Audrey Munson. In the center of the promenade once stood Mould's delicate, artful music stand originally intended to float on a barge so as to serenade New Yorkers along the Boating Lake. With Calvert Vaux he designed Belvedere Castle, the Casino, the graceful arches and bridges, and an elaborate, Oriental-inspired Conservatory for the Model Boat Pond but never realized. The stunning tiles on the ceiling of the Angel Tunnel are Mould's design; nearby are his greatest creations, the sandstone scrolls of birds, flora and fauna down the grand staircases of Bethesda Terrace. As a boy, sculptor James Edward Kelly "watched with wonder the carvers at work on...the Terrace," he wrote, "and to see a nugget of stone hewn into a life-like bird, or bloom into a graceful flower."

In the early spring of 1883, after having established a free school for science and art in the East Village, 92-year-old Peter Cooper died, and a Jewish-Italian mother across town in Greenwich Village nursed her infant son Fiorello who would grow to become an unimposing 5'2" and New York's most beloved mayor. That spring Alva Erskine Smith from Mobile, Alabama, (though quickly adding she was schooled in Paris) married Commodore Cornelius Vanderbilt's grandson William in one of the most spectacular parties ever seen in the city; live doves were arranged to flutter around her dress. The Metropolitan Opera House opened at Broadway and 39th Street with a production of Gounod's *Faust*, every 5,780 velvet-cushioned seat occupied with New York's wealthiest in glittering gowns and fine tuxedos. Meanwhile that year 405,909 immigrants staggered exhausted, overburdened, and grateful from the processing center at Castle Garden in Battery Park (Ellis Island would not open for another nine years) before being swallowed by the unimaginably congested tenements on the Lower East Side. And that year a young New Yorker composed a sonnet meant to raise awareness and funds for the Statue of Liberty's pedestal. Soon dying of Hodgkin's Disease, Emma Lazarus would never see the giant figure celebrated in her poem "The New Colossus."

1883 was "a year of universal distrust," wrote the *New York Daily Tribune*, "of terrible catastrophes and malignant tendencies…miscarriages of public justice…the acquittal of notorious murderers…and scandalous judicial failures." But on May 2nd the New York Giants played their first baseball game, defeating the Boston Red Stockings 7 to 5 on polo grounds just above the northeast corner of Central Park. After fourteen years of labor, sacrifice, loss, and courage, the Brooklyn Bridge opened on May 24. A few weeks later, a small gathering took place in Central Park around an American flag covering a sculpture set upon a ledge of rock along the East Drive near lamppost #E7701. The sculptor attended, accompanied by a pretty woman beneath a parasol. The sculptor's uncle was also there, as well as Park Commissioner Salem Wales, Park Superintendent Aneurin Jones, and several news reporters. After a few words, Commissioner Wales removed the flag (to a startled "Oh my!" from the woman with the parasol) to reveal a life-size mountain lion so true in form and spirit that it seemed in the sunlight nearly quivering for the attack. There in the base, as if written with a finger before the bronze hardened, the name of the artist above the imprint of the face of a wolf.

Edward Kemeys may have turned for a look at his lion's hollow eyes, its alert face and perked ears, the compressed muscles ready to uncoil. Perhaps he gazed across the molded landscape, toward the museum where three more of his works would be displayed, then to the tapered valley leading to the Conservatory Water. And with the late afternoon sun on his face he might try recalling how these acres, so artful that June day in 1883, were once nearly treeless, with foul swamps, poison ivy, battered shacks and their thousand inhabitants. Though his own life had changed immeasurably since then, he could never have imagined in his hard, young manhood how land so spiritless, desperate, and barren could evolve into something so sublime.

In the years to come, Alice and her zany crew from Wonderland appeared along the pond nearby, captivating generations of children as well as grown-ups reciting "Jabberwolky." Hans Christian Andersen sits close by, perpetually reading "The Ugly Duckling" to a bronze duckling as children gather at his feet to hear stories on summer days. But with its tense and brutal beauty *Still Hunt* remains silently absorbed in the park, often unnoticed and magnificently alone.

CHAPTER SEVENTEEN

A Special Luncheon

When my daughter was in fourth grade, each student chose, and not from a list, a famous person to research, then, in costume, present to the class a biographical report. Lily chose Frederick Law Olmsted.

"And why did you pick him?"

She replied as if the answer were so obvious and her daddy so silly: "Because he designed Central Park!"

Stubbornly independent, she resisted any help though did look through a book I placed on her bed marked where she'd find a photograph of Olmsted whom she had always referred to as Sir Frederick; his gravesite, we decided, was the Humming Tombstone in the Ramble. She took careful notes printed in several colors on large note cards, and at a costume store I found a cap, mustache, and a dark, curly wig similar to Olmsted's in the photograph. In these and wearing one of my dark shirts she stood before her class.

"Frederick Law Olmsted designed Central Park," she began only a little shyly through her friends' hushed giggles. "He had never designed a park before."

Though feeling more nervous than Lily appeared, I tried not to laugh at how adorable she looked, more Groucho than Olmsted though she soon spoke with authority. She told us about the big drawing Olmsted made called the Greensward Plan and that he worked on it with Calvert Vaux "that rhymes with hawks," she declared assuredly. She spoke of the Ramble, its woods and stream and waterfalls "with more birds than anywhere. And it was Frederick's" but then she hesitated, lowering her eyes and suppressing a smile, "I mean *my* favorite part of Central Park," then looked at us again. "Except for my home, it is my favorite place in New York City."

She received eager applause, my heart touched nearly to tears.

The next day a hand-addressed envelope for Lily appeared outside our front door. The envelope contained a note written in careful script.

"In gratitude for your class presentation, please join me and a few friends for lunch at the home of Mr. Calvert Vaux, 136 East 18th Street, on Sunday, March 21, 1858, at 2 PM. You may bring a guest."

Beneath the note, in a modest flourish, *"Frederick Law Olmsted."*

Lily was very excited and Sunday but two days away. She wondered what to wear and I suggested the costume from class but she wanted to be herself.

"Then a new dress?"

She thought that a wonderful idea, and the next day ("See, Daddy," Lily whispered as we stepped into the past, "like Osseo's log only backwards") we shopped at Macy's, a new department store that opened just below 14th Street on Sixth Avenue. She chose a cream-colored lace dress, and as we walked Fourth Avenue I felt very fine holding my child's hand that charming, chilly Sunday afternoon in 1858.

It was a graceful townhouse on a handsome block near Irving Place. We knocked at the door soon opened by a young maid who took our coats just as a short, stocky, full-bearded man in a brown wool suit and rimless eyeglasses entered the foyer.

"And you must be Lily," he said with an English accent, then took her hand and bowed slightly. "Calvert Vaux," he continued, "though I cannot imagine how such a pretty young lady could ever make herself resemble Mr. Olmsted."

He straightened himself before turning to me with dark and gracious eyes. "Mr. Wolf, welcome to my home."

He escorted us to the drawing room where several men and a young woman stood casually around a fire place and its small fire giving both warmth and fragrance to the room. Their friendly chatter ceased with our appearance and they smiled at us. We were introduced first to the young woman, Mr. Vaux's wife Mary who complimented Lily on her pretty dress.

"Yours is very pretty too," Lily replied.

The young man beside her was Mr. Clarence Cook, his dark hair parted on one side and his curly beard rather scruffy. I wanted to tell him how much I love his book on Central Park but he hadn't written it yet. Beside him was a tall, somber, bald man in a long black coat and tight collar, Mr. Henry Bellows, pastor of the First Congregational Church of New York. A sturdy, clean-shaven fellow came forward, a newspaper reporter, I believe, or a painter –perhaps both– Cormac O'Connor. He had strong hands and a wide, handsome face, and though appearing a year or two under thirty, his dark eyes owned the expression of an old soul, as if, despite his youthful appearance, he had actually witnessed a hundred years.

And finally Mr. Vaux stood beside a quiet, serious young man nearly a foot taller than himself. He had broad shoulders and a wide forehead beneath dark, unruly hair.

"Lily," Mr. Vaux said to her, "I believe you have already made the acquaintance of Mr. Olmsted."

Olmsted bowed slightly and took Lily's extended hand, a soft smile on his gentle, delicately featured face.

"Oh yes," Olmsted replied, though his blue eyes remained on Lily. "We are old friends. How nice to see you."

"And it's nice to see you, Frederick," she replied with similar cordiality. "How is the work going?"

"Very well, thank you, but very slowly. I fear we may not make the deadline."

"Then let's have lunch," she uttered, mildly distressed, "and you get right back to it."

When the maid invited us all into the dining room Vaux insisted Lily sit beside him. Mary excused herself to check on their young son Downing as we were served tomatoes and crisp, cold lettuce, then a fine onion soup. Mr. Bellows asked me if we had perhaps passed their new church on East 20th Street. "A truly splendid structure," he assured me, "designed by a strange and gifted man named Jacob Wrey Mould."

I said I had not seen it but would be sure to as we headed home.

"You can't miss it," added Cormac O'Conner with lively eyes and a slight Irish accent. "It's the one that resembles a zebra," then he turned to Lily and asked not what grade she was in or about her favorite teacher but rather what books she likes to read.

"Alice's Adventures in Wonderland," she replied, looking him in the eyes. "And the poems of poor Edgar Allan Poe. And stories of the ancient Greeks."

"Which story do you like best?" Cormac asked.

"The adventures of O-dis-ee-us," she pronounced carefully.

"I love that too," he said with growing animation. "And do you have a favorite episode?"

After a thoughtful pause when I laughed to myself as she briefly bit her lower lip and a small crease appeared between her eyes, Lily replied with assurance, "The Sirens."

Mr. Bellows grumbled with evident disapproval; "Even though he was advised not to listen?" he asked.

"Because he wants to know how everything feels," she joyfully said to him.

"Mr. Wolf," Vaux declared through hardy a laugh, "you certainly have been blessed with a child of her own mind. Good luck."

"Of your daughter," Cormac O'Connor said to me, "you must be right proud."

When Mrs. Vaux returned we were served thin slices of seared pork, roasted potatoes, broccoli with diced red peppers, yet despite the friendly atmosphere Olmsted seemed detached. He listened and laughed quietly but said nothing, and I sensed that, though physically with us, his thoughts were elsewhere.

"We shall have coffee and tea," Vaux said to the table in general, "and ice cream," he uttered to Lily, "in my study." And it was there, handsomely decorated with comfortable leather chairs and tall candlesticks beside them, with bookshelves filled with orderly, abundant volumes and paintings on the walls of a stately villa set in a meadow and another, smaller painting of a wintery forest clearing, that we discovered the true reason for this intimate gathering.

Since the previous autumn Vaux and Olmsted have met weeknights and Sundays in this room to design and redesign the acres the city had purchased for the intended park. There would be thirty-two additional entries by other landscape architects submitted on the April 1st deadline, and before the board of commissioners announced the winner on April 28, all entries will be on display at Stanford and Delisse's bookstore, 637 Broadway. Vaux and Olmsted's design would be accompanied by illustrations to indicate how their creation would appear, one future vision provided by Mary McEntee Vaux's brother Jervis, a gifted, somber painter of the Hudson River School; it was his painting of the forest that hung on the study wall. But as Olmsted had earlier indicated to Lily, the

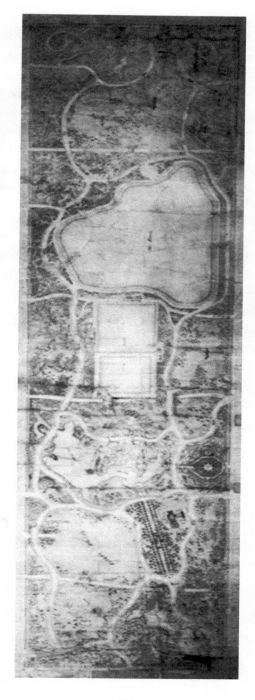

deadline for submission was rapidly approaching.

"Mr. Wolf, if you would assist me," Vaux asked while handing me one end of a thick scroll of paper perhaps four feet wide. As he unrolled a map eleven feet long he explained that lunch was only a ruse; what was needed were steady hands to help complete the design. Cormac O'Connor threw back his head and laughed again, and Mr. Cook wondered with one eyebrow lifted, "Are we to wash the lunch dishes as well?" After the map was unrolled to its full length, I saw it all spread before me.

Near my right thumb were the words "Principal Entrance"; with most of New York's three-quarters of a million people living downtown, the entrance at Fifth Avenue and 60th Street would be closest, would be "principal." At my left thumb was not the domineering *Maine Monument* where Bo and I would enter more than a century later but rather the quiet, winding entrance of MERCHANTS' GATE. I saw the rectangle of the Old Reservoir before it was drained to create the Great Lawn, that across Sheep Meadow were the words "Parade Ground," how far the Pond flowed into the park before a skating rink would be added, and on this map the park ended not at 110th Street but at 106th. Vaux and I spread the long paper across an even longer table, and after Olmsted gave her brush, green paint, and brief guidance, Lily carefully colored the trees on the Greensward Plan.

Epilogue

What spectacle confronted them when they...emerged silently...from a passageway...into the penumbra of the garden?

The heaventree of stars hung with humid nightblue fruit.

Ulysses, from "Ithaca"

It is a perfect summer day, a gift of a day. Low humidity, temperature in
the mid-80s with a soft, western breeze, foamy clouds scattered across
the vast blue sky. I am at the most northern edge of the Great Lawn, the
center of Central Park, in the center of Manhattan, which is the center of
the world. To the north, beyond the old reservoir's stone wall, a horizon
of tall green trees beyond which lies another whole half of the park: Lake
Manhattan, the North Meadow, the serene Pool and the Ravine winding
through the North Woods, the ruins of McGowan's Tavern and Saint
Vincent, the tranquil Conservatory Garden, and Harlem Meer. Trees at
the Great Lawn's perimeter block the apartments along Fifth Avenue and
Central Park West with a leafy veil just as Olmsted wanted. Only to the
south does the city intrude: rising ever higher, the daunting skyline of
Manhattan.

We first stood here during my maiden flight on a bicycle. Much
has been taken since then, much given, and much remains. Over three
decades have passed and I still cycle the winding walkways, spin along
their rises and dips, as close to feeling like a bird as I can get. Wheels for
wings.

Today on the Great Lawn's healthy grass a shirtless young man
repeatedly kicks up to handstands seeking elusive, unwavering balance. A
lazy softball game plays on the fine dirt diamond, and a little girl walking with her father pleads, "Can we come back another day?" Along
the walkway a summer camp straggles for the picnic tables under the

Pinetum's ever-green trees, and after watching a squirrel bury a peanut snatched from my fingertips, a chubby fellow mounts his trail bike and moans to the sky, "Central Park is awesome."

Nearby my son shoots hoops at the 96th Street basketball courts before a rinse in the sparkling spray of a cold sprinkler; when did he grow to be so tall? After riding to the park on her bike (a 'Bikes, By George!' sticker on the down-tube), my daughter sits beneath a tree reading the last, transcendent chapter of *One Hundred Years of Solitude*; she turns the page with a slender right hand, her index finger encircled by that old filigreed ring –the end of a fork or spoon and easily adjustable. High above on imperceptible string, a kite with undulant streamers like long tail-feathers of some exotic bird or tentacles of jellyfish, languid and hovering. Even higher, Pale Male with mighty, outstretched wings glides in effortless spirals over the park's glistening waters, its thick canopy of trees, above Bo's ashes, and the single tree growing miraculously from bedrock east of the promenade where I had kissed the mother of my children.

And just as we can see into the past when searching deep space with powerful telescopes, I imagine that the higher Pale Male soars the further back *he* can see in the park's story: when park visitors peddled like a bicycle a swan-shaped boat beneath Gapstow Bridge—Lohengrin Boats—and baffled hunters searched for puma, before villages vanish beneath the pick ax, back even to the Lenape trekking their ways through the forest, around that hill and along the pond.

Is this nostalgia, what Pete Hamill –our literary Springsteen—believes the most powerful New York emotion? Life in our city is chronicled with continuous change, he wrote in his historical memoir *Downtown: My Manhattan*, and New Yorkers possess "an almost fatalistic acceptance of the permanent presence of loss." But Pete's nostalgia is legitimate; he really did cheer in the stands of Ebbets Field, kiss farewells and reunions in the old Penn Station, scuttle with notebook and a keen eye in the shadows of the Twin Towers. I long for a park I've never seen, before epic entrance gates, automobile traffic, and when the art museum hadn't devoured a dozen acres of the city's finest work of art. And my look backwards will pass Clarence Cook's to the future and what the park's creators believed their most enduring gift: "We who are in the middle of life can never know all its beauty. That is reserved for those for whom we have planted these shrubs and trees, and spread these level lawns."

Already another generation of children skid with giddy delight down the Big Slide. Someday amid their tears and laughter my own children will scatter my ashes through the park (later, please, rather than soon) and a few on the Lower East Side. Hopefully selling and buying will have ended along the promenade, that cars pass through the park only by the burrowed transverse roads, that park lovers' desires become central to the Conservancy, and for *Webster* to be banished. Pale Male —immortal—will always soar above his domain.

While writing these memories of Central Park I often wished truly to relive them, that all those dear to me with whom I shared the park and others met in my imagination might gather once more beneath the heaventrees as Meta plays her golden harp and Bo wanders off awhile without a limp. We'd watch dragonflies skim the Model Boat Pond and dance in the shade of Sheep Meadow and my children will again splash in the Angel's restorative water. Even now, I stroll the promenade or the Ramble feeling far younger than I really am through a park that remains always unknowable, both fixed and ever-changing. Whether the park of wounds and neglect when I first followed Bo or amid the pervasive magic that bewitched my children, despite "Keep Off" signs and the crowds and commerce of today, the wonder of Central Park remains just on the other side of that low stone wall. And so in any season, whether it's frozen or steamy, in rain or at night, my unwavering desire will always be for that one more visit to the park.

Thank You

For the unrelenting effort and faith of my agent Robert Stricker; to Irene Silver, the godmother of this book; for the thorough, generous editing of Constance Rosenblum; to Lily for the cool maps; to Dave Smith upon whom I can count; to Lou Phillips who knows what matters; to my colleagues Steven Streeter, Heather Klomhaus, Richard Jackson, Filippa Modesto, and David Stoler at Berkeley College; to Dan Wakin of the West Side Hawks; to Sean Akerman who celebrates the magic of words; to Silvio Biasci who always asked how the book was going; to Paul for his careful readings and pastries; to Tom Gaffney who kept reminding me of tenacity; to Aurélie Duclos and her eye for adjectives; to Eric Bronson for a good reading; to Belle Chan and her skills in mysterious ways; to Gottlieb Pinball for use of the picture of 'Central Park'; to Zipporah Films for use of a still from Frederick Wiseman's *Central Park*; to the Fairfield Porter estate for use of the painting "New York City Skyline and Central Park"; to Dr. Catherine Diefenbach who saved my life; to the patience and good spirit of Kimberly Brooks at Griffith Moon; to Ernie, Champ of the Yard; and most dearly to my daughter Lily and my son Skylar whom I love even more than I love Central Park.

About The Author

Stephen Wolf is the editor of *I Speak of the City: Poems of New York* (Columbia University Press). His excerpt about the park's notorious Casino appeared in *The New York Times*, and his city portraits and histories appeared regularly in *The Villager*. His fiction has been published in *Playboy, Ploughshares, Shenandoah, Penthouse, The New American Library* anthology *American Families,* and his short story cycle *Intimate Articles,* with illustrations by Larry Rivers, was published by TenSpeed Press. Born in Chicago, he has been a truck driver, bike messenger, construction worker, gymnastics coach, received a Ph.D. in American Literature from the University of Illinois, and when not in Central Park teaches literature and humanities at Berkeley College in New York City.

photo by Heather Klomhaus

CPSIA information can be obtained
at www.ICGtesting.com
Printed in the USA
BVHW07s0631050718
520783BV00007B/390/P